Hanging Rock 1, 1991. Tim Jones, Wood engraving, 7.2 x 5.0 cm.

Hanging Rock - A History

Chris McConville

Drawing by Ian Scott, 2013.

A catalogue record for this
book is available from the
National Library of Australia

NATIONAL
LIBRARY
OF AUSTRALIA

First published by Friends of Hanging Rock Inc. in 2017

Copyright © Friends of Hanging Rock Inc. 2017

Every effort has been made to identify copyright holders of
material where appropriate. Friends of Hanging Rock Inc.
would be happy to hear from any copyright holders
who have not been acknowledged.

Title: Hanging Rock – A History
Author: Chris McConville
Designer: Wayne Rankin
Edited by: Chris McConville and Matthew Nickson
Printed in Australia: Southern Colour (VIC) Pty. Ltd.
Cover painting: © John Kelly - Hanging Rock (landscape V) 2016

Public Record
Office Victoria

VICTORIA
State
Government

Friends of Hanging Rock gratefully acknowledges the support
of the Victorian Government and Public Record Office Victoria
for making this project possible.

FSC
www.fsc.org

MIX
Paper from
responsible sources
FSC® C010983

Dryden's Rock, Mount Macedon c.1886 . Artist unknown, engraving 12.5 x 20cm,
based on Richard Daintree's photograph. *Drydens Rock, Woodend* c.1858.
Prepared for The Great Exhibition, Melbourne, 1886.

Courtesy Jennifer Clarke

T MACEDON,

Contents

Hanging Rock

There's been a renewed outbreak of the History Wars in recent times with attempts to at least metaphorically - tumble English notables from their pedestals. At issue, the proposition that James Cook 'discovered' Australia. This ignores the flotilla of European boat people who'd been in the neighbourhood before him – and infuriates the Aboriginal people who'd arrived 70,000 years ago.

In the same spirit let us make the point that my old friend Joan Lindsay did not 'discover' Hanging Rock. Nor did Peter Weir when filming 'Picnic'. Come to think of it, I made my first feature film at the Rock decades earlier, in the mid Sixties before Joan wrote the novel.

Nobody 'discovered' Hanging Rock. In a sense it discovered us. It was waiting for us a very long time. And it will outlive us, remaining a haunting presence when all humanity has vanished as surely as Miranda and the girls.

By eerie coincidence it is almost exactly the same age as the human species. Both us and it were born 6,000,000 years ago, so the Rock had to wait a very long time for our arrival.

This magnificent book is a testament to its geological and cultural significances – to indigenous, white and other hued Australians. It speaks on behalf of a monolith – specifically one of the world's most magnificent mamelons – that has in recent years needed human help to save it from human stupidity.

Hanging Rock has been part of my life for over half a century – a mere second of its existence. It brought Joan and I together in an enduring friendship and helped me rekindle a lost Australian film industry. I thank the author for this tribute. I thank the Rock for existing.

Phillip Adams

Acknowledgements

A grant from Local History Grants Public Record Office Victoria enabled this project to get off the ground. Michael Gudinski and others at Frontier Touring assisted with time, support, references and corrections. The Shire of Macedon Ranges allowed access to historical records held by the Shire.

The history has been actively supported by Friends of Hanging Rock. Several members of the Friends group provided information and reviewed chapters. In particular Nathan Alexander put aside time to check details of the text, illustrations and point to critical gaps in the writing and Jan Schapper provided valuable comment.

Members of local historical societies assisted with references and information; in particular Janet Hawkins and others at the Woodend and District Heritage Society, Phyllis Boyd and The Gisborne and Mount Macedon Districts Historical Society, as well as The Romsey and Lancefield Districts Historical Society and Kyneton Historical Society . All made archival sources in their collections readily available.

Tony Ingram generously allowed access to his archival material. Andrew Lemon assisted with horseracing information. Robyne Blee and the Kyneton & Hanging Rock Racing Club provided additional resources. Andrew McConville was an essential guide to otherwise obscure references.

Bruce Hedge and David Critchley provided a range of photographs and Euan McGillivray gave ongoing encouragement. The Newham Garden Club provided support and Simon Fenner was always available and helpful. Staff at the State Library of Victoria, the State Library of New South Wales, and Public Record Office Victoria were consistently knowledgeable and supportive. Geoff Laurenson at Geelong Grammar School was a wealth of information about the Clyde School at Woodend.

The project would not have been possible at all without the direction of Matthew Nickson from Friends of Hanging Rock. Matthew shaped the project, from first of all realising the need for a new history of Hanging Rock through to identifying sources and on to managing all stages of the production and distribution.

Chris McConville

5

Photograph by John Van Groningen, 2009.

Spectre in the Mist

As the year 1870 drew to a close, a band of holiday-makers set out on an adventure north of Melbourne. They had decided to climb Hanging Rock. After a trip out to the Rock from one of the towns nearby, they wandered around below its ramparts, until finally agreeing on the best spot for their ascent. Ignoring the easiest pathways, they clambered up the sheer rock wall, squeezing through 'loopholes' between boulders. Grasping broken branches, they hauled each other across loose and sliding stones, to reach the 'Summit' — in reality a plateau-like expanse — broken by rock columns. Dusting themselves down, and ignoring scratches and tears, they were finally able to wander across Hanging Rock's highest point. From far above the plains of central Victoria, they could peer down between huge rock pinnacles, picking out tiny specks of picnickers scattered below. The 'drone' of bagpipes drifted up to them, from where the holiday-makers of Kyneton, Woodend and Lancefield were celebrating Christmas holidays in the bush.[1] They could just possibly have made out the looping track of a very crude racecourse, as it curved, erratically, around trees.

Beyond the Rock and picnic grounds, the climbers could identify the greying skeletons of trees, where farmers had started to ringbark their way through woodland. They could gaze over paddocks on which imported grasses were replacing native ground covers. Clusters of timber houses, and the shingle roofing of a few stores, pubs or timber mills, marked the sites of local hamlets, Hesket and Newham. Further into the distance, and forested slopes filled their view, Macedon to the south; Cobaw to the north. And yet, it was Hanging Rock itself, rather than this vast panorama, which left them in awe. 'It has a weird and spectral appearance, something like that of a ruined castle' mused one of the climbers. He reflected as well, that he would dread getting stuck on the Summit of a moonlit night.[2] It is this image of Hanging Rock, as a spectral, perhaps malevolent, but always fascinating place, which has stayed with us ever since.

These adventurers were able to climb Hanging Rock because a public recreation reserve had been proclaimed there in May 1870 and placed under the control of the Shire of Newham. This Reserve simply enclosed a block of land alongside the Rock itself, and not until 1884 was the Reserve extended, to take in the massive outcrop and its rock walls. A little more than a century later, and Hanging Rock Reserve was expanded for a second time, to include the 'East Paddock'.[3] With each of these extended boundaries, places within the Reserve changed also. A thoroughbred racetrack was shifted from the western to the eastern side of the Rock after 1884. Half a century later, and sports ovals and tennis courts were laid out at the base. Near to these appeared a café, visitors' centre, and caretaker's house. Once the 'East Paddock' became part of Hanging Rock Reserve, global megastars took to an outdoor stage there, for rock music concerts.

The 'ruined castle' of the rock outcrop has though, barely changed. Hanging Rock was first thrust to the Earth's surface some six million years ago, in a time we know now as the Miocene. It took European natural scientists many years to understand its strange character, with vertical slabs of rocks forming sheer columns, and pinnacles of grey or red stone thrust above the plateau of the 'Summit'. They eventually agreed that a rare volcanic upheaval must have created Hanging Rock; one in which a thick mixture of lava and rock (magma) pulsed upwards through a vent in the Earth's surface, congealing as it rose. The magma then weathered over millions of years, becoming the weird vertical slabs, spire-like peaks, and cylindrical rock columns of Hanging Rock. The outcrop was eventually understood as a rare volcanic form, a mamelon.

Hanging Rock seems even more odd, even unsettling, since it appears suddenly over undulating paddocks. The rock columns rise up like cliffs from flat farmland. This landmark reaches to a height of seven hundred metres, more than one hundred metres above the surrounding farmlands.[4] It is not as high as neighbouring Mount Macedon, which stands at over one thousand metres. And it is Macedon, rather than Hanging Rock, which is routinely recognised as the dominant peak in the volcanic, mountainous ranges of central Victoria. In the deep history of volcanic Australia, Hanging Rock is, in any case, unlike Mt Macedon, or other older peaks along the Great Dividing Range. It differs too from the more recent calderas and low hills familiar to travellers in the Western District of Victoria. And although its character as a mamelon is widely recognised, its place in the evolution of the continent, as the bridge between ancient and very recent volcanic eras, is less well understood.

As the Rock cooled and weathered over millions of years, snow gums and other hardy eucalypts clung to crevasses on its steepled sides, some twisted and stunted, others grown tall and straight. At first home to Australia's megafauna, Hanging Rock eventually came to shelter the animal life we know today. But from the moment Europeans discovered Hanging Rock, they began to transform it. Climbers, including the party of 1870, cut branches from wattles as they clawed their way upwards. One leaseholder planted avenues of European trees. He then graded a roadway towards the Summit. Recreational shooters delighted in slaughtering slow-moving possums and koalas. On any weekend until well into the twentieth century, boys with pea rifles wandered around Hanging Rock, taking aim at all sorts of birds.

Even in the last decades of the twentieth century, shooters were still coming onto Hanging Rock Reserve to kill koalas.

The woodlands around the Reserve vanished even more speedily than fauna within its boundaries. In the 1850s gold miners drifted away from the diggings to the north and west of Hanging Rock. Several had sailed off from the Victorian finds to the new gold strikes in Otago, on the South Island of New Zealand. When they eventually made their way back to Victoria, they took up farming around the castle-like outcrop of Hanging Rock. Their farming families erased forest, planted English bushes as hedgerows, and sowed crops. The block gazetted as a recreation reserve in 1870 had been initially set aside to protect a water supply for their stock, so that, in dry summers, these farmers could drive cattle and sheep into the Reserve. Here, their livestock could reach water in Five Mile Creek. This stream ran southwards from Hanging Rock, before meandering north-west to meet the Campaspe River.[5]

By 1866, and feeling a little more secure about the future of their bush blocks, local farming families had begun to gather on flat land beneath Hanging Rock, for Christmas and New Year get-togethers. If they wanted to climb Hanging Rock, then they did so under the auspices of the proprietor of the Hanging Rock Hotel. The hotelier, and leaseholder of Hanging Rock, William Adams, was the energetic landscape designer who had driven a road towards the Summit, planted avenues of exotic trees, imported white swans, and filled up an artificial lake. By the time the Reserve grew to take in the Rock in 1884, and despite the limitations of William Adams's original 'improvements', Hanging Rock had become a spectacular summer fair ground. Much of this was due to the popularity of the Hanging Rock horse races, held each New Year's Day.

Massive raceday crowds started arriving at Woodend and Macedon railway stations in the 1890s, most of them from Melbourne or Bendigo, and some from as far afield as New South Wales (NSW) and South Australia. From the railway stations, they piled into dog carts, drays, or wagons, for the dusty trip out to the Hanging Rock racetrack. It took only a few years for this throng to spill out from the track, and spread across the Reserve. With them came all of the camp-followers of Melbourne's festival days. So one slightly suspicious visitor spied at the Hanging Rock races,

> Professor Skuthorpe who advertises himself as 'The Hero of Gordon's Famous Leap at Mount Gambier' [and] . . . gives exhibitions of buck-jumping. The old cry of 'The game's quite fair and the monkey don't care' rings through the crowd, and one is quite amused by the thriving business done by the owner of the monkey. The thimble and pea man and the three-card trick operator carry on their respective trades . . . a merry-go-round does a roaring trade, and the shooting galleries are numerous.[6]

The spectacle of three-card tricksters, buck-jumpers and shooting contests was hardly the recreation that nature-loving climbers had in mind for Hanging Rock. Visitors who came to enjoy the picturesque panorama from the Summit, who perhaps sought a quiet reflection on wildlife and native plants, or many who simply hoped for a natural haven away from the city, wanted little to do with sideshows and horse races. Over their objections, the Hanging Rock Racing Club extended its track and put up new buildings, so that the race meetings flourished. During the inter-war years Hanging Rock races were hailed as the most entertaining thoroughbred event outside Australia's major cities. By then, football clubs, the Hesket Cricket Club, tennis parties and motor-bike racers, were all setting out to enjoy a day at Hanging Rock. And because Hanging Rock stood just 75 kilometres north-west of Melbourne, more and more claimants began to jostle for space within the boundaries of Hanging Rock Reserve. After 1945, rock climbers, and cross-country runners all tried to claim a piece of the place for themselves. A petanque club hosted world championships at Hanging Rock in 2006.[7] Over the last two decades, massive crowds have begun arriving for rock concerts in the East Paddock. Global megastars like Leonard Cohen, The Eagles and Rod Stewart, all drew fans to Hanging Rock. Bruce Springsteen and his E Street Band took to the stage at Hanging Rock, for the third time, in 2017. From the mass

Dryden's Rocks near Mt. Macedon, 1858. A.H. Burkitt
Watercolour - 16 1/2 x 28 in.
State Library of New South Wales

Drydens Rock. c.1858. Photograph by Richard Daintree. State Library of Victoria

of fans who had enjoyed the spectacular event, 1743 faced police breath tests whilst driving home, and eight were found to have had too much to drink. Not quite the uninhibited wildness of raceday carnivals one hundred years earlier, but enough to disappoint Victoria Police.[8]

Recurrently, loud voices demand that the Reserve must be improved, in other words, modernised and commercialised. Intermittently, these modernising proposals have included schemes for a quarry, for a zoo, for a country club, and luxury resort. Others call for Hanging Rock to be returned to its 'natural' state, with as many of the modernising elements removed. The conflict between modernisers and nature's admirers has been played out by different interests over many years. But over and above these continuing disagreements, Hanging Rock always reappears, as a place of the imagination. Along with countless others, our climbers of 1870 were seeking out the 'picturesque' in their journey to the top. And when they thought of Hanging Rock as picturesque, they imagined some landscape whose pattern and order would attract a famous painter. The picturesque was simultaneously a place of great beauty and majesty. It inspired both admiration and awe, even fear. Such picturesque spots were typically understood metaphorically. Hanging Rock could become a ruined castle, a forbidding fortress, or a rough reflection of Stonehenge. It could be pictured, as one visiting journalist suggested, as an enchanted world, a place of

> Fairy-like grottoes completely shut in by rock, overlooking nothing but a wild and luxuriant mass of vegetation that descends on the hill slopes so suddenly and goes down so far that the sight makes one giddy to contemplate.[9]

When the Rock was brought to a global audience through Joan Lindsay's 1967 novel, *Picnic at Hanging Rock* and Peter Weir's 1975 film of the same name, older emotions of dread, of the Rock as a symbol of an overpowering perhaps malevolent nature, came to be shared around the world. Any visitors to the Reserve who have read the novel, or seen the film of *Picnic at Hanging Rock*, arrive with an expectation that they will be overawed and disturbed, in much

the same manner as were our adventurous climbers in December 1870. No doubt the new television series of this much-celebrated St Valentine's Day picnic, to be shown in February 2018, will bring another generation of mystery-seekers. Like excursionists before them, they will arrive, intent on climbing Hanging Rock, and subjecting themselves to the thrill of its 'weird and spectral' character.[10]

Fortress-like rock ramparts, picnic spots and sports fields, the racetrack, neighbouring farmlands and hamlets, a concert venue and a place of mysterious disappearance, even distant forests, all share in both the landscape and history of Hanging Rock. Many of the artists central to the landscape tradition in Australia, from Eugene von Guérard to Fred McCubbin, have painted Hanging Rock. Several of Australia's famous nineteenth-century photographers tried to reproduce its material reality, whilst at the same time hinting at the superhuman ambience of Hanging Rock. Richard Daintree took photographs here as an employee of Victoria's Geological Survey. Later in the nineteenth century, Nicholas Caire and Charles Nettleton came as commercial cameramen, to record and then market this unique monument. Joan Lindsay drew on artists' images of the Rock in shaping her *Picnic at Hanging Rock*. Lindsay's classic tale, in turn, was refashioned by scriptwriter Cliff Green into Peter Weir's magical film.[11] So the Rock, no longer simply a natural phenomenon with its creek, freshwater spring, a Christmas party ground, or New Year's racetrack, is now a celebrated locale in a global cinematic culture. Its place in the spectacular world of modern, mediated culture has been further cemented by the likes of Bruce Springsteen and Leonard Cohen, through their performances in the East Paddock of the Reserve.

Travellers on the backroads threaded through Hesket and Newham get used to sloping paddocks, stands of eucalypts and swampy lowland. Then, a climb over the most gentle of rises, or a turning through some slight road bend, will reveal the wall of grey, or perhaps red; stone columns, with trees and bushes clinging to odd crevasses; the unheralded emergence of Hanging Rock. Suddenly, these grey ramparts can just as easily disappear, hidden by a morning mist or lost as the backroad turns once more. The farms and trees seem ordinary once again, as if this massive rock pile never existed. Hanging Rock lives on then, as a both natural, material place, as metaphor, and as ethereal mystery. The volcanic rocks, the flora and fauna, the farms, towns and sportsgrounds, all form material layers visible to anyone passing by Hanging Rock. Each of these varied layers reflects one or other aspect of Hanging Rock's imagined and material history.

Some 150 years after our 1870 holiday-makers made their epic ascent, a vast panorama still opens for anyone atop Hanging Rock. To the north and east, farmlands undulate around windbreaks, broken now by clusters of suburban houses and sheds. Distant forests still frame the view, although grassed paddocks or vineyards rather than oat crops and timber mills now fill the foreground. The small towns nearby have shrunk, just as the public reserve around Hanging Rock has expanded. Visitors intent on climbing the Rock now pass between a café and discovery centre. And instead of hauling themselves up rock walls, and across loose stones, they can follow a gentle asphalt pathway as it curls up towards the Summit. Steeper sets of steps pass under the rock formation that gave this landmark its name. The 'Hanging Rock' is a fallen boulder jammed between rock pinnacles, and forming an archway below the Summit.

As the holidaying climbers descended from their adventure in 1870, the noise from picnic parties below grew louder. And once they reached the base of the Rock they couldn't help feeling dismayed. The wild solitude of their Hanging Rock was under threat, from crowds wanting little more than a raucous day out around campfires. Today, this contrast can be drawn even more sharply. Designated picnic spots have brought a certain formality to the Reserve, which, to nineteenth-century climbers, remained, by and large, a wilderness. And yet, perhaps because of this sharpened contrast, between the wildness of the rock formations above, and the frivolity of the picnic grounds below, it is Hanging Rock's otherworldy aura, or, in the words of our 1870 climbers, the Rock's 'weird and spectral appearance', which picnickers and climbers continue to hold in awe.

Historians have tried to answer many questions about the image and material reality of Hanging Rock. The historical societies in Woodend and Gisborne hold rich collections relating to Hanging Rock. Local writers have drawn together careful chronologies of changing land ownership at Hanging Rock and around its base. Marion Hutton has given us a meticulous reconstruction of changing tenure and boundaries in the Reserve.[12] The stories of neighbouring towns and farms are captured through oral history, and a close reading of local manuscripts and newspapers.[13] A few historians have tried to go beyond the occasional glimpses of Aboriginal history.[14] Macedon Ranges historians have produced a fine collection of photographs, supported by careful historical descriptions. These neatly combine many of the more significant metaphorical images of the Rock, with rare and intimate portraits of family outings in the Reserve.[15] Cinema critics and book reviewers, as well as biographers, have gone to the imagery of the Rock, and the lives of novelist and film-maker, hoping at the same time to connect these life journeys to Hanging Rock as a material site.[16] We now have access to a series of bureaucratic histories, shaped to meet requirements of heritage listing and land management more broadly, and which present a detailed sequence of changes in landform at Hanging Rock.

Both the ancient and modern histories of Hanging Rock are then being reconstituted, at the same time as the imagined Rock, through a novel, a film and musical performance, now appears as an iconic reference point in global popular culture. And yet, the mysteries remain. The eerie monument, the ruined castle, a fortress, or in one early account a giant porcupine, and many other images, are all part of the story of Hanging Rock. Gradually, this imagined Rock has come to overshadow the natural and social history of the place. One of the very few thorough attempts to measure the fictional tale of Hanging Rock against historical facts was undertaken by Sarah Frith. Her 1990 thesis carefully assessed Joan Lindsay's fictional Appleyard College against the curriculum and structures of Clyde School. She was able to show just how far the imaginary Rock had become distanced from historical reality.[17]

Stereographic view of Hanging Rocks (Dalhouse [sic] Plains). 1862.
Photograph by John H. Jones, digital reproduction of original stereographic view.
Collection Bendigo Art Gallery. R. H. S. Abbott Bequest Fund 2009.

Top of the "Hanging Rock."

Top of the Hanging Rock. c.1854 – c.1862. In collection. Cogger album of photographs. State Library of Victoria

Between its global image and its natural history, Hanging Rock remains embedded in a more communal story. Its old picnic celebrations, its continuing race meetings, and even the raids made by desperate farmers on its water and grass, all remind us of people who lived around the Rock. Hanging Rock possessed a rare capacity to draw them all together, even if only for a few days each year. Perhaps that social significance explains the strange majesty that writers, photographers, film-makers and popular music performers have sought to capture. There is though, another deeper and more elusive history of Hanging Rock.

Long before any shooting parties, field naturalists, or rock stars ventured out to Hanging Rock, it was a place for gatherings of Aboriginal peoples. The Rock stands at the juncture of lands familiar to three distinct peoples of Aboriginal Australia. It was always a place for their ceremonial events, a meeting place of different networks, and the site for bartering for greenstone, the crossroads for trade routes that extended across what are now state borders, into the centre and the north of the continent. Hanging Rock might now be encircled by farms, sports grounds, a racetrack and visitors' centre. It may have recently won global acclaim for its cinematic image. A new generation knows of it as a unique site for spectacular rock concerts. Hanging Rock remains, even after all of these events, a place to be respected for its role in an ongoing Aboriginal life.

Modern reflections on local Aboriginal life sometimes isolate a 'last' gathering, or dwell on broken traditions and lost memories. No doubt there are reasons for pronouncing such a finality. It is though, impossible to prove that any one gathering of Aboriginal people was the 'last' such coming together. For local custodians defied the invasion of the sheep barons of the 1830s to the extent that they were singled out by squatters as the fiercest of resisters. When expelled from their own country by troopers and Aboriginal 'Protectors' in the 1840s, the 'Mount Macedon tribes' as they were defined, made every effort to return to the lands around Macedon and Hanging Rock until, eventually, they were able to win over some colonial officials.

When colonial authorities again forced them away from their lands later in the nineteenth century, some managed to return. Farmers around Hesket and Newham employed Aboriginal farm workers between the wars. A band of Aboriginal musicians and craftspeople travelled through the area in the 1930s. They demonstrated their skills in hunting and told their stories of the land to interested locals. When Hanging Rock Reserve was first entered onto the Register of the National Estate, it was Hanging Rock's place in Aboriginal history that carried weight. And in more recent times, Aboriginal spokespeople have won a place for themselves in the management of Hanging Rock. Current attempts to reconcile a European history with Aboriginal connections to place are, of course, far from straightforward. But there has been no 'last' Aboriginal engagement with Hanging Rock.

We have reached a point in the Rock's history where it is subject to concerted official regulation. In this controlled place, the bureaucratic procedures of local and state government set down a way forward. Official land use planning standards contain the Rock within a structure of formal complexity. But in seeking to protect Hanging Rock into the future, neither natural history nor metaphorical image provide, when isolated, the most solid foundation. The Rock will always be a place of great cultural significance to Aboriginal people. Managing Hanging Rock also means coming to terms with its role in social networks, in the first instance those of neighbouring farm families, and then extending to those of the racetrack, the Hanging Rock Hotel, and the cricket ovals and tennis courts of the Reserve. The history of Hanging Rock is an ongoing story, but one which needs to be respected in any decisions about the future of the Reserve.

Where nineteenth-century observers often floundered in trying to comprehend the natural history of the Rock, we are today confident about resurrecting this aspect of its past. The stages of the Rock's formation, and its critical place in the geography of Australia's volcanic era are documented. Despite the fact that its history of flora and fauna is less clear, management of The Rock in the 21st century involves embarking on yet another stage in reshaping the Reserve.

THE HANGING ROCK, NEAR WOODEND.

Of all the places of holiday resort for pic-nic purposes open to the choice of the pleasure-seeker, there is none at once more interesting, picturesque, popular, and readily accessible than the Hanging Rock, which lies some four or five miles from Woodend. Its situation and surroundings are interesting and picturesque. All around its base stretch farm clearings, cutting the forest into alternate squares, like the white and black squares of a chess-board. Away to the north and east lie bold hills scattered in groups, or linking themselves into regular chains of ranges, some covered with farm holdings, others dark with the almost unbroken forest. To the south rise high and dark the sombre masses of the Mount Macedon range, and in the middle of the crowning ridge stands up bare and rugged the rocky, roughly fissured cone of Mount Diogenes.

The Hanging Rock itself is a hill of rudely conical form, from 300ft. to 400ft. in height, and crowded in its upper part with an enormous mass of rugged trap rocks, broken and riven and weathered into the most fantastic forms. The shape most affected is the pinnacle, but in places the rock solidifies into a wall of perpendicular precipice, rising to 50ft. or 60ft. In other parts it resembles the rough cyclopean masonry of an earlier world. The path generally followed up the hill passes under the foot of a frowning, lofty, overhanging cliff, on the broken face of which rock-ferns and musk bushes struggle for life. It then ascends between the walls of an enormous portal, formed by an immense boulder of some scores of tons in weight, lying jammed between the side walls of rock. Beyond this the path climbs up a grassy ascent, out of which stand up strangely-shaped crags, some scooped and hollowed out by the weather into mere shells, others crowned with great toppling boulders, only held in place by vast wedges of rock. And amidst all grow graceful white gum trees, with their clean white stems and green drooping foliage, casting delicate, gently waving shadows on the grey surfaces of the lichen-grown rocks. Above this rises the second cone or citadel of what seems a grey defaced ruin, of such antiquity that all trace of form is lost. The strange shapes of the rocks and the curious alliances of stone and tree everywhere arrest attention. Here there is a singular hollow in a vast crag, out of which something like a wild petrified head of the earlier ages of the world seems to look. Then another rock is split in two, the split suspending and being kept open by great stones, which have fallen into it, and showing large orifices, through which the eye ranges out and gets charming views of the surrounding country enclosed in the rough rock frame. The most difficult and perpendicular part of the outer rampart is riven with deep crevices, which extend down low into the heart of the hill. To go down one of these is one of the correct things to be done by all visitors to the rock, and the journey is worth the squeeze and the difficulty it involves for the sake of the queer sensation given to the passer, by finding himself in a mere crack between immense flat walls, formed by an enormous rock, which had once divided, and might—horrible thought—again close.

THE HANGING ROCK, MOUNT MACEDON.

The Hanging Rock, Mount Macedon.
Wood engraving.
The Illustrated Australian News.
30 December, 1874.

State Library of Victoria

Unknown photographer,
(possibly Nicholas Caire).

Image courtesy of
Douglas Stewart Fine Books,
Melbourne.

At the Hanging Rock, The Hanging Rock Races.
The Leader 12 January, 1907.
State Library of Victoria

Some funds are set aside for repairing environmental damage, planting swamp gums and removing weeds. Older picnic furniture will be replaced. Restoration, especially when driven essentially by a desire to recapture the wild and natural Hanging Rock, has yet to find a balance with either the Rock as a playground for sports clubs and racing enthusiasts, or with that overarching popular sense of the Rock: as an awesome somehow magical place, but at the same time an arena for having fun with friends and family, a locale for spectacles and carnival.

Is history a useful guide to the difficult choices facing those charged with safeguarding Hanging Rock? The chapters that follow explore distinct themes in the Rock's life. Its deep history of volcanic eruption, plants and wildlife. Its role as both a node for local farming families, and as a nice spot where city folk could enjoy a day in the bush. The efforts to maintain a racing club and picnic race meetings beneath the Rock continue to this day, and form a central part of the history. The images created by film-makers, photographers and writers are also crucial to the Rock's history, as are efforts to plan and manage the Reserve, whilst simultaneously opening it up to the global culture surrounding rock music megastars.

The Rock's history points us towards the underlying tension in its recent past: a tension between the urge to modernise and commercialise the place, and an alternative commitment to seek out its wildness and in so doing, to return to some unmodernised, natural environment. The images of Hanging Rock, composed over many years reflect this instability. Routinely, popular lines from *Picnic at Hanging Rock*, about the material world as no more than a dream, are reiterated, as if that is all that needs be said about Hanging Rock. More often than not, such imagery has confused, rather than explained, the wide appeal of Hanging Rock as a real place, to be enjoyed and explored. To understand at least some of the Rock's historical reality, and to be able to assess popular imagery against that record of the past, must surely offer a useful starting point for decisions about the Rock's future. But wherever this story leads, Hanging Rock will remain a special place.

A place that we still approach with a sense of awe. In the finish, no matter how many mundane events a written history unearths, the mystery and the awe will remain. And the special character of Hanging Rock can never be understood without first reflecting on Hanging Rock's unique place in Aboriginal cultural life. ✸

At the Hanging Rock, near Kyneton

Looking over and under the Hanging
Rock towards Mount Macedon.
At the Hanging Rock Near Kyneton. c.190
Shirley Jones collection
of Victorian postcards.

At the Hanging Rock,
near Kyneton

Looking through the Window Rock. *At the Hanging Rock Near Kyneton.* c.1907.
Shirley Jones collection of Victorian postcards.

Endnotes

'The Hanging Rock', *South Bourke Standard*, 30 December 1870: 2.

[2] *South Bourke Standard*, 30 December 1870: 2.

[3] Expanding the Reserve seemed to go hand-in-hand with expanded local government authorities. The Shire of Newham was the first manager. Newham expanded to become the United Shire of Newham and Woodend, until further amalgamations created the Shire of Macedon Ranges, the current responsible authority.

[4] Heritage Council Victoria, Victoria Heritage Database Report, Hanging Rock Reserve, VHR number H2339, Overlay H088, registered 12 March 2015, Government of Victoria, http://vhd.heritagecouncil.vic.gov.au/places/12533/download-report, (viewed 20 April 2017).

[5] North Central Catchment Management Authority, Victoria, *Five Mile Creek Waterway Action Plan*, Government of Victoria, 2004.

[6] 'Winchester', 'At Hanging Rock', *Australasian*, 10 January 1903: 36.

[7] Hanging Rock Petanque Club File, Woodend and District Heritage Society, Woodend, Victoria.

[8] Andrew Jefferson, 'Bruce Springsteen Fans caught Drinking and Driving at Hanging Rock', *Herald Sun*, 13 February 2017.

[9] 'The Hanging Rock', *Illustrated New for Home Readers*, 30 December 1874: 219.

[10] On the television series, see Foxtel Press Release, 6 September 2016 https://www.foxtel.com.au/got/whats-on/foxtel-insider/foxtel/picnic-at-hanging-rock.html, (viewed February 2017).

[11] Cliff Green, *Picnic at Hanging Rock: a film, photographs by David Kynoch*, Cheshire, Melbourne, 1975.

[12] Marion Hutton, The Hanging Rock, Mt Macedon Historical Society, Mt Macedon, 1991. See too, Vera P. Clemens, *Interesting Facts of the Hanging Rock near Newham and Woodend*, Kyneton, Vic., 1974.

[13] Colin McKenzie, *Newham Primary School Centenary*, C. McKenzie, Newham Vic, 1977. Woodend and District Heritage Society, *Memories of Newham*, Woodend and District Heritage Society, Woodend, 1999; Valerie Roberts, *Scottish Settlement in Newham*, Valerie Roberts, Melbourne, 2009; Jannyse Williams, *Echoes of the Past: A history of Newham and Cobaw*, Woodend and District Heritage Society, Woodend, 2004; Jane Holth, illustrated Jocelyn Moreland, *Forging History: a history of blacksmiths in the Woodend and Newham Districts*, Woodend and District Heritage Society, Woodend , 2008; Betty Jean Barned, *My Side of the Mountain: a history of Hesket, Cherokee and Kerrie*, Lowden, Kilmore, 1983; Jocelyn Moreland, *Time Gentlemen Please: Hotels of Woodend and surrounding district*, Woodend and District Heritage Society, Woodend, 2013.

[14] Jim Poulter, *Sharing heritage in Kulin Country: lessons in reconciliation from our first contact history*, Red Hen, Melbourne, 2011.

[15] Gisborne and Mount Macedon Districts Historical Society Inc., *Pictorial Hanging Rock: A Journey Through Time*, Gisborne and Mount Macedon Districts Historical Society Inc., Mount Macedon, 2012.

[16] See most recently The National Film and Sound Archives online exhibition, (https://www.nfsa.gov.au/collection/online-exhibition/picnic-at-hanging-rock, (viewed January 2017). Amongst the several reflections, to either resolve or stimulate new interest in the vanishing at the picnic in 1900, see Yvonne Rousseau, *The Secret of Hanging Rock: Joan Lindsay's Final Chapter* with an Introduction by John Taylor and commentary by Yvonne Rousseau, Angus and Robertson, North Ryde, 1987; See too, to read further on the novel, the novelist, film-maker, or later adaptations, Yvonne Rousseau, *The Murders at Hanging Rock*, Scribe, Fitzroy, 1980; also Barbara Lynch and Valerie Heath, *Picnic at Hanging Rock: playscript*, Lyncon, South Yarra Vic, 2003; Janelle McCulloch, *Beyond the Rock: the Life of Joan Lindsay and the Mystery of Picnic at Hanging Rock*, Echo, Bonnier Publishing, Richmond, Vic., 2017; John C. Tibbets, *Peter Weir: Interviews*, University Press of Mississippi, Jackson, 2014; Theo Peeters, *Peter Weir and His Films: a critical bibliography*, Australian Film Institute Research and Information, Melbourne, 1983 and Jonathan Rayner, *The Films of Peter Weir*, Continuum, New York and London, 2003.

[17] Sarah L. Frith, 'Fact and Fiction in Joan Lindsay's Picnic at Hanging Rock', Master of Education thesis, University of Melbourne, 1990.

W. H. and Mrs W. H. Wilson with friends under the Hanging Rock. c.1910. Unknown photographer.

The Romsey and Lancefield Districts Historical Society

DRYDEN'S ROCK, near Mount Macedon

Dryden's Rock near Mt Macedon. Robert Bruce. Wood engraving.
The Illustrated Melbourne Post. 25 January, 1865. State Library of Victoria

First People

'The Australian Aborigines are more a law-abiding people than is generally supposed; in their natural condition, their daily domestic and social life was regulated by well-understood and strictly observed rules. Examples illustrative of this might be multiplied indefinitely'

Report of the Committee inquiring into the Present Condition of the Aborigines of this Colony,

Legislative Council, Parliament of Victoria, 1858-9: xii.

For thousands of years Aboriginal custodians cared for Hanging Rock. Over the last 150 years, both visitors to Hanging Rock and its image-makers first of all ignored the role of Aboriginal people in protecting the place. They preferred to picture the Rock as 'natural', a wilderness rather than a cultural landscape. They then made belated, occasionally romanticised, and often poorly substantiated attempts at reconstructing an Aboriginal image of Hanging Rock, and neighbouring sites. Finally, in the 21st century, the Aboriginal custodians of Hanging Rock have been acknowledged in arrangements for managing the Reserve, and in accounts of its significance as a cultural landscape. The same cannot yet be said for many historical reflections on the Reserve. There are, of course, real obstacles facing any historian hoping to comprehend the deep history of Hanging Rock and its first people. Hanging Rock lies within the lands of the Kulin nation although close to the margins of lands occupied by several Aboriginal groupings — generally defined in recent accounts as the Wurundjeri, Dja Dja Wurrung and Taugurung clan networks — within this nation. The environment immediately around Hanging Rock is thought to have lain within the lands of the Gunung Willam Bulluk clan. European attempts to fix boundaries to these clan networks and to their territories have proven unstable. Since historians have to rely on the incomplete accounts, often from squatters fearful of local inhabitants, Hanging Rock cannot yet be placed accurately within the known history of one or other Aboriginal clan network. Secondly, the 1830s invasion of sheep barons to the north of the Port Phillip settlement quickly concealed pathways and trading routes, along which Hanging Rock occupied a central place. So, any European writing down impressions of Aboriginal life in and around Hanging Rock, faced great difficulty in reinterpreting its cultural centrality, let alone rediscovering the deep history of the place. Thirdly, the first Europeans who travelled through the area in the 1820s and 1830s, along with later administrators of Aboriginal missions, had only the most confused grasp of the networks and connections between distinct Aboriginal peoples in the lands to the north of Melbourne. Intermittently, those living in and around the Port Phillip settlements were described as the Yarra Yarra tribes, those to the north as the

Campaspe tribes. Around Hanging Rock observers could be a little more accurate in identifying the 'Mount Macedon tribe'. Tribe might not be the best description of a localised social system, but most of this writing was no doubt referring to the Gunung Willam Bulluk. One government official, seeking permission to resettle Aboriginal people from Macedon to the Loddon, referred to the 'country' of the 'Mount Macedon tribe' as extending '20 to 30 miles to the North, West and South of that mountain'.[1] When the Gunung Willam Bulluk were manouevred into settlements such as Acheron, any ongoing ceremonial and trading, or exchange use of Hanging Rock was hidden, to become apparent as scattered traces in the later twentieth century. The deep history of Aboriginal life and culture in and around Hanging Rock is, however, not lost, as some superficial accounts may claim. The history of the first people who made use of Hanging Rock, reveals itself only gradually. Alongside the role of Aboriginal representatives in managing the Rock, this history will continue to change, and no doubt reframe future accounts of this special place.

INVADERS

Aboriginal clan groups recognised the weathered volcanic outcrop of Hanging Rock as a culturally significant place over many thousands of years. It played a role in ceremonial life as well as in maintaining sophisticated inter-tribal agreements. Marriage and initiation ceremonies were thought to have taken place there regularly. The inter-clan practice of exogamy — marriages across clan and territorial boundaries — made Hanging Rock critical to ensuring stable, inter-group connections. Richard Broome has reminded us that British bureaucrats in Victoria were confronted by a 'managed landscape [that] was invisibly divided into dozens of discrete Aboriginal traditional countries, each with their own stories, sacred sites and clan owners to care for them'.[2] Very few European observers could grasp the complex role of Hanging Rock in this managed landscape. It may have been a handy lookout for comprehending the undulating lands to the east and west. Around it, probably in what is now the East Paddock, there were sites for regular trading in greenstone and other prized items.[3] The trading routes for these materials extended from the nearby greenstone (diabase) quarry at Mt William (or Wil-im-ee Moor-ing), to Hanging Rock and Macedon.[4] They then spread across western Victoria, reaching at least to the Gariwerd (Grampian) mountains. They ran further to the north-west, across what is now known as the Murray-Darling River system, and probably beyond. As archaeologists remind us, this trade in greenstone had its practical material side; distant groups prized the strength of the stone blanks from Mt William, which could be on-traded after sharpening and shaping in a sandstone block at the base of Mt Macedon. At the same time, trade had its symbolic role. Isabel McBryde, and Alan Watchman, amongst others, pointed to the exchange system's ritual significance for local peoples, and for the distant nations, amongst whom these artifacts were prized. As McBryde indicated, 'exchange and distribution' explain the activities around greenstone articles far better than modernity's trade or supply. Such terms lead us to the complex inter-connections of ritual and material culture by which neighbouring clans engaged with another, maintaining co-operative networks, rather than remaining isolated and rival 'tribes'.[5]

Even though these complex interactions extended across the continent, they meant little to the first British land grabbers. Some Aboriginal groups encountered European explorers, travelling south from Sydney in the 1820s and 1830s. More often their first contact was in the 1840s, with the squatters (pastoralists), men hoping to make their fortunes from running sheep across Aboriginal lands. When squatters such as Edward Dryden and Charles Peters first saw Hanging Rock, they liked the fact that it had a spring and freshwater creek at its base. They also knew it would be useless for grazing, although they recognised, as had Aboriginal people, that it could serve them well as a survey point. Hanging Rock commanded the surrounding landscape. From Hanging Rock a lookout could spy approaching British or Aboriginal travellers. There are some recollections that Dryden had, in fact, placed a signal beacon at the Summit. All the same, neither he nor Peters demonstrated any detailed knowledge of the trading or spiritual roles of Hanging Rock. Nor did they or other squatters take much notice of the artifacts produced and exchanged around them.

Only once small farmers began to unearth axeheads, as they put in fences or built foundations to farm sheds, did Europeans begin to grasp the importance of this ceremonial, trading world.

If these first Europeans were ignorant, or at least uncaring about Hanging Rock as a ritual and exchange site, they were equally blind to the managed landscape around them. The overland explorers imagined themselves setting off southwards, into a trackless wilderness. And yet, the British official who catalogued the lands of what became Victoria, Thomas Mitchell, has left behind accounts of a meadow-like expanse in central Victoria. It seems now, highly unlikely that this open, grassed and rolling vastness, with its occasional copse-like wooded slopes, was anything other than a carefully tended environment, one created over many, many thousands of years. Some sharp-eyed European observers were able to recognise the human element in this landscape. The surveyor of the new British colony of Victoria, Robert Hoddle, painted a scene of Aboriginal figures and Europeans working the same land near the Macedon Ranges. He also remarked on the environment to the north, which included Hanging Rock. Here he was struck by the park-like, carefully tended character of the trees and grasses. Even rivers and creeks seemed managed and controlled. So Hoddle, in reflecting on what he had seen, wrote that,

> The country north of Mount Macedon . . . is of the most fascinating description, consisting of open forest country — park-like in its appearance, and open plains where soil is a rich black loam . . . abundantly supplied with good water in chains of large ponds of great depth which open occasionally in long reaches abounding with wild fowl.[6]

Whereas the first European explorers imagined that they were setting off into a trackless wilderness, they were in fact traversing a sequence of well-understood landscapes. The European travellers were reliant on Aboriginal knowledge of the lands in their path. And these paths were carefully selected by their guides. Confusing to the British explorers, they were always legible to Aboriginal mentors. So, these Aboriginal leaders of European expeditions used boundaries, or the blurred and shared margins between distinct clans, to direct their naïve companions. The explorers found themselves drawn to the very same campsites and water sources discovered, visited, and monitored by Aboriginal people. This custodianship had survived for so long as to remain beyond the comprehension of modernising Europeans. Hamilton Hume and William Hovell, recognised as the first overland explorers from Sydney to Port Phillip, were following pathways trodden for years before them. Sometimes they set out along tracks that they eventually assumed were shaped by kangaroos and Aboriginal hunters. More likely they were following routes established for trading, and used by extended-family kin groups, circulating through several sites within one clan region. As they headed south, along a network skeined through a precisely managed landscape, they were further directed by Aboriginal use of fire. These early overlanders remarked on the way that Aboriginal watchers tracked their route, and then set fire to the lands ahead, so as to redirect their journey.[7]

Bill Gammage highlighted the Aboriginal maintenance of those open 'downs', the grassed expanses that so impressed the 'discoverers' of Victoria, Thomas Mitchell, Hamilton Hume and William Hovell. He reminded us that Europeans entered into no undisturbed 'nature' or 'wilderness' when they set out to travel overland to the settlement of Port Phillip. In fact it would be irrational to imagine that several thousand people, even if living at a low density, could occupy a place for perhaps 40,000 years without engaging in regular and thorough manipulation of their environment. To think otherwise is to fall into the trap of picturing the European as the active environmental shaper, and the first people as passive occupants. Gammage noted the depictions Hoddle made of approaching Mt Macedon during his survey work. He reconstructed the general park-like characteristics of the lands depicted by Hoddle and others, Mitchell included. As he explains, in drawing on these illustrations, the Aboriginal people around Macedon Ranges had 'linked forest hills to grass and scrub belts on plains and left dense timber on colder south slopes but north slopes open enough to ride horses up'.[8] This cultural landscape, which squatters overran, was then, neither wilderness nor trackless. Instead

it was the product of careful management. It was intimately known, cared for, and invested with symbolic power.

The Europeans who first passed by Hanging Rock were not always ignorant of Aboriginal cultural practices. Thomas Mitchell's travels had taken him through the lands of many clan networks. In these he was always conscious of tradition and custom. For much of his journey southwards he depended on Aboriginal intermediaries. Mitchell acknowledged that, once outside the convict settlements, both he and his men were the uncivilised and incapable, whereas their Aboriginal companions had sophisticated understandings of their environment. He knew that the men and women he came across were superior to his crew in these, and in many ways, and he was keen to record respect for them as human beings. On his return to Sydney, Mitchell tried to set out his views of various customs, as well as systematically listing a series of Aboriginal words and expressions he encountered along the journey.

At the same time, Mitchell saw himself as leading a military expedition, referring to his group as a 'small army'. He was always ready for altercation, and his trips to Victoria and elsewhere in Australia resulted in confrontations with Aboriginal warriors. In a number of incidents his men fired their weapons, wounding and killing several in the bands challenging them.[9] Once back in Sydney, Mitchell found that respect for his Aboriginal companions was increasingly undermined by pastoralists overrunning Aboriginal lands. He eventually concluded that Aboriginal hunting grounds would have to be restricted to wild, back country, unused by farmers. Mitchell sadly came close, as one biographer suggested, to 'being reduced to the hope that government policy might, at best, merely smooth the pillow of the dying race'.[10]

A few European scientists also tried to understand connections to place. William Blandowski, the German naturalist who will reappear frequently in the story of Hanging Rock, was one who took Aboriginal social structure and land management seriously. He sought, alongside

Aboriginal axe factory remains, Mt. William, Victoria. c.1875 – c.1938.
Photograph by John Henry Harvey.

State Library of Victoria

Greenstone Axe. Collected Hopetoun, N-W Victoria. Blanks from the
Mt William quarry were polished into axe heads such as this one at
Mt Macedon (X 27143) Photograph by Rodney Start

Museums Victoria

his studies in natural science, to convince British authorities to come to some agreement with Aboriginal people. Blandowski left a careful account of the greenstone quarries near Hanging Rock for example. Needless to say, few took his warnings about the social collapse of the pre-European world seriously. Blandowski worked hard to communicate this deep local attachment in Aboriginal life. He even went further than had Mitchell in his enthusiasms for what he understood to be Aboriginal social and religious structures. The German-born Blandowski, both in his political stance and in his research work, was far more inclined to defend Aboriginal rights than were British military men like Mitchell. He often spoke forcefully in Melbourne, to support a somewhat idiosyncratic version of indigenous rights. He made concerted attempts to promote respect for Aboriginal culture and arts, winning few British friends in the process. He then used sketches of Aboriginal life to demonstrate the destructive impact of colonial expansion. His drawings from the Murray demonstrated fundamental respect for Aboriginal practice, whilst his sketches of Hanging Rock pictured Aboriginal figures in the foreground, overwhelmed in typical romantic trope by the immensity and the threat of the Rock itself.[11] Blandowski's romanticism may well have registered with a wide audience and undoubtedly coloured later reflections on Hanging Rock. It certainly suggested to him that he could use Aboriginal figures to heighten a sense of the majesty of nature, crucial in his sketches of Hanging Rock. His championing of Aboriginal rights won less lasting interest. The Rock as a place of deep meaning to traditional owners was barely noted by later visitors to Hanging Rock and its Reserve.

RESISTERS

The first squatters remained, by and large, unconcerned by any of this. Several were intrigued by Aboriginal custom, whilst simultaneously converting traditional landscapes into commercial sheep runs. Adulated in some local histories as vanguard settlers, surrounded by nomadic Aboriginals, the opposite was more often the case. Squatters exchanged runs, moved their flocks in search of better pasture, and roamed nomadically across woodland and open plain. In contrast,

the Aboriginal people they encountered, had settled in localised landscapes for thousands of years. For the most part ruthless and mercenary, these squatters had defied colonial rule in manufacturing their runs across the Port Phillip District. Driven by European prices for wool and mutton, they were hardly likely to translate curiosity about Aboriginal customs into respect for indigenous environmental practice. For theirs was a venture in meeting the demands of a globalising and modern market, for meat, leather and wool. Their livestock constituted a massive capital investment and good, well-watered grazing land was the prerequisite for turning a profit. They had also come, in many cases, including that of Hanging Rock's principal pastoralists, Dryden and Peters, from a Tasmania scarred by a campaign of extermination. Port Phillip, in the eyes of one observer, barely escaped the same terrible circumstance.[12] And even if the murderous strategies of Tasmania could be avoided, disease had already decimated the Aboriginal societies of Port Phillip. Richard Broome pointed out that, some time before the sheep barons set foot on the land of the Kulin, smallpox had spread through the Aboriginal clans living south of the Murray. In 1790 and again in 1830, smallpox pandemics cut a swathe through the population, perhaps killing every second Aboriginal adult. This spread of smallpox may have been made easier because of the very exchange and distribution networks centred on Hanging Rock and its greenstone routes.[13] The squatting invasion then, suddenly thrust a crude element of modernity and a marginal market economy, into a moment of disruption and social stress through disease. Over a little less than a decade, commercial modernity shaped a new Port Phillip, one to which older ways were adjusted, and against which, the people who were custodians of the land, chose to respond decisively and imaginatively.

The land grab spreading from NSW and Tasmania forced, as Richard Broome notes, 'Aboriginal traditional owners and European settlers [to] interact in complex and varied ways during this frenzied decade of settlement'.[14] Of course the threat and the actuality of lethal violence was never far from these exchanges. Around Aboriginal people, as disease cut down their own numbers, and diminished social and cultural structures, the number of sheep owners constantly rose. But away from Melbourne, and along what for a time was the northern frontier of the Port Phillip District, around Macedon and Hanging Rock, the reverse was often the case. Isolated in a hut in the midst of an environment that he neither understood nor properly owned, the squatter often felt himself dangerously exposed, to still tightly organised Aboriginal networks. Of these, the Mount Macedon tribe, as they were vaguely defined (and more clearly identified by Rachel Tanner as the Gunung Willam Bulluk) seemed the most capable of resisting the pastoralists' advance.[15] They knew the rocks and woodlands, the best routes through sub-alpine forests, they could judge the onset of snow and ice on the mountains, or distances to the nearest water in summer. According to colonial journalists, they were, as well, guided by the most far-sighted Aboriginal leaders. In such circumstances, a number of options were open to both squatter and traditional owners. What historians have seen as an unstable peace and a mutual wariness, which may have varied from curiosity to fear, was typically shaped by Aboriginal 'measured behaviour' towards those who had set themselves up as masters of the land.[16] And despite the governing system of Aboriginal Protectors, day-to-day contacts on runs like Dryden's or Peter's, around Hanging Rock, were always delicate and uncertain. Such encounters could sometimes stem from a mutual respect rather than suspicion. Squatters traded with Aboriginal people, an activity that must have begun very early in the history of Port Phillip, since Mitchell had seen cuts in trees when he passed through the area north-west of Hanging Rock. He knew that these could only have been made by steel axeheads. A few Aboriginal men worked on sheep runs, and on occasions as guides for parties headed inland. But violence was never far from the surface. The squatters, outnumbered, insecure in both their place in British imperial law, and in relation to Aboriginal ownership, but in possession of firearms, could easily claim self-defence in shooting outrages.[17] Their shepherds might have been ex-convicts, men transported for crimes often involving serious violence. The lightly modulated sadism of a British penal system irredeemably brutalised many. Such men, dispersed to rough huts as shepherds, or as stock

nightwatchmen, were placed in isolation, out on the margins of a sheep run. Here, alone but for their kangaroo dogs, they were hardly likely to seek a partnership, in preference to threatening violence, when confronted by local Aboriginal men.

Edward Dryden may have later claimed that he had good relations with local Aboriginal people, but it is certain that on neighbouring runs, conflict rather than co-operation was, at least for several years, the dominant aspect of European-Aboriginal relations. Broome and Tanner both recorded Aboriginal resistance at Aitken's run, close to Dryden's Mount Macedon. These conflicts led to a series of reprisals and investigations, with Aitken justifying his use of firearms.[18] As historians have pointed out, the ability to take sworn evidence from Aboriginal men involved was always hampered, and violent events that wound up in court were invariably weighted in favour of white settlers. With no clear witnesses, shootings on isolated stations and attacks by Aboriginals on stock, were confusing to both police and courts. Just who initiated violence and who defended themselves, was understood automatically by investigators, as Aboriginal attack and European resistance. The opposite was more often the case, although it took an alert mounted trooper or extreme circumstances for that fact to be recognized in legal proceedings. Even where shepherds may have been at fault, interpretations in the Port Phillip settlement fundamentally twisted evidence so that it favoured those rough, marginalised men working alone in the bush.

To take one example from an incident on the Mt Macedon Road in 1841, and which involved a shepherd named Slattery. One Friday morning that May, an injured Aboriginal man was brought into Melbourne by Captain Oxley of the Mounted Police. Five hundred men from the local clan had gathered around Slattery's hut and according to police 'came upon him with threatening gestures'.[19] Slattery ran into the bush but one of his dogs turned back to the hut. Once police arrived, the dog guided them through the bush. There they discovered Slattery's body, 'stripped naked, transfixed with seven spears and his head cloven by a tomahawk'.[20] Police found an Aboriginal man

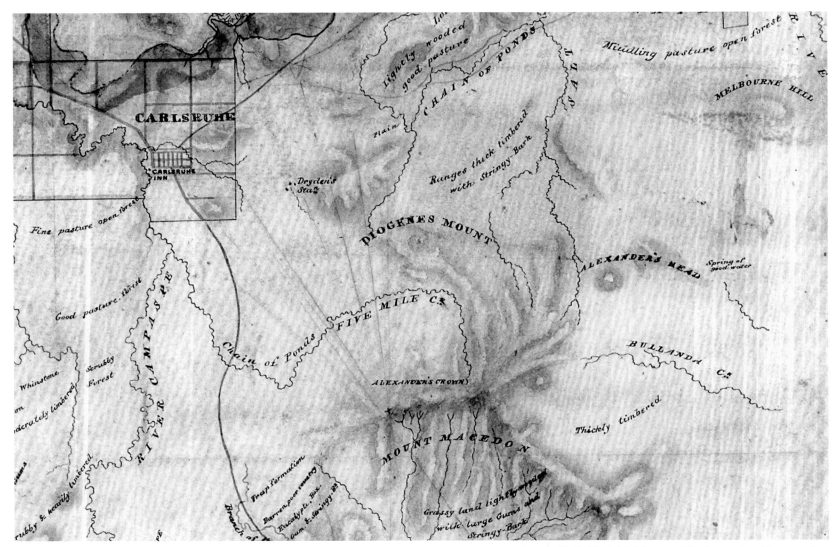

Section of R. Hoddle & A.R.C. Selwyn, 1852. *Feature plan with some geology,
for parts of the Counties of Dalhousie, Talbot and Bendigo, with notes on natural features.*
Plan No 2053/M/2. Geological Survey of Victoria.

Based on Robert Hoddle's map of 1844. (see page 60)

nearby, with a musket wound to his leg. The police surmised that Slattery had fired his rifle as 'a last resort', and with one hundred sheep now missing, neighbouring squatters were clamouring for greater protection. In turn their demands led to further repression of local people, cutting off any chance for co-operation or trade between squatters and local clan. Incidents such as these could be interpreted in many ways. But presenting Aboriginal men as the initiators of violence, and the shepherds as the resisters, was the most common, though not necessarily the most accurate, response. For pastoralists responding to these conflicts, the theft of stock seemed to count as 'outrages', far more than did attacks on their expendable shepherds. And the Mt Macedon tribes were typically depicted as aggressive and very successful raiders of the pastoralists' flocks.

In one such 'outrage' in 1838, Mt Macedon Aboriginal men made off with between eight and nine hundred sheep from Captain Brown's station. Brown's workers set out to recover the sheep. To do so they shot and killed thirteen of the Macedon Aboriginal men. The local Assistant Protector had taken time off to go to Melbourne. In his place, a second local official set out for Brown's station, recording the details of the massacre matter-of-factly, and emphasising the prior rights of pastoralists to recover their prized stock. The outrage, like so many other such conflicts, was interpreted as stock theft by Aboriginal men, rather than as murder by pastoral workers.[21]

Other incidents involving the Mt Macedon men included a confrontation between hunters and pastoral shepherds to the north of Hanging Rock, near to Mt Alexander. The 'Mount Macedon tribe' were seen around one of the outstations, on Henry Munro's run in 1840. Brandishing spears, they forced the shepherds into the hut under Aboriginal guard, before making off with food, and driving sheep into the forest. When one of the station overseers followed the flock, and brought back 135 sheep, he found that the Mt Macedon men had taken over the hut and 'were busily regaling themselves on damper and mutton'.[22] The official Aboriginal Protector, Robinson, then intervened. Christie, the supervisor, slaughtered a sheep and presented the meat to the Mt Macedon men. Munro charged the cost to the Aboriginal Protectorate.

This sort of sensible resolution seemed all too rare. And even in this encounter, good relations were speedily undermined. Dissatisfied with the role of the Aboriginal Protector, Christie had then gone to Melbourne to report the incident, and to demand further protection. As result, the Mt Macedon people were singled out as dangerous marauders, to be kept under surveillance for the remainder of the Protectorate. These Aboriginal warriors from around the Macedon Ranges were blamed for other attacks on flocks. 'Savages', 'Marauders' or 'Ruffians' were the common ascriptions given to Aboriginal resisters in newspapers. Even though squatters had no compunction about stealing land, they could not countenance theft of their livestock.

SURVIVORS

Resistance in the face of the onslaught of the sheep barons, the catastrophe of disease, and loss of traditional land did not necessarily lead to murderous confrontation. Aboriginal people managed to find avenues to survival, even whilst the cataclysm of European modernity reshaped more and more of the lands around Hanging Rock. One response of Aboriginal men had been to engage with the imperial state rather than attack it. Several men of the Gunung Willam Bulluk joined the Native Police, with some of the group eventually selected as leaders in this force.[23] Even though the first attempts at shaping a Native Police proved dismal failures, at least for a short time, this force enabled Aboriginal men to cross between the two cultural worlds co-existing in Victoria. When Henry Dana arrived in Port Phillip in 1842 events took a more promising turn. The Native Police of the 1830s had been subject to dissolute British officials and the force disintegrated to the lasting detriment of its Aboriginal members. When reformed in February 1842 under Henry Dana, a close associate of Governor La Trobe, the new native police took on some of the most expansive law and order campaigns in the colony. The force lasted until Dana's death (he contracted pneumonia whilst chasing bushrangers) and was disbanded soon after, leaving loyal Aboriginal officers isolated,

Self portrait of William Blandowski. Leaf 22, verso from album 1995.26.1.a-1995.26.60. Albumen silver photograph. 22.3 x 17.4 cm.

National Gallery of Victoria, Melbourne
Purchased, 1994. (1995.26.22.b)

(Blandowski logo). From Wilhelm von Blandowski. *Australien in 142 photographischen Abbildungen nach zehnjährigen Erfahrungen zusammengestellt. Gleiwitz*, 1862.
(Australia in 142 photographic. illustrations from 10 years' experience).

Haddon Library, Faculty of Archaeology and Anthropology,
University of Cambridge

Foot of Diogenes Monument. 4 miles N. from Mount Macedon, 40 miles NNW from Melbourne 1855-56. William Blandowski, print after James Redaway & Sons, engraver active Australia 1852–59. From the unpublished folio *Australia Terra Cognita* by William Blandowski. 1855-56 etching, engraving and lavis, printed in black ink, from one copper plate printed image 16.8 x 21.6 cm, plate-mark 21.4 x 28 cm, sheet 36 x 27 cm.

National Gallery of Australia. Canberra

>

Effect & Engraving by J. Radaway & Sons

Foot of Diogenes Monument
4 miles N. from Mount Macedon
40 miles N.W.N. from Melbourne.

cut off from their own people, and never accepted in the new Victoria Police.[24]

Within a decade from this abandonment, Aboriginal people around Hanging Rock had come into contact with a new wave of invaders — the gold diggers. The survival strategies available to them were radically altered, when the squatters themselves found their runs invaded, this time by gold miners. Roads to the major diggings ran north past Hanging Rock. Along these, diggers rushed to gold finds across Aboriginal lands, and over the runs claimed by squatters. From 1851 onwards, one gold strike after another brought a surge of mining hopefuls to the woodlands to the west and north of Hanging Rock. The diggers' intense swarming to new strikes, the rise of sudden town structures and their equally sudden collapse, suggest a different response from Aboriginal people to European modernity. Fred Cahir has pointed to the active engagement of Aboriginal clans with the first wave of diggers around major mining fields.[25] Aboriginal men and women guided diggers, bartered food, and educated the newcomers in killing, skinning and curing possum skins. Used as both rugs and coats, these skins became the hallmark of Victoria's itinerant gold seekers.

As the golden decade of the 1850s drew to a close, several observers had convinced themselves that the people of the clans, who not so long before used Hanging Rock as a ceremonial site, had vanished. When a committee of the Victorian parliament set out to trace Victoria's Aboriginal people in 1859, reports from towns near Hanging Rock assumed that all of the local families had gone. They had disappeared, not through the violence of squatters, but because of the chaos caused by a seemingly endless criss-crossing of frantic digging rushes in Aboriginal lands.

'As a race their history is a tale of the past', confidently asserted W.H.F. Mitchell before a Legislative Council Committee in 1859.[26] Mitchell had lived in and around Kyneton, to the north-west of Hanging Rock, until 1842. In those days he recalled, hundreds of Aboriginal families gathered together with at least fifty children. When he returned to the district in 1852, he could find no Aboriginal families at all, blaming the disappearance entirely on the gold rushes.[27] Another witness, William Lavender, recalled his travels in and around the Macedon Ranges, where he too thought that Aboriginal clans had entirely disappeared. 'Even in the forest of Mount Macedon . . . I have never heard of one being seen in my time' he announced.[28] Invariably, witness after witness simply assumed that the Kulin had vanished from the landscape. If witnesses were associated with pastoralism, they were generally inclined to blame this disappearance on gold miners. They may have found some support in Edward Dryden's communication with governor La Trobe. Dryden wrote that Aboriginal groups had visited his station on their travels through the district. About 150 local people were moving across traditional lands between Macedon and Mt Alexander, and Dryden claimed he always had good relations with the local people in the 1840s. A decade later, and European observers assumed that all of these 150 people had vanished, a consequence, or so it was understood, of gold mining.

But digging for gold was a short-term, highly mobile activity. The miners were transients, like the first sheep barons, and swarmed around a gold strike suddenly, to only disperse, with equal alacrity. It is not surprising then, to come across later recollections that pointed to several Aboriginal settlements in and around the towns on the Mt Alexander Road. These survived for long after the miners themselves had moved on. Tanner noted that in Gisborne in the 1870s residents recollected Aboriginal camps in some of the streets of the town.[29] The Europeans who claimed Aboriginal people had vanished were no doubt assuming that the survivors of the squatting and mining decades could not have simply retreated into a familiar landscape, hidden away from the few urban centres and roadways. When the Legislative Council's committee came to assess numbers of Aboriginal survivors in 1859, they concluded that there were nearly 500 Aboriginal people across Victoria gathered together and confined to missions. Those from around Macedon were initially placed at Acheron or Western Port, before being moved to Corranderk. Many others still lay beyond the reach of the missions. As Richard Broome pointed out, Aboriginal people found ways to survive in and around the colonial settlements of Victoria. According to Broome,

> Aboriginal battlers and 'wanderers' within the wider white society fought in their own way to be free aboriginal people: free to think, to move and to live as they wished.[30]

In 1859 the Legislative Council's committee concluded that all of these wanderers ought to be coerced into one or other of the colony's mission stations. 'No false sentimentality as to the supposed hardship of gathering in the Aborigines should be allowed to interfere with this step' asserted the committee members.[31] If the drive to bring all Aboriginal survivors onto such stations was commenced in 1859, then it was slow to produce results. A later inquiry in 1877 included a report on Aboriginal numbers in Victoria. Of just over one thousand Aboriginal individuals counted, little more than half were on the mission stations, with 135 at Corranderk, the station closest to Hanging Rock.[32] One Aboriginal man was listed as living in Romsey, to the east of Hanging Rock.

Many years later, well into the twentieth century, some of these Aboriginal people returned to traditional lands as itinerant workers. Recollections of farm life in Newham and Hesket included accounts of Aboriginal figures who turned up for harvest work or fruit picking. They lived with farming families each year, walked around the lands of their clans, and told stories of their history to fascinated local children. In the 1930s a troupe of Aboriginal people reached Romsey before heading towards Hanging Rock, and performing traditional skills for an interested local audience.

Places central to Aboriginal life remained constant reminders of a deep connection with the landscape. Nowhere was this more so that at Mt William (Wil-im-ee Moor-ing), a site closely linked to Hanging Rock through the greenstone trade. Some forty years after Blandowski's campaigns for fair treatment of Aboriginal people, greenstone artifacts were discovered in quarries at nearby Mt William. The discoveries set off a renewed, if sometimes patronising concern for the Aboriginal history of lands around Hanging Rock. Baldwin Spencer representing the Museum of Victoria, and members of the Historical Society of Victoria had tried to persuade the state government to buy the quarry in 1910. Before long however, the Mt William discoveries, and knowledge of their integration into the ceremonial and trading spaces around Hanging Rock, were subsumed under a drive to once again erase any memory of Aboriginal prior ownership. One anonymous poet in 1913, for example, had published his tribute to a prehistoric, volcanic Hanging Rock in a local newspaper. He rounded out his verse by reflecting on Aboriginal occupation of the landmark. The Rock, he wrote, had witnessed Aboriginal people 'disappear from their country's bright face' so that Hanging Rock was ultimately 'a monument to the departed race'. Then the poet concluded with a sense of dread and guilt:

> Let us hope nature won't seek to avenge the dead
> And people this land with a dark race again.[33]

There are no doubt traces of a romantic and sublime terror in this imagery. And the verse was written soon after renewed awareness of local Aboriginal culture, derived from the Mt William quarry. The reflections of A.W. Howitt on Aboriginal Victoria had also turned attention to local trade in axeheads and other stone tools.[34] The Aboriginal quarries at Mt William, together with the finds of other artifacts at the Camel's Hump, inspired further reflection on the cultural role of Hanging Rock in Aboriginal networks, of which twentieth century Europeans in Australia had only a limited grasp. The quarry however, once seen in connection to Hanging Rock, provided tangible evidence of Aboriginal industry and trading structures.

Early in the twentieth century, the 'Mt William Stone Quarry' was acknowledged as a gathering place for Aboriginal trading from as far afield as Geelong and Corio Bay.[35] As knowledge of the extent of trading in the greenstone artifacts from the quarry became better known, with greenstones from the Macedon Ranges and Mt William

SCENERY AT MOUNT MACEDON.—SEE PAGE 8.

Scenery at Mount Macedon. Wood engraving. The Illustrated Melbourne Post, 25 April, 1863. State Library of Victoria

discovered as far away as Warrnambool, the Mt William greenstone quarry won interest as far more than a curiosity. Allen Cameron, manager of the Commercial Bank at Romsey and Lancefield, and for a time licensee of the Romsey Hotel, was elected as the Liberal Party member for Dalhousie in 1914. Cameron had heard many stories about the stone quarry and its greenstone axeheads. He demanded over and over again that the state government buy the site, and open it up to the public, to be a 'monument...and a landmark of great historic interest'.[36] Concern to recognise Aboriginal history no doubt drove Cameron in his campaign. He was, though, just as keen on using the 'landmark' to build up local tourism.

Cameron died before this proposal won any support from local councillors. His plan for an historic monument to Aboriginal culture died with him. Later visitors, aware of the cultural and industrial significance of Mt William as of Camel's Hump and Hanging Rock, noted the destructive impact of white 'civilisation' on such indigenous industries. Typically they then went on to extol the tourism qualities of the broader landscape rather than the quarries themselves.[37] Delegates to the Centenary Science Congress in 1935 visited both Mt William and Hanging Rock, their interest partly piqued by the unique geology, although extended to the Aboriginal history of the region. In the previous year a small band of Aboriginal people travelled through the district and talked to interested white listeners about the history of the quarry, the trading networks and cultural role of places like Hanging Rock. But the local newspaper reported that the quarry

> Is rapidly losing its attraction as a historic locality. It is many years since operations were carried on there by the first inhabitants of Australia, and to the present day tourist the quarry is just a place from which stone has been taken, no matter by whom, or for what purpose.[38]

'The up-to-date sightseer yearns for something more than a deserted quarry' insisted the reporter, before advising motorists and hikers to head to Kilmore and the 'fern creeks of Tantaraboo'.[39]

CUSTODIANS

For many years this continued connection, even if occasionally obscured, was ignored by historians and others. Many were quick to see Aboriginal society as completely overwhelmed and tradition and knowledge lost. The forced removal of local people to distant mission settlements seemed to spell the end of attachment to traditional land. Yet, as early as 1840, Mount Macedon Aboriginal families, who had been pushed out to the coast of Port Phillip, were demanding that government officials return them to their own lands. William Thomas had taken several Mount Macedon families to a settlement at Arthur's Seat, along with Aboriginal clans from Western Port. No sooner had they arrived at Arthur's Seat, than the Mount Macedon families were asking to go back to their own lands. Thomas seemed convinced by their deep attachment to country. Allowing for the problem that the families could only travel eight or nine miles each day 'having their food to procure', he proposed that he might go with them, across the ninety miles to their own lands.[40] Such a powerful attachment to place can never fully disappear. Some European observers reflect on Aboriginal occupation and then turn to asserting that all local Aboriginal people have vanished, or that the last inter-tribal gathering at Hanging Rock had taken place, perhaps, in 1851. But then Blandowski's writings seem to suggest that local traditional practices had continued into 1854 at least. Aboriginal figures were depicted in etchings of Hanging Rock in 1865. Aboriginal returns to the district were noted in the inter-war years. And from the time of new legislation for Aboriginal ownership of former missions in Victoria in 1970, attention has been turned to continuing Aboriginal connection to place. The greenstone hatchet quarrying and trading drew the interest of archaeologists such as Isabel McBryde from 1976 onwards. Then, an initial listing of Hanging Rock on the Register of the National Estate proposed that the contemporary popularity of the place, could not be understood without acknowledging, at some deep level, the Aboriginal cosmology of the site.

Nor have Aboriginal people vanished from the localities around Hanging Rock. Whereas nineteenth century census takers could only

W. v. Blandowski, Australia.

Effect & Engraving by J. Redaway & Sons

Browns Dos a Dos,
near Mount Macedon 45 m. N by W from Melbourne

find one thousand Aboriginal people across the whole of Victoria, in 2011, census takers estimated that there were over 200 Aboriginal residents in the Shire of Macedon Ranges alone.[41] As with other local government areas across Victoria, the shire now has a set of protocols for engaging with Aboriginal people, and for cultural protocols as regards Aboriginal cultural heritage sites.[42] In 2012, the Wil-im-ee Moor-ing/Mount William stone hatchet quarry was returned to its traditional owners.

Fascination with the quarry, and with the wider cultural networks which embraced Hanging Rock, may have fallen away not long after the centenary year of the State of Victoria (1934). But within five decades interest in the cosmology and industry of the quarry, Camel's Hump and Hanging Rock had certainly revived. [43] Both the quarry and Hanging Rock are recognised in official heritage databases for their significance to Aboriginal people; a cultural importance without which other assessments of significance cannot be made. The most recent management proposals for Hanging Rock acknowledge the rights of traditional owners to have a strong voice in the future of the Rock. Professional heritage studies now take Aboriginal history seriously. In 1859 the Kyneton witness to Aboriginal life around Hanging Rock and across the wider Macedon region, could confidently assert that the history of Aboriginal people was 'a tale of the past'. In the 21st century, no such assertion can be made. There may well be broad gaps in our knowledge of the Aboriginal history of Hanging Rock. But this deep and enduring story, can no longer be put to one side as an entirely lost history. ✪

Browns Dos a Dos, near Mount Macedon 45m N by W from Melbourne. 1855-56.
William Blandowski, print after James Redaway & Sons, engraver active Australia 1852–59. From the unpublished folio *Australia Terra Cognita* by William Blandowski. 1855-56etching, engraving and lavis, printed in black ink, from one copper plate printed image 16.8 x 21.6 cm, plate-mark 21.4 x 28 cm, sheet 36 x 27 cm.
National Gallery of Australia, Canberra

<

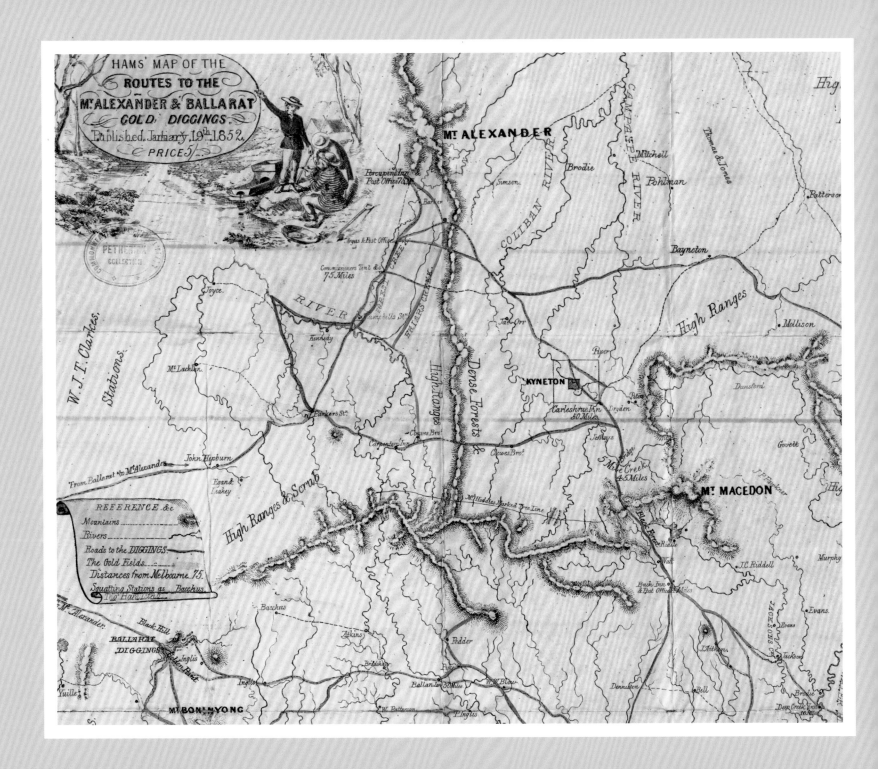

HAMS' MAP OF THE
ROUTES TO THE
Mt ALEXANDER & BALLARAT
GOLD DIGGINGS
Published January 19th 1852,
PRICE 5

Mt ALEXANDER

CAMPASPE RIVER
COLIBAN RIVER

Thomas & Jones
Mitchell
Brodie
Pohlman
Patterson
Simson
Bayneton
Porcupine Inn &
Post Office 74 M

Barker

Ingas & Post Office

Joyce
Commissioners Tent &c
75 Miles
Jas Orr
High Ranges
Mollison

RIVER
Campbells Sta
Kennedy
Piper
Dunsford

FREESTONE CREEK
FRIARS CREEK

W.J.T. Clarkes.
Stations
McLachlan
High Ranges
KYNETON
Peter
Dryden

Parkers Sta
Carlesbrue Inn
50 Miles
Jeffreys

Clowes Bro
Govett
Carpenters Inn
Clowes Bro
5 Mile Creek
45 Miles

From Ballarat to McAlexander
John Hepburn
Egan &
Leahey
Mt MACEDON

High Ranges & Scrub
Mt Hoddles Marked Tree Line
Black Pore
Riddle
Watt

REFERENCE &c
Mountains _____
Rivers _____
Roads to the DIGGINGS _____
The Gold Fields _____
Distances from Melbourne 75 _____
Squatting Stations as Bacchus _____
The Ham Lith

Bush Inn
& Post Office Miles

Mt Alexander
Black Hill
Bacchus
J. Atkins
Evans
BALLARAT
DIGGINGS
Zikins
Padder
J.C. Riddell
Murphy
Inglis
Golden Point
Bridekirk
Port
Jackson
Inglis
Ballan Inn 30 Miles
W.W. Blow
Dennison
Yuille
W. Patterson
T. Inglis
Bell
Brodie
Mt BONINYONG
Deep Creek Inn

Road making in the Black Forest near Mt. Macedon, Victoria, N.S.W., 1853 – Morning.
T. G. Taylor. Oil on canvas. 39.5 x 55.2 cm.

State Library of Victoria

Section of *Hams' map of the routes to the
Mt. Alexander & Ballarat gold diggings.*
Thomas Ham & Co. 1852.

National Library of Australia (Bib Id 3572503)

<

Printed in Colors by

Hamel & Ferguson Melb.ne

NATIVE POLICE.

Last of Victorian Aborigines — Corranderk

Endnotes

[1] Assistant Protector Barker to G.A Robinson, Chief Protector, 26 October 1840, Inwards Correspondence, Chief Protector of Aborigines, VPRS 11/P0000/4/146, Public Record Office Victoria.

[2] Richard Broome, *Aboriginal Victorians: A history since 1800*, Allen and Unwin, Crows Nest, NSW, 2005: 69.

[3] See Dr Vincent Clark and Associates, 'Hanging Rock Archaeology', http://vincentclark.com.au/2013/11/archaeology-at-hanging-rock/ (viewed April 2017).

[4] Mount William Stone Hatchet Quarry, Australian Heritage Database, 105936, 30 January 2007, Australian Government, Department of Environment, Water, Heritage and the Arts.

[5] I. McBryde and A. Watchman, A., 'The distribution of greenstone axes in southeastern Australia: a preliminary report', *The Australian Journal of Anthropology*, vol. 10 no.3: 163, 1976; and I. McBryde, 'Kulin greenstone quarries: the social contexts of production and distribution for the Mt William site', *World Archaeology*, vol. 16 no. 2, 1984: 267-85.

[6] Robert Hoddle, 'A chapter on Port Phillip', *Port Phillip Gazette*, 31 July 1841: 7

[7] W Bland, ed., *Journal of Discovery to Port Phillip*, Queensberry Hill Press, Carlton South, 1985.

[8] W. Gammage, *The Biggest Estate on Earth*: 219, Allen and Unwin, Crows Nest NSW, 2011.

[9] Thomas Mitchell, *Three Expeditions into the Interior of Eastern Australia: with descriptions of the recently explored region of Australia Felix and of the present colony of New South Wales*, T.W. Boone, London,1839.

[10] D. W. Baker, *The Civilised Surveyor: Thomas Mitchell and the Australian Aborigines*, Melbourne University Press, Carlton, Vic., 1997: 195

[11] Harry Allen, *William Blandowski's Illustrated Encyclopaedia of Aboriginal Australia*, Aboriginal Studies Press, Canberra, 2010, plate 48. See too Khadija von Zinnenburg Carroll, 'What would Indigenous Taxonomy Look Like? The Case of Blandowski's Australia', *Arcadia*, 12, 2014 Rachel Carson Center for Environment and Society, http://www.environmentandsociety.org/node/6292 , (viewed March 2017) and Mary Mackay, 'Singularity and the Sublime in Australian Landscape Representation', *Literature & Aesthetics*, 8, 2011.

[12] 'The aborigines of Victoria', *Age*,19 October 1854: 8.

[13] Richard Broome, *Aboriginal Victorians: A history since 1800*, Allen and Unwin, Crow's Nest NSW, 2005.

[14] Broome, *Aboriginal Victorians*: 55. The decade referred to is that roughly from 1836 to 1845.

[15] Rachel Tanner, '"What Aborigines". The History of the Gunung Willam Balluk of the Macedon Region: Pre-settlement to the Year 2001', Bachelor of Arts Honours Thesis, Monash University, 2001, Box 4668/13, held at Manuscripts, State Library of Victoria.

[16] Broome, *Aboriginal Victorians*: 75.

[17] For more detail see Broome, *Aboriginal Victorians*.

[18] See generally Tanner 'What Aborigines' and Broome, *Aboriginal Victorians*.

[19] 'Melbourne', *Geelong Advertiser*, 22 May 1841: 4.

[20] *Geelong Advertiser*, 22 May 1841:4.

[21] James Dredge to G.A. Robinson, Chief Protector, 23 July 1839, Unregistered Inwards Correspondence, Chief Protector of Aborigines, VPRS 11/P0000/1/25, PROV.

[22] *South Australian Colonist and Settlers' Weekly Record and Melbourne Patriot*

[23] Tanner, 'What Aborigines'.

[24] Robert Haldane, *The people's force: a history of the Victoria Police*, Melbourne University Press, Melbourne, 1986.

[25] Fred Cahir, *Black gold: Aboriginal people on the goldfields of Victoria*, 1850-1870. ANU Press, Canberra, 2013.

[26] W.H.F. Mitchell, Minutes of Evidence, *Proceedings of the Committee Inquiring in to the Aborigines, Legislative Council*, Victoria, 1859: 85.

[27] Mitchell, Evidence: 85.

[28] William Lavender, Evidence, *Committee on Aborigines*: 85.

[29] Tanner, 'What Aborigines'.

[30] Broome, *Aboriginal Victorians*:165

[31] *Report of the Committee on Aborigines in the Colony*, Legislative Council, 1859: xii.

[32] Census Return, 15 March 1877, in *Royal Commission on the Aborigines, Report, Minutes of Evidence and Appendices*, Parliament of Victoria, 1877.

[33] Anon (C.W.L.), *McIvor Times and Rodney Advertiser*, 25 December 1913: 3.

[34] A.W.Howitt, *The Native Tribes of South-East Australia*, Macmillan London, 1904.

[35] *The McIvor Times and Rodney Advertiser*, 14 June 1906: 2.

[36] 'Perambulator', *Kilmore Free Press*, 10 March 1921: 2.

[37] ' Mount William Visited', *Kilmore Free Press*, 26 April 1928: 2.

[38] *Kilmore Free Press*, 25 October 1934: 4.

[39] 'Mount William Visited', *Kilmore Free Press*.

[40] William Thomas, Assistant Protector, Western Port, to G.A. Robinson, Chief Protector, 3 July 1840, Unregistered Inwards Correspondence, Chief Protector of Aborigines, VPRS 11/P0000/7/315, Public Record Office Victoria.

[41] Australian Bureau of Statistics, *Census of the Commonwealth of Australia, 2011*, Regional Data Macedon Region.

[42] Macedon Ranges Shire Council, *Organisational Protocols for Recognising Traditional Owners/Custodians*, n.d.

[43] Gary Presland, 'How Aboriginal Studies ceased to be part of natural history',*Victorian Naturalist*, 124, no. 3, 2007: 157, and Isabel McBryde, 'Exchange in south eastern Australia: an ethnohistorical perspective', *Aboriginal History* , 1984: 132-53. See too Jim Poulter, *Sharing Heritage in Kulin Country, Lessons in Reconciliation from our First Contact History*, Red Hen, Melbourne, 2011.

Mt William greenstone axe head, partially ground.
Photograph by Matthew Nickson.
The Romsey and Lancefield Districts Historical Society

Diogenes Monument "Anneyelong" looking Sth towards Mt Macedon. W. V. Blandowski. Effect & engraving by J. Redaway & Sons.
From the unpublished folio *Australia Terra Cognita* by William Blandowski. 1855-56. plate mark 20.8 x 27.7 cm. State Library of Victoria

Volcanic Wilderness

Relic of an age long past

The Hanging Rock on its pedestal passive

Through the terrestrial upheavals sat fast

One of nature's curious massive

At one time washed by the ocean

But still it kept its place

In the huge waves' powerful motion

While the sea surged round its base

Anon (C.W.L.), McIvor Times and Rodney Advertiser, 25 December 1913: 3

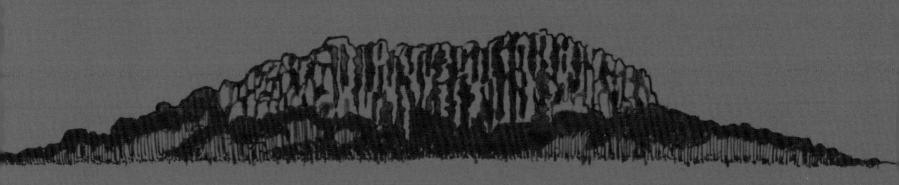

Once Wilhelm von Blandowski, newly-appointed official Victorian Zoologist, had set up camp in the Macedon Ranges in 1854, he rode off towards nearby Hanging Rock. As the Rock came into sight, Blandowski, like visitors ever since, was struck by its pinnacles and rock walls. He left the first detailed description of Hanging Rock as

> One of the most remarkable spots in the country . . . an almost perpendicular wall of dolerite, of deep somber hue, rising above the most lofty of the trees, imparts a strikingly picturesque character to the view. Approaching the monument, the interest increases at every step . . . at the foot of the monument, about a thousand pyramidal columns rise in bold relief from the surface, giving to the hill, which is about one mile in circumference at the base, a kind of giant porcupine appearance.[1]

Blandowski later recalled that gaps between the rock slabs were so narrow that he had to dismount from his horse to get through. Like the NSW-based explorers of the 1820s and 1830s, he recorded wildlife and plants in the ranges around the Rock. Unlike these exploring overlanders, who had by-passed Hanging Rock in their rush to the southern coast, he tried hard to explain its odd characteristics. Blandowski eventually decided that Hanging Rock had been thrown up in two distinct volcanic explosions, an idea which resonated through geological accounts of the Rock for more than half a century.

Hanging Rock certainly continued to fascinate observers over the decades that followed, although they too struggled to explain its origins. Like the anonymous bush poet whose words appear at the start of this chapter, many imagined that Hanging Rock was once an island in some vast prehistoric ocean. They were not alone in this theory of 'Neptunism', or the belief that the planet had been entirely covered by oceans, above which volcanic peaks took millions of years to surface. Only in the early twentieth century did the geological history of the Rock become clear. It took even longer for natural scientists to recognise the value of the flora and fauna of the Rock and its Reserve. Today, Hanging Rock itself, and any surviving wildlife

and plants on the Reserve, are highly valued. The Rock is not under any immediate threat, although not so long ago it was viewed as a useful site for excavating construction materials. Trees, cut down unthinkingly in the past, are now being replaced. Today it is the wildlife of the Reserve, especially the smaller marsupials, which are under stress.

Blandowski had sought, in his later writings, to understand connections between plants, animals and Aboriginal beliefs. Such a radical respect for an indigenous taxonomy probably contributed to his eventual falling out with others in the tiny scientific community of gold rush Melbourne. Is it possible that in the 21st century, his views on Hanging Rock's natural environment can be resurrected? Might they enable a reconciliation of Aboriginal and European connections to the cultural landscape of Hanging Rock? An answer may perhaps be found in the way Europeans have tried to comprehend the natural history of Hanging Rock, its geology, its vegetation and its animal life.

SURVEYORS

In 1824, the expeditioners Hamilton Hume and William Hovell pushed southwards from the frontiers of NSW's European settlements. Between October 1824 and January 1825, with their horses, bullock teams and servants, they left British outposts behind, and rode in what they trusted was the general direction of Port Phillip, far away to the south.[2] Hume, the adventurous Parramatta-born bushman, and the Englishman, Hovell, a one-time ship's captain, were intent on locating a clear pathway for the invasion of British sheep owners.[3] Following tracks beaten down by Aboriginal families and hunters, they travelled with dogs for killing wildlife. They loaded packsaddles onto their cattle, and commanded a staff of bearers. They recorded the water flows of rivers and estimated the heights of mountains, bestowing their or their relatives' names on several such landmarks. The explorers fought with each other, at one time over a frying pan. They shot kangaroos and snakes, and left at least one loyal dog behind in the bush. Hume and Hovell's expedition eventually brought them near to Hanging Rock. Journeying southwards they climbed Mt

Disappointment, to the east, and then, on their return northwards, they passed closer to the Rock, finding a way through the Great Dividing Range at the 'Kilmore Gap'. As with many who followed them, their eyes turned to Hanging Rock's higher neighbour, which they named Mt Wentworth (later to be renamed Macedon). Their mistakes in confusing Westernport with Port Phillip only compounded the deep-seated contempt they held for each other, amplified in rival journals of the expedition, which they separately published.

A more meticulous survey of Australia Felix, or the lands settled over many thousands of years by several Aboriginal peoples to the south of the Murray River, was carried out a decade later, under the guidance of an assistant surveyor and later Surveyor-General of NSW, Major Thomas Livingstone Mitchell.[4] Mitchell owed his colonial career to his standing as a veteran of the Iberian campaigns against Napoleon, for which he had made military maps.[5] He too passed by Hanging Rock and climbed Mt Macedon instead. He had set out from Sydney with 24 men, at least two of whom were transported murderers, and a second-in-command whose company he loathed. Each one of Mitchell's ex-criminal staffers was equipped with pistol and carbine. One band he detailed solely to carry barometers, and like Hume and Hovell before them, these expeditioners travelled with a full animal complement, including packhorses, sheep, bullocks and cattle. As this cavalcade trundled south, Mitchell grew more estranged from the men under his soldierly command. Instead of their advice, he came to rely for almost every decision on his Aboriginal mentors, in particular Piper, who had been with him since he set out from Bathurst.[6]

Mitchell, rather than his adviser Piper, is routinely revered in local histories. And he almost certainly was the first European to venture into the Macedon Ranges, although, even if he did see Hanging Rock, he did not give it a great deal of thought. Mitchell left his main party in September 1836, to find a vantage point from which to view Port Phillip. He was then able to climb a gradual slope up Mt Macedon, where unlike Blandowski at Hanging Rock, he realised that he could reach the summit without even getting off his horse.[7] Once there, Mitchell found that mountain ash and tree ferns were blocking his view southwards. So he spent the night on the plateau, and next morning set up his theodolite. Standing on a flat rock, he thought he could make out Port Phillip, even though the view to the distant coast included 'no stockyards, cattle, or even smoke'.[8] Some white shapes suggested tents and a rough settlement. So, Mitchell concluded his measurements, took in the view southwards for a last time, and set off to resume command of his 'small army'. Thomas Mitchell continued his return journey to Sydney and a celebrated colonial career. Heading northwards, he recorded mountains and hills between Macedon and the Cobaw Range, perhaps seeing, although not making any special reference to Hanging Rock.

Preferring Aboriginal names for his discoveries, Mitchell nonetheless named the peak he had climbed Macedon, in deference to the elusive vista of Port Phillip, and the classical Grecian hero, Phillip of Macedon. It was left to a later surveyor, and one with little love for Mitchell, to name Hanging Rock as 'Diogenes Mount'. Robert Hoddle had worked under the NSW Surveyor-General, John Oxley, for more than a decade. But when Mitchell arrived in the colony as Oxley's replacement, he made his disdain for this deputy, Hoddle, plain. ' A man who can scarcely spell' he raged. Hoddle correctly surmised that he had little future in Sydney and took up the position of government surveyor in Port Phillip.[9] Lauded, perhaps a little too generously for his role in setting out the Melbourne city grid, Hoddle also mapped the Macedon region as a part of the task of setting boundaries to the County of Bourke.[10] Hoddle may well have been a man who could 'scarcely spell'. But it was he, rather than his overbearing superior, who first fixed Hanging Rock in the British topography of Australia. Hoddle set out on a survey march from Carlsruhe, heading north. His line took him to the east of Hanging Rock which he surveyed in late March 1843.[11] And Hoddle turned, as had Mitchell, to classical Greece, to name Hanging Rock as Diogenes. His allusion seems unlikely to have been a mark of respect for his old boss. For the Diogenes after whom Hanging Rock was named had invented philosophical 'Cynicism'. Diogenes spent most of his adult life ridiculing celebrated heroes of classical

Map of the south east portion of Australia, shewing the progress of discovery, in the interior of New South Wales, by Major Mitchell, Survr. Genl. of the colony. Australia Felix is probably the first reference to the term "Lucky Australia" and refers to the lush pasture of western Victoria and its potential for sheep grazing. Drawn & engraved by J. Arrowsmith. 1837.

State Library of New South Wales

Portrait of Sir Thomas Livingstone Mitchell, c.1830s.
Oil on canvas, artist unknown, frame 103 x 87 cm.

State Library of New South Wales

Silver coffee pot presented to Major Mitchell on his discovery of Australia Felix
by London merchants. 1839. State Library of New South Wales

Inscription reads 'On the discovery of Australia Felix 1836'. State Library of New South Wales

Greece, Phillip of Macedon included. Not that any of this mattered all that much. Hard-bitten Victorian colonists displayed scant respect for the classics. Since Edward Dryden had grabbed a sheep run around Hanging Rock in the 1830s, this odd outcrop was soon known popularly as Dryden's Monument or Dryden's Rock.[12]

Scientific interest in Macedon, the surrounding ranges and eventually Hanging Rock/ Dryden's Monument remained centred on trigonometric accuracy. Hoddle and others turned to the relatively new technique of 'triangulation' (Great Britain's major triangulation exercise, the Ordnance Survey was only completed in 1853) to plot these and other locations.[13] In passing they noticed the character of rocks and soil. Mitchell, more thoroughly than others, recorded weather, water sources and animal life. Intermittently he remarked on rock formations referring generally to the volcanic origins of 'traprocks', or what we would now regard as basalt. More detailed understanding of Hanging Rock came from Alfred Selwyn. Selwyn had worked on the massive Ordnance Survey of Britain, studied glaciation in Wales and then surveyed British coalfields.[14] He arrived in Melbourne in 1852 as Geological Surveyor to the new colony of Victoria. Quickly training a small staff, he set about producing a set of detailed geological maps, later rated as equal in quality to any produced in the world for that time. Selwyn mapped out the region around Hanging Rock, emphasising the differences in geological formation between the rocks and soils to the north and the south of the Great Dividing Range. His summary essay pointed to the distinctive volcanic character of Hanging Rock as 'varieties of feldspar and quartz-porphyries'.[15] Yet, within a decade of his writing this report, the Victorian government terminated the survey.[16] Selwyn left Victoria, eventually taking up the position of director of the Geological Survey of Canada. It was left to Blandowski, another, later disgruntled employee of the Geological Survey, to leave us with a more complete picture of Dryden's Monument.

GEOLOGISTS

William Blandowski, like Selwyn, would eventually abandon Victoria, after disputes with colonial superiors and fellow scientists. Professor Frederick McCoy of the then very new University of Melbourne was amongst his most bitter opponents. Blandowski worked for a while as an assistant to Selwyn on the Geological Survey, before winning the post of official colonial zoologist and founding Director of the Museum of Victoria (although that role was never made entirely clear, to Bandowski's later detriment). He described Dryden's Monument for a popular readership (his travel notes of 1854 were syndicated through a series of newspapers and magazines) and for scientific gatherings in his role at the museum, and in lectures to Melbourne learned societies. Blandowski had hoped as well, to publish his drawings through a book that would take 'Unknown Australia' to the world. The man who so eloquently pictured Hanging Rock was born in Gliewitz, Silesia (Germany and later in Poland) in 1822. For a time he studied in a military academy before dropping out, turning to geology, and setting himself up as a mining engineer. Caught up at least on the periphery of the 1848 revolution in Berlin, he fled to Australia. William Blandowski arrived in 1849, to eventually find his way to the goldfields. Once there, unlike most other gold-diggers, Blandowski made a small fortune at mining.[17] Whilst on the Mt Alexander goldfield he even found time to invent a new type of water pump.[18] As a naturalist rather than miner, Blandowski's most celebrated expedition was to the Murray region in 1856-57. But before then he had spent several months recording the environs of Macedon, Cobaw and Hanging Rock.

William Blandowski was intent on collecting plant and animal specimens and gathered more than 17,000 in one expedition alone. But he is better remembered for rare and valuable drawings of local Aboriginal life. He included Aboriginal figures in at least one of his scenes of Hanging Rock. These, and other illustrations, many of which were the work of his assistants, Gustav Mützel and Johann Krefft, rather than Blandowski himself, he had converted to engravings by John Redaway in Melbourne (and later by engravers in Germany).[19] Blandowski's dream was to produce a richly illustrated volume of

Australian landforms, bird and animal life. More importantly, he had hoped to create a full record of Aboriginal life and arts, at a moment when he feared these would be lost forever. After a series of disputes, he was removed as museum director. McCoy snatched much of his collection, removing the bounty to the new university. Blandowski did though manage to take a cache of drawings and specimens with him to Germany. Eventually, some results of his work were published, although by then Blandowski had little hope of either making a fortune from this books, or resurrecting his geological career. He was committed to a psychiatric institution in Silesia, where he died in 1878.

Blandowski's survey of Dryden's Monument, and of the surrounding countryside, led him to conclude that the Rock's unusual character could be explained by successive volcanic upheavals. Like others he began by explaining the broader geology of the region:

> The basalt formation extends about four miles westwards of Lancefield, but is then interrupted by slate and milky quartz, strongly indicative of auriferous strata. Still further westward these are succeeded by dolerite, which extends over Alexander's Head, Mount Macedon, and Dryden's Monument.[20]

Blandowski went on to reflect on what seemed the unique volcanic origins of Hanging Rock. He thought that the shape of the Rock could be traced to two distinct eruptions. He further proposed that the 'plasticity' of whatever material was hurled upwards in the two magma upheavals failed to spread into a lava flow and instead settled and cooled in the one place 'That this hill was formed by subterraneous agency, acting at two separate periods, there can be little doubt', he asserted.[21]

The unique cylindrical columns of the Rock's walls he imagined were shaped by water flowing into the softened volcanic stone, which then hollowed out the cylinders before spreading around the base. Blandowski did come close to discovering the critical aspect of Hanging Rock's rare history. Rather than lava and rock being forced

to the surface through a subterranean chimney and forming a peak or elevated crater, Hanging Rock's thick magma had congealed and so held rocks in a pile around a vent at ground level. This strange form had only been defined in 1798, by the French naturalist, Jean Baptiste Bory de Saint-Vincent.[22] Hanging Rock was thus the product of rare volcanic processes; a surface vent, thick lava flows and piled rock; a process that produced one of the planet's rare 'mamelons'.[23]

Mary Mackay remarked that Blandowski's engravings of Hanging Rock suggest that 'geological understandings in the fifties (1850s) had not totally overcome strongly held beliefs of the power of unstable forces ruling the earth'.[24] If, as she proposed, Hanging Rock was 'a mystery that science (had) not yet penetrated', there were clear reasons for such uncertainty. Geological science was in a state of constant revision in the nineteenth century, and not until the first radiometric dating experiments in 1907, by the Yale scientist Bertram Boltwood, were disputes about the age of the planet dispelled, and the nature of volcanic activity modified.[25] Just a few years before Mitchell set out for Australia Felix, Charles Lyell's *Principles of Geology* (1830-33) opened the way for new geological perspectives.[26] Lyell, for example, was the first to define the epoch in which Hanging Rock was formed, some six million years earlier, as the Miocene.[27] Lyell also succeeded in turning some volcano experts away from the then dominant view of 'catastrophism', sometimes Neptunism, in which massive aquatic events, possibly deluges such as Noah's Flood, shaped the globe.[28]

Disputes about the age of the planet raged on into the second half of the nineteenth century. Since Lyell was an associate of Charles Darwin, his geology could seem tainted by the Darwinian notion of human origins in the 'monkey world', rather than in Almighty God's instant creation. So, some Australian clergy and their flocks clung assiduously to the six-thousand-year span of the Bible, as the age of the planet. Others were prepared to accept a history of millions, if not billions of years. Around the gold fields to the north of Hanging Rock, one self-taught mining analyst claimed that electric arcs linking up around the globe, had produced both volcanic eruptions and rich gold deposits.

Portrait of Robert Hoddle, c.1840s.
Unknown photographer. Papers of G. B. Pritchard.

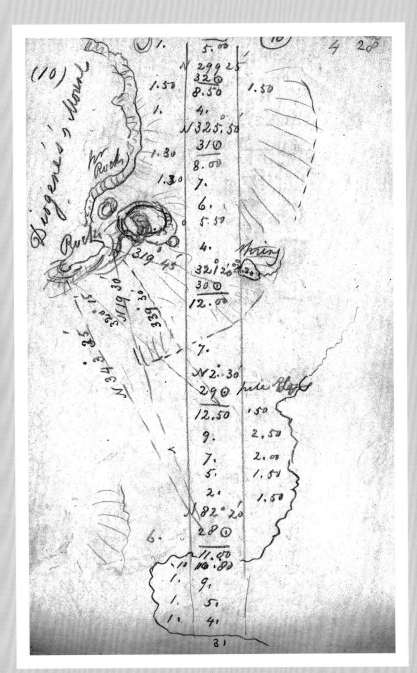

First recording of Diogenes Mount. Robert Hoddle, March, 1843. Robert Hoddle, Field Book, Bundle 79, Book 1155, page 31-52, VPRS 16685/P0001, Survey Department, PROV.

Mt Macedon and surrounding area. Robert Hoddle, March, 1843.
Robert Hoddle, Field Book, Bundle 79, Book 1155, page 31-52, VPRS 16685/P0001, Survey Department, PROV.

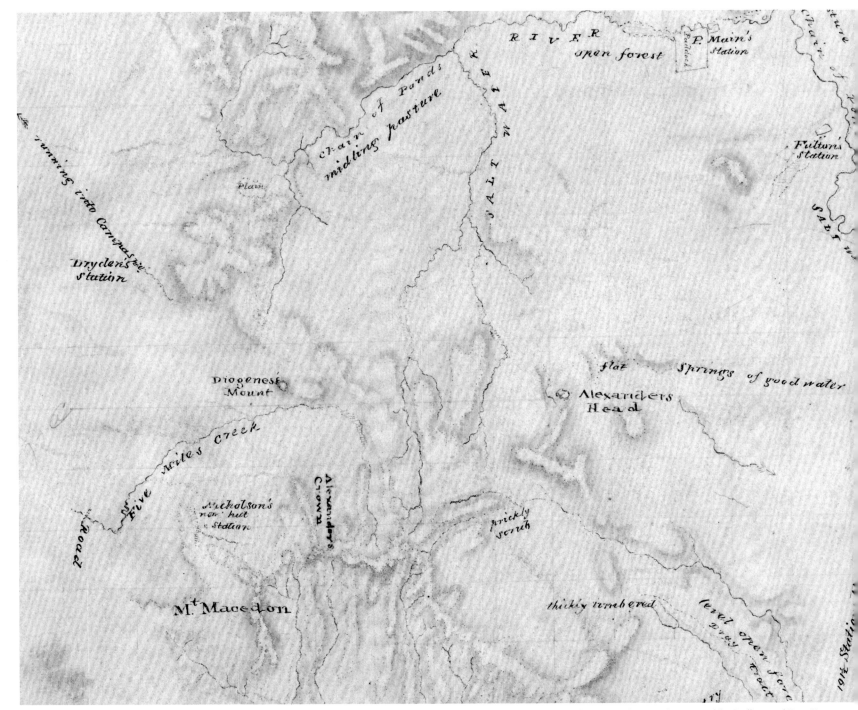

Section of *"Plan shewing the Ranges from Mount Macedon to Kilmore which separates the waters of Saltwater River Campaspe & also the Dividing Ranges between the waters of the Goulburn and Yarra Yarra Surveyed and drawn by Robert Hoddle 1844"*. 15899 Loddon 72 C Macedon Ranges , VPRS 8168, Survey Department, PROV. Public Record Office Victoria

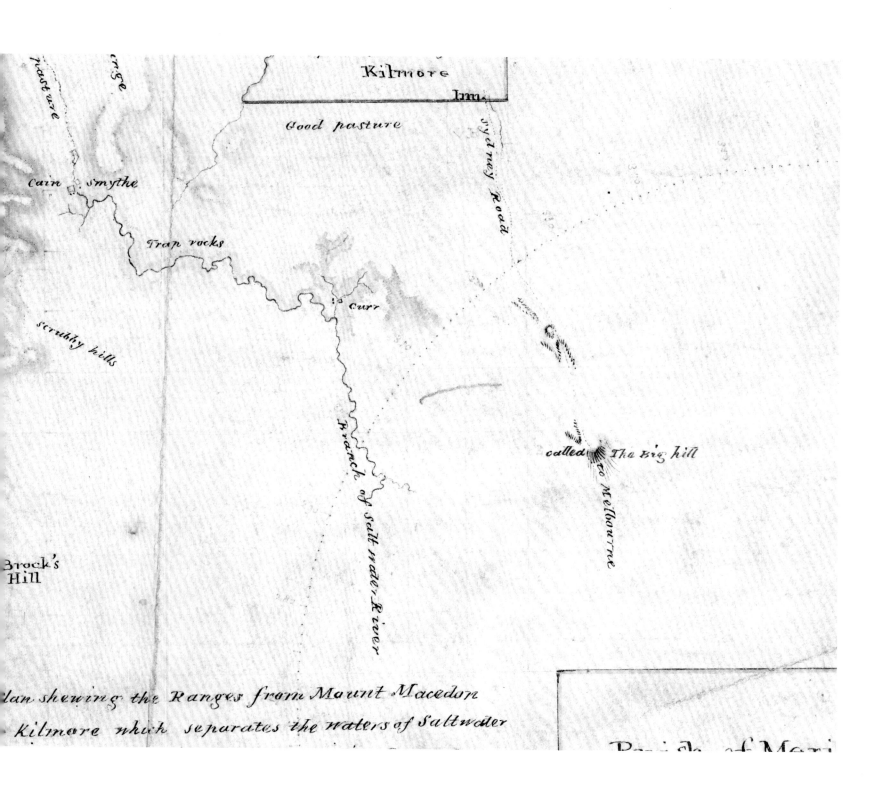

Kilmore

Inn

Good pasture

Sydney Road

Cain Smythe

Trap rocks

Curr

scrubby hills

Branch of Salt water River

called to Melbourne

The Big hill

Brock's
Hill

Plan shewing the Ranges from Mount Macedon

Kilmore which separates the waters of Saltwater

Parish of Meri

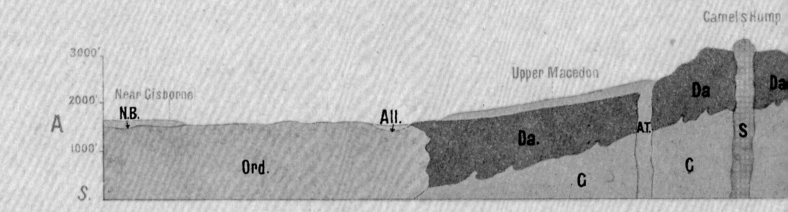

Camel's Hump

Upper Macedon

Near Gisborne

3000'

2000'

1000'

A

S.

N.B.

All.

Da.

Da.

Da.

Da.

AT.

S.

Ord.

G

G

G

SCALE { Hori
        { Ver

REF.

Alt.	H.W.	K	Ord.	
Alluvium.	Hill Wash.	Kainozoic. Grits and Quartzites.	Ordovician. Slates, Sandstones and Conglomerates.	Buc

A.B.2.	A.B.I.	B.T.	S.T.	
Macedonite.	Anorthoclase Basalt.	Olivine Anorthoclase Trachyte.	Anorthoclase Olivine Trachyte.	S

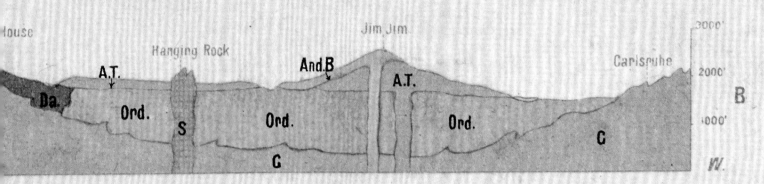

HROUGH Mt MACEDON

House

Jim Jim

Hanging Rock

And.B

A.T.

A.T.

Carlsruhe

Da.

Ord.

Ord.

Ord.

S

G

B

W.

3000'

2000'

1000'

iles to 1 inch
eet to 1 inch

NCE

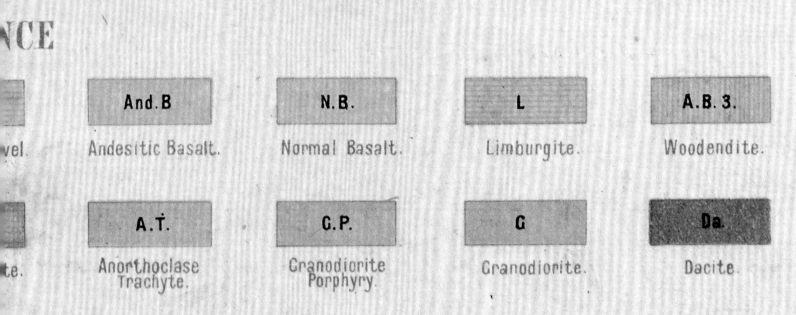

And.B	N.B.	L	A.B.3.
Andesitic Basalt.	Normal Basalt.	Limburgite.	Woodendite.

A.T.	G.P.	G	Da.
Anorthoclase Trachyte.	Granodiorite Porphyry.	Granodiorite.	Dacite.

Geological Map Of The Macedon District. Geologically Surveyed By E. W. Skeats And H. S. Summers. Geological Survey of Victoria, 1912. State Library of Victoria

These debates raged around Blandowski and other early interpreters of Victoria's surfaces and depths. Eventually, Blandowski found himself defending his theories from no less a critic than Selwyn, who disputed his account of volcanic formations near Melbourne. Despite these and other attacks, his scientific perspective survived. In fact Blandowski's account of Hanging Rock continued to be published in local newspapers into the twentieth century.[29]

In part, Blandowski was able to sway popular perceptions because natural scientists at the University of Melbourne had not shown much interest in places like Hanging Rock. Blandowski's nemesis in the 1850s, Professor Frederick McCoy, undermined his collecting at the museum, whilst taking almost no interest in his accounts of Aboriginal life. Gradually though, Edwardian geologists were able to modify Blandowski's double explosion theory about Hanging Rock. McCoy, described by one of his biographers as 'a naturalist who stayed indoors', was eventually succeeded at the university by John Gregory.[30] Gregory compiled a thorough geological and geographical account of Victoria.[31] He began research around Hanging Rock and identified the distinctive rock content as sölvsbergite. His brief career in Melbourne was ultimately shaped, not by local oddities like Hanging Rock, but rather by his fascination for the vast expanse he dubbed 'The Dead Heart': the inland deserts of central Australia.[32] In any case, dismayed by the failure of the state government and the university to fund geological studies, he only lasted four years in Melbourne. Once Gregory had left for Glasgow in 1904, his successor, Ernest Willington Skeats, was able to turn geological research back to central Victoria, and to places like Hanging Rock.

In 1910, E.W. Skeats defined the composition of Hanging Rock within a broader survey of Victorian geological history. After analysing Hanging Rock in a series of papers, he then summarised his findings in his presidential address to the geology section of the Australian Association for the Advancement of Science in Brisbane. Hanging Rock, he stated, was distinctive because of its age and composition,

rather than for the cylindrical columns that had so struck Blandowski. After reconstructing the billions of years of Australian geological change he described Hanging Rock:

> . . .The late volcanic rocks, nearly all basalt areas near Melbourne have been referred to the older series . . . older volcanic vents are flanked by agglomerates and tuffs. Dating in time between the older and newer basalts are the peculiar plugs of volcanic rock called sölvsbergite, which occur in the Camel's Hump and at Hanging Rock forming masses projecting about 200 ft above the surrounding flows.[33]

This peculiar material, sölvsbergite, contained silica and sodium, which accounted for the porous character of the rock's 'bladders' as surmised by Blandowski. It also distinguished the Rock and the Camel's Hump from both older and more recent volcanic peaks in Victoria, with, according to Skeats, the only larger formation of this material found in Norway.

In conjunction with a university colleague, Hubert Summers, Skeats examined Hanging Rock in closer detail, for a paper published for the Geological Survey in 1912.[34] Skeats and Summers acknowledged that Gregory had completed detailed work on Victoria's geology, although they noted that he never completed his analysis of Hanging Rock and the Camel's Hump. They singled out a local geologist, E.G. Hogg for his 1899 work on Hanging Rock.[35] Skeats and Summer now proposed that the 'well-known Hanging Rock' between the Jim Jim and the Camel's Hump was 'a conical shaped hill composed of sölvsbergite, probably consisting of a mamelon or boss'.[36] This was too solidified to exude outwards and instead eventually settled around the vent, piling upwards until it formed the rare spectacle of a mamelon, to be then weathered down over millions of years.[37]

The most distinctive feature of Hanging Rock, its strangely symmetrical and cylindrical columns, they explained through 'the strongly pronounced vertical joints, together with the weathering [which] have given rise to a rude columnar structure'.[38] The rock they

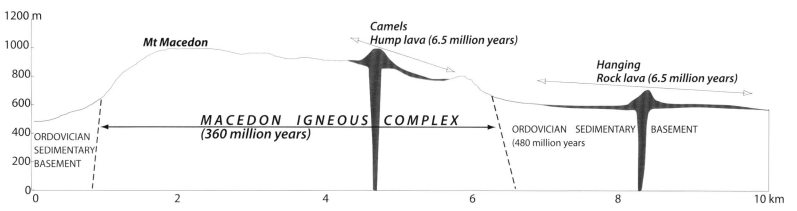

Geological cross section Macedon and Hanging Rock. N. Rosengen, 2017.

thought 'somewhat greenish in colour, but is generally altered to a greyish or brownish tint as a result of weathering'.[39] In passing, Skeats and Summers reflected on the two-phase volcanic process imagined by Blandowski. They pointed out that it was difficult to determine which was the older formation, the unique material of Hanging Rock, or its surroundings, composed of 'anorthoclase trachyte'. The sequence they thought unclear since

> the only place where the two abut against one another is at the Hanging Rock... here, however, the actual junction is obscured by material fallen from the higher part of the hill.[40]

'We picture' they went on 'the extrusion of the anorthoclase trachytes followed by the formation of the mamelons or bosses of sölvsbergite'.[41]

If Skeats was confident about the mamelon's material, as well as its volcanic origins, he also suggested an additional layer of significance to Hanging Rock. Hanging Rock seemed important in Skeats's reading because it provided a bridge between older and more recent volcanic activity. Later geologists, after identifying soda trachyte as a basic material in major volcanoes along the eastern range of Australia, have taken up this idea and proposed Hanging Rock as the southernmost extremity of a volcanic chain extending south from Hillsborough in Queensland. Tectonic movement of plates had caused the emerging Australian land mass to inch its way northwards until it separated from Antarctica and collided with the islands of East Asia. As it did so, over a period of 33 million years, the continent passed over volcanic hot spots. These forced magma to the surface. By the last decades of the twentieth century, Hanging Rock was recognised as a product of the most recent phase of this movement, occurring as the continent reached its northernmost position, rather than for any distinctive mamelon form, or rare material.[42]

NATURALISTS

About the time at which radiometric dating commenced, educationists and scientists, if not the broad public, had come to accept the enormous historical depth of the Australian continent. Over billions of years, the land mass had formed and reformed into Gondwana and Pangaea, the super-continents of the Southern Hemisphere. Super-volcanoes had thrown rock from eastern to western Australia. In the more recent Miocene Epoch (commenced about 10 million years ago) the continent inched its way over regions of volcanic activity, detaching from Antarctica, drying Bass Strait and crushing into Asian islands. Megafauna appeared, herds of giant wombats, giant kangaroos and enormous flesh-eating birds. Then, the rainforests retreated, and Australia grew both dry and brown. And near to Hanging Rock in the Lancefield swamp this drying has left a vast array of remains of the megafauna that once wandered through the landscape as Hanging Rock was formed.[43] Over the course of their dominance of the land, Australia was becoming a recognisable, separate continent, with its own flora and fauna, and a dry, warm climate.

Europeans arrived in this landscape long after the disappearance of megafauna, and once volcanoes had fallen dormant. Hanging Rock we now know as a fine example of a volcanic site for its mamelon or plug like form, the nature of its magma, and more significantly, as a link in our understanding of plate tectonics. Not much of this was understood by the first Europeans who had set out into what is now central Victoria. Neither did the vegetation which grew up around the new volcanic sites interest many of the first sheep owners, whose real concern was access to water and the ability to replace tough native grasses with imported and more easily edible grasses for their livestock.

In their first survey, map-makers noted that the Rock stood amidst an open woodland. On their maps, Messmate and Ironbark were recorded as common trees. Blandowski further saw, as he approached the base of Dryden's Monument, that this open woodland grew denser and the eucalypts grew taller. The higher he went up the Rock then the thinner and more sparse became this forest. Eventually the Summit gave footholds to only a few eucalypts, hanging off the rock walls at odd angles. He described the surrounds as an 'exquisite harmony' between the dark eucalypts and the deep hues of the rocks above.[44] Daintree's photographs of a few years later, also captured a relatively open woodland with scattered eucalypts, fallen branches across the grass, and suggestions of a thicker forest directly beneath the Rock itself.[45] After half a century of change, climbers who reached the top of the Rock, were able to survey the land around. From here they could make out dramatic European marks on the landscape. One climber in 1903 was struck by gorse bushes growing across farmland and within the Reserve. In the distance he could make out rich fields of white flowers marking potatoes, and the golden swards of wheat. The native

vegetation seemed to make no impression on him at all.[46] Blandowski's stay in and around Hanging Rock had also produced a rather predictable catalogue of Australian birds and mammals. He recorded the annual arrival of black and mountain ducks. He described the gang-gang cockatoos, the magpies and the 'laughing jackass', all common to the forest and woodland. Blandowski sought to distinguish birds seen in the ranges all year round from those that migrated annually. He and his Aboriginal companions had tried to capture wombats along local streams. They were aware of platypus in the creeks, and Blandowski contrasted the large number of gliders to the absence of the grey kangaroo, which had been so plentiful only a few years earlier.

In the years immediately after Blandowski's trip, European birds had begun to colonise the Macedon ranges. Sparrows and other imports were quick to make their presence felt in the woodlands at the Rock's base. Other English birds were eventually discovered higher up on Hanging Rock. In 1863 one visitor to Hanging Rock recorded his thrill at hearing an English thrush. Augustus Greeves had been climbing up the Rock when 'near the summit sheltering in one of the many open caves formed by the rocks lying upon the top of others, was a full grown English thrush'.[47] The bird seemed quite tame and in the distance he thought he could hear another thrush singing. Greeves though was concerned that shooters out to slaughter native game might decide to take aim at this 'delightful songster'. He described the thrush for *Argus* readers, and then went on to remark that he felt obliged to warn the 'numerous sportsmen who frequent the neighbourhood' and especially 'juvenile sportsmen' that they needed to protect the alien thrush. Of course they were free to continue slaughtering native game.[48]

Nearly a century after Blandowski's expedition, another ornithological field trip took place in the ranges and now cleared farmland around Hanging Rock. One enthusiastic bird watcher spent a holiday at Macedon, from where he recorded Flame Robins on their annual return 'migration back to the ranges for the warmer months'.[49] The robins could be seen in flocks of up to fifty birds with 'the green pastures dotted with Flame Robins making a most pleasant sight'.[50] Scarlet robins were more likely to be seen in pairs and to stick to the timbered slopes. Lorikeets of several types as well as honeyeaters were found in 'box' trees, although the ground-dwelling birds noted by Blandowski, and seen on a few occasions across the later nineteenth century, had become a rare sight.

If European destruction of the native plants and animals transformed nature at Hanging Rock, a more powerful change came about as European plants and animals spread across the land around the Rock, and within the Reserve itself. As early as 1851, the Shire of Newham was warned about infestations of scotch thistles. Thistles reached Hanging Rock and spread along the roads around the Rock by 1870. The shire kept up a constant war against the invader, so that thistle control remained a major aspect of council expenditure for decades (later in the century other common local weeds were also brought under the Thistle Act).[51] Then the first owner of the Hanging Rock Hotel, William Adams, decided that he would 'improve' the landscape of the Rock. This meant clearing away undergrowth, taking out some trees and planting tree ferns all the way to the peak. Over the years, a rough ornamental entrance avenue was shaped for visitors, between rows of conifers and other imported trees. One local account painted a picture of the elaborate landscaping at Hanging Rock

> Mr Adams went to considerable work and expense to develop the Rock as a pleasure resort. The Five Mile Creek was weired to make a lake several acres in extent, on which rowing boats were available. Swans and other water birds were imported. A road was constructed almost to the top of the Rock. This road started at the foot of the Rock on the western side and climbed around the southern side into the large open area at the top of the Rock just below the final peak. It was wide enough for a cab to be driven up with safety. Ornamental trees were planted and beds of flowers laid out.[52]

William Adams, Hanging Rock Hotel licensee and lessee of the Rock,

had begun the process of modernising Hanging Rock, with all the hallmarks of a European pleasure resort.

There were to be many later schemes intended to continue with that commercialised modernity. The racing club made some attempt to restore natural vegetation, buying seedlings and saplings from the State nursery in nearby Macedon. Not that all raceday spectators were committed to restoring natural landscapes. In 1905 one racing enthusiast had imagined that the Rock might be stripped of trees altogether and turned into an 'admirable stand', a vast viewing platform to watch horseracing![53] Even he had second thoughts, and decided that a neatly forested backdrop would more easily enhance the charm of racing beneath the rock walls. So racing enthusiasts proceeded with their reforesting plans. The club's annual meeting in 1915 thanked the State Nursery for all the plants they had put in, and asked for the same sort of support in 1916. They were envisioning these as part of a wider beautification, which would include better grass in the members enclosure, and putting a flock of sheep onto the track to keep the grass down.[54] In the 1930s gangs of unemployed men were put to work cutting back timber and undergrowth at Hanging Rock.[55]

The sparse woodland identified in the first maps around Hanging Rock had by then been gradually cut down. Skeats noted that what was left of forest cover was extensively ringbarked and dying in 1912. Not that this was surprising. For decades Newham and Woodend councillors had given speedy permission to anyone wanting to 'fell timber'. Steam mills worked away in the forest. Council engineers were intent on taking trees out of road bends and from intersections near to Hanging Rock. The demise of forests though did little to deter shooters, anglers and trappers. Any remaining timbered public lands at Hanging Rock, and around Kyneton or Woodend, were favourite places for city hunting parties. If they went to Kyneton in 1900, they were advised that besides the excellent shooting, they ought to taking in the spectacle of Hanging Rock, 'a magnificent sight'. They could then move on to the main attraction, shooting pigeons and sparrows

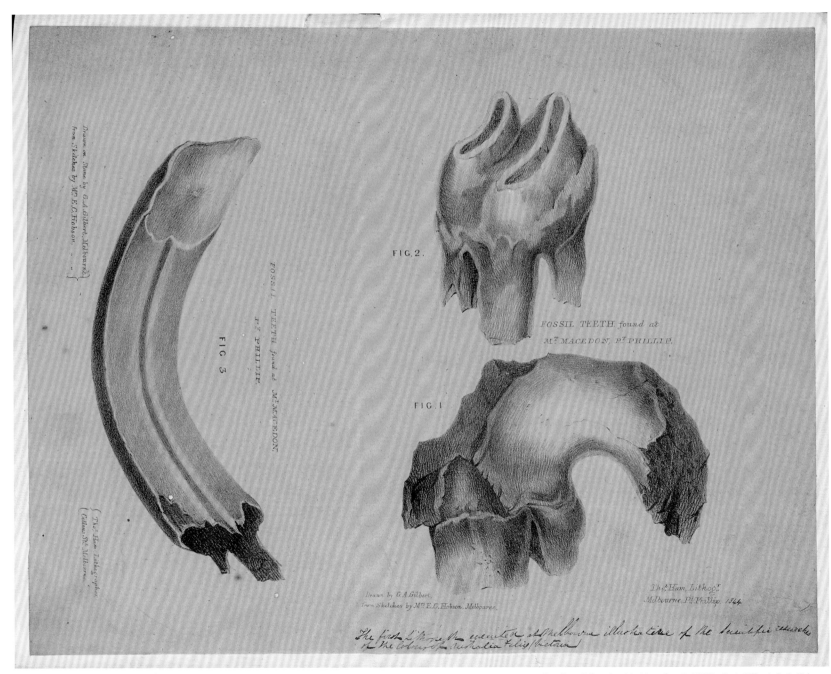

FIG. 2.

FOSSIL. TEETH. found at
M^{T.} MACEDON, P^{T.} PHILLIP.

FIG. 1

FOSSIL. TEETH. found at M^{T.} MACEDON,
P^{T.} PHILLIP.

FIG 3

*Drawn on Stone by G. A. Gilbert, Melbourne,
from Sketches by Mr E. C. Hobson.*

*Thos Ham Lithographer,
Collins St Melbourne.*

*Drawn by G. A. Gilbert,
from Sketches by Mr E. C. Hobson, Melbourne.*

*Thos Ham, Lithog^r
Melbourne, P^t Phillip. 1844.*

*The first Lithograph executed at Melbourne illustrative of the scientific researches
of the Colony of Australia Felix / Victoria*

Pig-footed Bandicoot. Artist. Gerard Krefft. Blandowski River Murray Expedition. 1857.
Wood engraving on paper, registration no. BA 509.

Museums Victoria

Red-capped Robin. Blandowski River Murray Expedition.1857.
Registration no. R 9307. Photograph by Rodney Start.

Museums Victoria

at the sports grounds every Wednesday and Saturday.[56] From time to time anglers wanted to have local streams stocked with fish. When the local angling club was offered fish stock in 1914, however, they rejected the opportunity. The flow in the Five Mile Creek from Hanging Rock Reserve to the south had become so low that the water was 'detrimental to the fish'.[57]

Organised excursion parties from Melbourne as well as farmer's children armed with pea guns hunted hares and rabbits around the Rock, with rabbit shooting continuing as a popular pastime into the middle of the twentieth century (the first rabbits were supposed to have been released by a Newham farmer who had been sent them as a present).[58] The Hanging Rock Committee of Management hired hunters to shoot rabbits on several occasions.[59] Foxes turned out to be more of a threat than other imported animals. One young girl growing up on a farm near Hanging Rock described how foxes were always after their poultry. But when they closed gaps into the chookyard, or their farm dogs were on guard, the foxes retreated to Hanging Rock or the Jim Jim range, where they survived on rabbits.

More of a Hanging Rock mystery than a living threat to farmers and their stock, was a near legendary beast sighted between Hesket and Hanging Rock in 1895. The mysterious Tantanoola Tiger was supposed to have escaped from a circus near to the South Australian border, before setting out on a meandering trek into central Victoria. One night in March 1895, two men drove wildly up to the door of the Newham pub, claiming that they had seen the tiger, or at least an animal about the size and colour of a tiger, 'lying on its side in a gutter or culvert and busily scratching away with its claws at the earth'.[60] Despite a fevered hunt by pub patrons, and then a search of Hanging Rock and around Macedon the next morning, nothing was to be found of the tiger.

Within a few years of this hunt, more measured explorations drew school groups to Hanging Rock. These followed on from new certainties about the Rock's origins and the continent's age, so that excursions to Hanging Rock became a useful adjunct to school nature studies. The Lancefield and Romsey Districts Teachers' Association took students from 25 schools to Hanging Rock towards the close of the school year in 1907.[61] Directed by J.A. Leach, the Education Department's Organising Inspector of Nature Study, over one thousand students and 'friends' were gathered at the Rock. They were joined by enthusiasts from the Field Naturalists Society. Professor Skeats and an associate walked from Monegeetta and on through Hesket to meet the crowd. Leach then explained the rarity of the rocks' geological composition to all and sundry, and went on to reprise the process by which soda and rain together had worked the columns into such curious contortions.[62] The Field Naturalists also organised the occasional excursion to Hanging Rock, although they showed far more interest in less 'managed' mountain areas.[63] H.W. Wilson led one such field trip to Hanging Rock in 1909. Fifteen members joined in, 'a good attendance . . . considering the distance from town', he reported.

RESTORING NATURE

By the middle of the twentieth century, an expanded racetrack, additions of sports ovals, picnic areas and tennis courts had transformed the open woodland in Hanging Rock Reserve. Much of the flat area of the Reserve is now shaped by these later uses and the constant transformations to accommodate car parking. Recent surveys of bird life and assessments of flora and fauna have divided the Reserve into distinct zones.[64] Areas with three vegetation layers (canopy, shrub and ground-story) cover approximately one quarter of the Reserve. The two principal such sites are within the racecourse and on the slopes of the Rock. Some areas such as the picnic sites share poor indigenous ground cover but do have a surviving tree canopy, whilst broad areas of imported and mown grasses, cover most of the Reserve.[65] There remain in addition 'riparian' areas along the creek, contours where some indigenous species have been replanted. Isolated to a few small spots, especially in crevasses near to the Summit, snow gums and silver banksia survive, their rarity adding botanical interest to the Reserve.

Curiously, the most significant patch of remnant vegetation is protected by one of the major modernising land-uses, the racecourse.[66] Ironically, patches of Leavy Fireweed have only escaped destruction because they are growing in the centre of the Reserve's spectacle place. They are found in the centre of the Hanging Rock racecourse. Within the Reserve, surveys sighted a number of significant bird and animals, many of them under threat.[67] These include grey goshawks, rare waterbirds, owls and the swift parrot. The greater glider has become a permanent resident of the Reserve. Alongside these surviving native fauna, were recorded a range of imported threats including deer, rabbits and feral cats. Blackbirds were regarded as pests as were the black rats attracted to picnic areas, along with the occasional fox.

It is clear that threats from imported plants and from animals have grown since the nineteenth century. At the same time the Reserve continues to support native sometimes threatened or rare species. It is cared for now through management plans and an attempt to tighten controls on just what visitors can bring onto the Reserve. Dogs are no longer allowed on the Summit for example. Blandowski, modern assessor of the Rock's nature, has left us with a far less detailed account than exists in these systematic recent surveys. Nonetheless his account remains both distinct and imaginative, and probably does need to be brought to bear on any attempt to restore pre-European flora and fauna. For a pre-European restoration effort cannot pretend the Rock was anything other than a humanised landscape before the 1840s. Aboriginal interventions in the landscape may not have been as transformative as those imposed by Europeans over a very short period of occupation. But as Blandowski understood, Aboriginal people lived actively rather than passively within the environment. They managed it, developing their own unique taxonomies over a far broader span of time than have Europeans.

When William Blandowski travelled around Hanging Rock and the nearby ranges he relied on his two Aboriginal companions to guide him through the complexities of relations between animal life, climate, vegetation and landform. When he compiled his vast collection, and

drew the limitless ire of British scientists, McCoy in particular, this could have been dismissed as simply a personal dispute, between bitter and isolated professional men. But Blandowski was analysing and categorising the environment of Victoria and trying, as he did so, to adapt to an Aboriginal perspective.[68] It has been argued that Blandowski's collecting was structured around an Aboriginal local knowledge specifically rejected by British scientists. His work 'fell into obscurity and failed precisely because he tried to foreground Aboriginal classification', claimed one recent account.[69] Hanging Rock, recognised as a meeting ground for several Aboriginal peoples, a crossroads for Aboriginal artifact exchanges, and for ceremonial moments, seems the perfect site for a restoration derived from these indigenous taxonomies. Such an approach may better reflect the site's history than any contemporary European 'conservation'; conservation of a nature which, independently of human management, may never have existed. ✺

Bridled Nail-tail Wallaby. Blandowski Murray River Expedition. 1857. Registration no. C 27925.
Photograph by Heath Warwick.

Museums Victoria

Horsfield's Bronze-cuckoo. Blandowski River Murray Expedition. 1857. Registration no. 30097.
Photograph by Rodney Start.

Museums Victoria

Endnotes

[1] 'Dryden's Monument and Mount Macedon', *The Age*, 14 September 1855: 6.

[2] Hamilton Hume, *A Brief Statement of Facts in Connection with an Overland Expedition from Lake George to Port Phillip in 1824*, J. J. Brown, Yass, NSW, 1874, and W.H. Hovell, *Answer to the preface to the second edition of Mr Hamilton Hume's 'A Brief Statement of Facts' in connection with an overland expedition from Lake George to Port Phillip in 1824*, J. Ferguson, Sydney, 1874.

[3] Hume, *A Brief Statement of Facts*.

[4] Mitchell's name for the lands to the south of the Murray River, Australia Felix, was a grand advertising slogan. By using 'Felix', Latin for fortunate or successful, he hoped his label would attract pastoralists to the Aboriginal pastures that had so impressed him.

[5] Lyndsay Gardiner, *Thomas Mitchell*, Oxford University Press, Melbourne, 1962.

[6] Thomas Mitchell, *Three Expeditions into the Interior of Eastern Australia: with descriptions of the recently explored region of Australia Felix and of the present colony of New South Wales*, T.W. Boone, London, 1839, ch. 8.

[7] Mitchell, *Three Expeditions into the Interior of Eastern Australia*, ch. 8.

[8] Thomas Mitchell, Journal entry, 30 September 1836.

[9] Marjorie J. Tipping, 'Hoddle, Robert (1794–1881)', *Australian Dictionary of Biography*, National Centre of Biography, Australian National University, http://adb.anu.edu.au/biography/hoddle-robert-2190/text2823 , published first in hardcopy 1966, (viewed online 15 September 2016).

[10] Maitland Mercury and Hunter River *Advertiser*, 13 December 1845.

[11] Robert Hoddle, Field Book, Bundle 79, Book 1155, page 31-52, VPRS 16685/P0001, Survey Department, PROV.

[12] Dryden's pastoral activities will be discussed in detail in a later chapter.

[13] Rachel Hewitt, *Map of a Nation: a biography of the Ordnance Survey*, Granta, London, 2010.

[14] D. F. Branagan and K. A. Townley, 'Selwyn, Alfred Richard (1824–1902)', *Australian Dictionary of Biography*, National Centre of Biography, Australian National University, http://adb.anu.edu.au/biography/selwyn-alfred-richard-4556/text7473 , published first in hardcopy 1976, (viewed online 19 December 2016).

[15] Alfred Selwyn, *Notes on the Physical Geography, Geology and Minerology of Victoria*, Blundell and Ford, Melbourne, 1866: 28.

[16] J. Dunn and D. J. Mahony, 'Biographical sketch of the founders of the Geological Survey of Victoria', Victorian Geological Survey, Bulletin, no. 23, 1910.

[17] Harry Allen, ed., *'Introduction' in William Blandowski's Illustrated Encyclopedia*, Aboriginal Studies Press ANU, Canberra, 2012.

[18] William Blandowski, *Personal Observations in Victoria*, Goodhugh and Trembath, Melbourne, 1855.

[19] Many of these illustrations and specimens are available on the website of the State Museum of Berlin, Germany, http://www.smb.museum/en/home.htm .

[20] Blandowski, Personal *Reflections*: 8-9. Alexander's Head refers to the nearby mamelon of Camel's Hump.

[21] Blandowski, *Personal Reflections*.

[22] Bory de Saint-Vincent had been assigned to the role as naturalist on Baudin's expedition to Australia but left the ship to explore the volcanic landscape of Reunion Island, where the mamelon formation seemed unique, until knowledge of Hanging Rock spread to Europe.

[23] A. Peltier, Aline, Frédérick Massin, Patrick Bachèlery, and Anthony Finizola. 'Internal structure and building of basaltic shield volcanoes: the example of the Piton de La Fournaise terminal cone (La Réunion).' *Bulletin of volcanology*, vol. 74, no. 8, 2012: 1881-97.

[24] Mary Mackay, 'Singularity and the Sublime in Australian Landscape Representation', *Literature & Aesthetics*, vol. 8, 2011:120. See too M. Mackay, 'Sleeping Tigers of the South: Volcanoes and the Sublime', *Australian Journal of Art*, vol. 13, no. 1, 1996: 93-113.

[25] For one broad survey of the state of volcanology at the end of the century see T. G. Bonney, *Volcanoes*, London, 1899.

[26] Charles Lyell, *Principles of Geology: or the modern changes of the earth and its inhabitants as illustrative of geology*, John Murray, London, 1833.

[27] The Miocene is generally accepted as the initial epoch of the Neogene Period. It extended to about 5.333 million years ago. Hanging Rock's origins lie in the late Miocene between 5.5 and 6 million years ago.

[28] Charles Lyell, 'On craters of denudation, with observations on the structure and growth of volcanic cones', *Quarterly Journal of the Geological Society*, vol. 6, no. 1-2, 1850: 207-34. See too, M. J. S. Rudwick, 'Lyell and the Principles of Geology', *Geological Society, London, Special Publications* vol. 143, no. 1, 1998: 1-15.

[29] See for example 'Geological Observations', *Ballarat Star*, 23 September 1905: 5.

[30] G. C. Fendley, 'McCoy, Sir Frederick (1817–1899)', *Australian Dictionary of Biography*, National Centre of Biography, Australian National University, http://adb.anu.edu.au/biography/mccoy-sir-frederick-4069/text6491 , published first in hardcopy 1974, (viewed online 16 April 2017).

[31] J.W. Gregory, *The geography of Victoria, historical, physical and political*, Whitcomb and Tombs, Melbourne, 1903.

[32] J.W. Gregory, in *Proceedings of the Royal Society of Victoria*, vol xiv, New Series Part 2, 1902: 201. See too *Annual Report for the Secretary of Mines*, Victoria, for 1907.

[33] 'Victoria's Volcanic Rocks: Professor Skeats's views', *Argus*, 12 November 1910: 7.

[34] E.W. Skeats and H.S. Summers, 'The Geology and Petrology of the Macedon District', Bulletins of the Geological Survey of Victoria, no. 24, Department of Mines, Melbourne, 1912.

[35] E.W. Skeats and H.S. Summers, 'The Geology and Petrology of the Macedon District': 7.

[36] Skeats and Summers: 'The Geology and Petrology of the Macedon District':12.

[37] On the nature of mamelons and their historical interpretation see: Laurent Michon, Andrea

Di Muro, Nicolas Villeneuve, Cécile Saint-Marc, Pierluigi Fadda, and Fabio Manta. 'Explosive activity of the summit cone of Piton de la Fournaise volcano (La Réunion island): a historical and geological review', *Journal of Volcanology and Geothermal Research*, no. 264, 2013: 117-33.

[38] Skeats and Summers: 12.

[39] Skeats and Summers: 21.

[40] Skeats and Summers : 49.

[41] Skeats and Summers: 53.

[42] P Wellman and I McDougall, 'Cainozoic Igneous Activity in Eastern Australia', *Tectonophysics*, vol. 23, 1974: 49-65; E.S. Hills, *The Physiography of Victoria*, Whitcombe and Tombs, Melbourne, 1940; Peter Wellman, 'Hotspot Volcanism in Australia and New Zealand: Cainozoic and Mid-Mesozoic', *Tectonophysics*, 1993: 225-43.

[43] 'Unearthing Lancefield's Megafauna', Latrobe University News, November no 11 2016, http://www.latrobe.edu.au/news/articles/2016/release/unearthing-lancefields-megafauna (viewed February 2017).

[44] W. Blandowski, 'Personal Observations', *Proceedings of the Philosophical Society of Victoria* 1855: 57.

[45] Richard Daintree, Hanging Rock, 1859, State Library of Victoria Photographic Collection.

[46] Winchester, 'At Hanging Rock', *Australasian*, 10 January 1903: 36.

[47] Augustus Greeves, 'The thrush', *Argus*, 18 August 1863: 8.

[48] 'The thrush', *Argus*, 18 August 1863: 8.

[49] Roy Wheeler, 'Bird Notes from Macedon Victoria', *Emu*, vol. XLIII, 1944: 187. One of Blandowski's specimens held in the Berlin collection is a Flame Robin.

[50] Roy Wheeler, 'Bird Notes from Macedon Victoria, *Emu:* 187.

[51] Minute Book Shire of Newham, VPRS 14325, Public Record Office Victoria.

[52] Wilfred Jones, 'Newham', in Shire of Newham and Woodend, *A Century of Local Government*, 1962, no page numbers.

[53] 'Hanging Rock Races and Picnic', *Weekly Times*, 7 January 1905: 18.

[54] 'Hanging Rock Racing Club', *Woodend Star*, 15 May 1915: 2.

[55] Expenditures, 1931-34, Shire of Newham, Hanging Rock Cash Book, Shire of Macedon Ranges.

[56] 'Kyneton', W*eekly Times*, 1 December 1900: 5.

[57] Kyneton *Guardian*, 26 February 1914: 4.

[58] McKenzie, *Looking Back Newham Primary School*.

[59] Hanging Rock, Cash Book, Shire of Macedon Ranges.

[60] ' The Tantanoola Tiger', *Launceston Examiner,* 14 March 1895: 7.

[61] 'Excursion at Woodend', *Age*,18 November 1907: 11.

[62] 'Excursion at Woodend', *Age*,18 November 1907.

[63] 'Reports, Field Naturalists Club of Victoria', *The Victoria Naturalist*, 15 April 1909, vol. 25, no. 304: 189.

[64] Practical Ecology, *Hanging Rock Reserve Environmental Management Plan Part 1: Background Report*, Macedon Ranges Shire Council, October 2015.

[65] Practical Ecology, *Hanging Rock Reserve Environmental Management Plan*.

[66] Practical Ecology, *Hanging Rock Reserve Environmental Management Plan*.

[67] Practical Ecology, *Hanging Rock Reserve Environmental Management Plan*, Table 6.

[68] On his collection see Peter Menkhorst, 'Blandowski's Mammals: Clues to a Lost World', *Proceedings of the Royal Society of Victoria*, vol 12, no. 1, 2009: 61-89

[69] Khadija von Zinnenburg Carroll, 'What Would Indigenous Taxonomy Look Like? The Case of Blandowski's Australia', Environment & Society Portal, *Arcadia*, 2014, no. 12, Rachel Carson Center for Environment and Society, LMU, Munich, http://www.environmentandsociety.org/node/6292 , (viewed online January 2017).

North view of the Hanging Rocks from Adams Shanty Woodend roall [sic].
Sir William Wiseman. *Sketches in Australia, New Zealand, Fiji and New Hebrides, after 1863.*
Mitchell Library, State Library of New South Wales

Around the Rock

Here, at Rochford, one, without becoming a recluse, could renounce the false glitter of this capricious world and live tranquilly, surrounded by a few sincere friends, to a ripe old age

'Reposeful Rochford', Romsey Examiner, 29 May 1914: 2

Little places such as 'Reposeful Rochford', or Hesket, Newham, Cherokee, and Kerrie are intimately entangled with the story of Hanging Rock. These hamlets, never more than clutches of houses, a few stores, the occasional pub, perhaps a public hall or school, often with a sawmill and church, and with too few residents to register with the first national census takers in 1911, gave occasional shelter to itinerant fruit pickers and timber cutters. They also brought together the farming families from amongst whom were drawn the self-proclaimed protectors of the Hanging Rock Reserve, and stalwarts of the Reserve's sports clubs.[1] The paddocks and barns of their farms spread under the shadow of the Rock, to be dusted with winter snows. Here too, in dry years, fires could burn through paddocks, before racing on to threaten towns. Farmers and townsfolk routinely argued about rights to water in the Hanging Rock Reserve, or were at odds about cattle grazing there. For Hanging Rock was always more than just a pleasant spot for picnickers and climbers. It was after all, both a water and recreation reserve, where farmers jealously guarded rights to its creek, and sometimes the lake. Local townspeople played sport at the Rock, and clung onto key posts in managing the Reserve. Summer visitors came to the Rock perhaps once a year for a day out. In contrast, for farmers, Hanging Rock stood as a familiar landmark in their day-to-day lives. These farms have been an integral part of the story of Hanging Rock. A cloud though hangs over their future. How many of their connections to Hanging Rock can survive the near disappearance of towns, and the accelerating northwards march of Melbourne's suburban fringe?

TASMANIAN LAND GRABBERS

Years before any of these towns sprang up in the midst of forests, squatters had made a charge for land around Hanging Rock. Although their 'sheep runs' changed boundaries between 1837 and the 1850s, in the eyes of these pastoralists, Hanging Rock itself was more or less worthless. They might have used its outcrop of rocks and trees as an orienting point. Perhaps they saw it as last resort when other water sources dried up. Mostly though, these 'squatters' were fixed on running their sheep across Aboriginal land, defying Crown authorities in Sydney, and defending their estates from any incursion by small-scale agriculturalists. Charles Ebden was amongst the first of these overlanders. His grasp on good pasture, around Carlsruhe in 1837, may have also led to deadly conflict with local people. But Ebden quickly set off for Melbourne. He speculated on city land, grew in his own words, 'disgustingly rich', and turned to a career in politics, most often as a defender of the rights of once rival squatters.[2]

Whereas Mitchell, Hume and Hovell envisioned that pastoralists would, like Ebden, reach Australia Felix from north of the Murray, men from the south spearheaded the invasion around Hanging Rock. The story of Hanging Rock itself cannot be told without recalling some of these young graziers, and in particular, Edward Dryden. With sheep and cattle in tow, Dryden set out from Launceston in the colony of Tasmania in the 1830s.[3] He sailed across Bass Strait to Port Phillip and arrived in Melbourne on New Year's Day, 1837.[4] With him on his journey was Charles Peters, already the holder of an estate, 'Garth', in Fingal, Tasmania. Dryden also had as a partner and sometime sponsor, his uncle Thomas Dryden, who, like Peters, owned a Tasmanian estate, at Haggerston. Eventually these connections proved more of a burden rather than benefit to Hanging Rock's first European, Edward Dryden. At first, however, these partnerships allowed the two young men to anchor their pastoral adventures on a firm financial footing. After unloading their livestock, Charles Peters, Edward (and perhaps Thomas) Dryden set off inland, seeking out the rich pastures reported widely in Tasmania. Intent on taking over as much grazing land as they could, they scarcely acknowledged Aboriginal prior occupation. Nor did these freebooters show much respect for British imperial rule, invading territory without regard for any legal restriction. Peters and Dryden stayed initially with John Aitken at Killamaine, near to present-day Kilmore, intermingling their sheep with his flock. Edward Dryden then settled on a campground on the banks of the Garden Hut Creek. Following the course of the creek, he came to the spot that he chose as a homestead. The two budding sheep barons then took up Mount Macedon Ranges Station, in June 1839. Here, one official visitor found Dryden living by himself, his home no more than a bark hut, tacked together in the depths of a forest.[5]

Only once ensconced on the acres they had claimed, was their squatting given quasi-legitimacy, in the form of pastoral leases, and then pre-emptive rights. Dryden was issued with a license for grazing in 1844, at which time he employed fourteen shepherds and farm labourers, he had cultivated seven acres, had two horses, eight cattle, 3,500 sheep and was living in a slab hut. Peters had settled for the northern half of what was the Mount Macedon Ranges Run. He called this enormous stretch of grazing land Garth, after his Fingal estate. Dryden christened his southern section Newham, after the Northumberland village where he had been born in 1808.[6]

Dryden was not the first of the cattle and sheep barons, although he did arrive in the Port Phillip District early enough to grasp a huge land-holding, to the north of Melbourne's then crude Yarra bank outpost. It was not until the 1840s that authorities in Sydney were able to bring some order to this illegal pastoral invasion. They issued the buccaneering pastoralists with 'Depasturing Licences' at £10 per run. This was the basis for Dryden's initial control of Hanging Rock, with his first Depasturing License issued on 1 July 1840.[7] When he renewed this lease in 1848 it covered an estimated area of 25,000 acres.[8] Dryden took up the lease (no. 75), through the agency of his uncle, Thomas, with a grazing capacity for 9,000 sheep. His run was bounded on the north by his travelling companion and former partner, Peters' Garth estate, and ran to the west as far as the Melbourne and Jeffries or Mount Macedon Road. It was bounded on the east by Cain's run. All in all, the boundaries were ten and a half miles, by nine miles, by eleven, by nine and a half miles. This vast estate extended over, as one letter writer to the Argus pointed out, an area far larger than the 25,000 acres paid for by license.[9] When Edward Dryden completed his return of land-holding in 1849 he had listed the extent of his squatting run as covering an area of almost one hundred square miles.[10] In 1851, Dryden was paying a licence fee of £24 for the use of less than half of his original run.[11] Again in 1853, Dryden listed his lands as covering only 24,000 acres (less than fifty square miles).[12] On this much reduced land-holding, Dryden ran 12,000 sheep, thirty cattle, and eighty horses. By 1854 Dryden was running one hundred horses,

thirty cattle, and now, only 4000 sheep.[13] Then, in 1855, Dryden listed his pastoral holding at less than 20,000 acres.[14]

In 1843, Dryden married Anne Robertson, whose brother, Francis Robertson, was to emerge as a significant politician in Victoria's Legislative Council.[15] Edward and Anne's six children were raised in their Newham homestead, and went on to play prominent roles in the farming and civic life of the district. When he died in 1886, after fifty years in and around Hanging Rock, Dryden was recalled as a man 'respected by all who knew him for his upright, honourable conduct during his long residence in the district'.[16] Unlike other squatters, Dryden had moved on from sheep and cattle. During his half a century around Hanging Rock, he took a lead in stock breeding, and extended his interest to horses, both thoroughbreds and riding hacks. He also bred cart and plough animals, and sold horses into the Melbourne hansom cab trade. Unsurprisingly, in later years, he (and later his son William) emerged as great patrons of the Hanging Rock races.[17] When Dryden died, he left his livestock to William, so that their breeding enterprise would continue. The estate he passed on included the bay colt, Peter the Great, and the filly Admiral, both valued at £50. His mares, Madame, Lady Victor (in foal) and Lady Darling were worth £100 each, with other horses marked down to between £30 and £40. A price of £69 was put on his hacks. Seven geldings, probably kept for racing, were listed at £150.[18]

Whereas other squatters stuck to the wool and mutton trades, Dryden invested consistently in horses such as these, breeding mainly for the Melbourne market. Equine experts of the later nineteenth century typically dismissed colonial stock horses in Victoria as a declining breed.[19] They did though respect the stud horses around Hanging Rock, and saw Dryden in particular, as a shrewd and improving breeder. In 1865 for instance, Wallace's Auctioneers were advertising '20 head of colts direct from the station of Edward Dryden' for sale. Half of the draft was composed of 'heavy' workhorses, the other half of 'strong upstanding hacks'. Anyone buying these horses need have no fear about their durability, since Dryden was already well-known as 'the breeder of Mazeppa, Ellis and other Celebrated Horses'. Auctioneers thought no further comment was necessary, and Dryden was so confident of his reputation as a breeder that he put no reserve price on the sale.[20]

Successful and respected Dryden may have been, but many years of his life at Newham were marred by disputes over property. He repaid the hospitality shown him by John Aitken by finding work for a relative, Robert Aitken. Aitken often stayed over at the Dryden homestead, where one night after a rowdy day at the races, he died in his sleep.[21] Peters and Dryden contested elements in the will to argue that some sheep deemed the possession of Aitken were rightfully theirs, and that over the years the three men had often intermingled their flocks. When his uncle Thomas died, Dryden found that he had left no legal will. Disputes with cousins, and, it appears, his own brother, continued in the Supreme Court of Victoria through to at least Dryden's own death.[22]

In his own will, Edward left his property (Pre-Emptive Section, Parish of Newham) to his wife and eldest son William. They inherited his four roomed stone house, with a thatched stable, land cleared of trees, although fenced only with an 'old post and rail and brush fence'.[23] The remaining children would inherit half of the property of 640 acres when their mother died. This was a greatly diminished land-owning empire. When he initially took on a Newham small-holding of 640 acres at the first Woodend land sales, he also had over 1000 acres, which he leased out to tenant farmers. On his death he held, from the vast sheep run of the 1840s, only his purchased land of 640 acres. His beneficiaries also inherited a mortgage debt to James Feathers of £1,700.[24] Dryden did though fare better than his unfortunate partner, Peters. Across Bass Strait, Peters' Garth estate became a ghoulish shrine in Tasmanian ghost stories, because of three mysterious deaths there.[25]

Hanging Rock may have been known for decades as Dryden's Rock or Dryden's Monument. But Dryden himself saw little use for the

craggy pile around which his sheep and horses grazed. The spring at the foot of the Rock, and the water cascading through the Rock, and then through Smokers Creek and the Five Mile Creek, was valued far more highly than the Rock itself. In February 1857, T.L. Jones, a Kyneton solicitor, took up 170 acres including Hanging Rock.[26] In 1860, Alexander Archer bought 100 acres within which stood the Rock itself and William Adams then bought Jones's remaining 70 acres.[27] Adams also bought the future site of the Hanging Rock Hotel, in 1866, with a portion to the east of the Rock then set aside as Crown land reservation. By then William Adams had acquired the land which covered most of Archer's original purchase and William Anderson owned the remaining southern portion. In 1884 Crown Land was extended further into Anderson's holding. Over these decades, more and more of Dryden's original run was divided up, so that the forest around Hanging Rock was cleared for a range of small farms serviced by hamlets beneath the Rock itself. Crown reserves were again sub-divided in 1891 and 1923 in Closer Settlement Schemes.

The road to the Castlemaine diggings and on to Bendigo had become one of the busiest routes out of Melbourne by the 1860s. The Sydney Road, further to the east of the Rock, remained the major inter-colonial route throughout the later nineteenth century. Railways reached Woodend in 1861, and Lancefield two decades later. The fortunes of local farmers may well have looked up, and Hanging Rock become a national tourist centre much earlier, if plans for a local railway had gone ahead.[28] The most promising scheme was for a spur line from Woodend to Hanging Rock and possibly running on to Lancefield, from where the Railway Department could transfer rolling stock between inter-colonial main routes. Useful to farmers on the rich 'chocolate soils' of the district, the line would primarily

> accommodate a large number of people to the Hanging Rock, 4 miles from Woodend, where two or three times a year, race meetings, picnics annually are held; from 5 to 10 thousand people annually resort to this popular place.[29]

Instead, farmers and the Newham councillors supported rival plans for a branch line from Lancefield north-west to Deep Creek and Cobaw, and then on to Heathcote and the Goulburn Valley; a proposal stymied because of the challenges faced in crossing the Great Dividing Range.[30] So, railway engineers spent years constructing an even more tortuous route across the range to Kilmore, and away from Hanging Rock. The line proved an immediate failure. It was closed due to lack of patronage after carrying trains for a very few years in the 1890s.

The drays, horses, bullock carts and wagons that plied the roads northwards, by and large ignored Hanging Rock and its surrounds. This meant that the arc of forest and farmland between major roadways was left more or less to its own devices, a secluded farming world with dense family, religious and community networks, lasting through generations. Farms were small, and farmers supplemented harvests and stock sales with timber cutting. Several small blocks, often on the least productive land, were leased out to tenant farmers. Most of the local hamlets bordered onto steam-driven timber mills. When Melbourne suburbs boomed, sawn timber handed farmers a lucrative windfall. In the small chapels and churches of townships, farming families intermarried for two to three generations. They shared cultural events at socials and dances. And for such a secluded district, the surrounds of Hanging Rock produced a remarkable sequence of technical advances in farming and, eventually, a unique political organisation of farmers. These technologically-adept and politically-aware farmers were also the source of ongoing conflict about the Hanging Rock Reserve.

WATER, SNOW AND FIRE

By the time a reserve was declared at Hanging Rock, land in the surrounding area had been sold at public auction or included in land selection laws. Extensive Crown land was still covered by forests to the north, at Cobaw, and to the south of Hanging Rock. There were always disputes about rights to timber in these forests. Then, once a section of the original Dryden run was declared a public reserve, it became a source of dispute between farmers and other users, largely because in dry years, Hanging Rock remained a reliable place to

collect water. When eventually announced in 1884, Hanging Rock Reserve was actually described as a recreation and water reserve. Before then, maps from 1867 included a water reserve alongside the Rock itself. Any rights to water however, remained uncertain. Peter Knights reviewed Victoria's water and river catchment laws in 1996, and pointed out that 'no matter what notation appears on the Parish plan regarding the reservation relating to a particular river' it was not until 1881 that official reservation boundaries were established; by an Order-in-Council of 23 May 1881.[31] When Hanging Rock was purchased by the state in 1884 this change in ownership only confused local farmers, so that Hanging Rock's water remained a much disputed resource.[32] For, whilst holiday-makers and publicans emphasised the recreational joys of the new Reserve, farmers were far more interested in Hanging Rock as a reliable supplier of summer water.

Blandowski had noted that water percolated through the Rock, before flowing out in clear surges. Several later observers were struck by its reddish tinge (earning the sobriquet 'Morgan's Blood' after the bushranger who was supposed, to have had a lookout on the Rock). Farmers took a more prosaic view. Here was public land and a source of water from both a creek and a lake. Long before the 1884 reserve was declared, farmers treated the site as a grazing commons. For much of the year, outside of one or two racedays, or New Year picnics, they, their cattle and sheep, had the Rock and its surround to themselves. After an 1871 inspection, shire councillors insisted that they would leave access for farmers unchanged, by fencing the Reserve on two sides only. Unsurprisingly, farmers liked to assert their right to uninterrupted access to water in the Reserve. They then called for an easy route for moving cattle from the Reserve further down Five Mile Creek, for the times when water ran low in the Reserve itself. Newham council seemed prepared to excise some of the hard won recreational land to make way for this cattle road, until townsfolk in Woodend objected.[33] They were also planning to burn off dead timber and kept an eye on the stone in the Reserve, which, they noted, could in the future be of 'considerable value' for road or building materials.[34]

30 feet diameter MacDonald & Scotts Law [sic] Mill nr Hesket Mount Macedon.
Sir William Wiseman. *Sketches in Australia, New Zealand, Fiji and New Hebrides, after 1863.*

None of this satisfied land-owners around Hanging Rock. Richard Adams and Eli Jones, prominent in almost every dispute on almost every potential use of Hanging Rock for forty years, complained in the summer of 1875 that they were being denied access to the Reserve's water.[35] As the following summer approached, Jones and Adams took the shire to task once more, claiming that they had a perfectly legal right to water in Five Mile Creek.[36]

Eli Jones, was still complaining in the following autumn. As he tried to get to the creek, the 'lessee' approached him, 'brandishing at the time a big shillelagh'.[37] The worthy lessee (of Hanging Rock) seemed 'determined to die knee deep in blood rather than let me have a drop of water' wrote Eli with a flourish by then familiar to shire officials. He demanded a detailed inquiry as to the rights of local residents to water at Hanging Rock. For, whilst he was barred, he knew of at least three families who routinely carted buckets of water from the Reserve to nearby homes. Regulations seemingly allowed for this, but water-carriers often left the gate to the Reserve open so that their cattle could wander in at night. If he could not get to the water, then Eli demanded that council had to be more vigilant about keeping the gate closed.[38]

After the 1884 government purchase of Hanging Rock, Eli's farming neighbours, perhaps even those who picnicked there on New Year and Christmas, demanded, conversely, that the Reserve be left unfenced, so they could get stock to water. Petitions were sent to the Lands Department asking that the Shire of Newham be prevented from any fencing at all on land around the Rock. Once made aware of plans for an expanded reserve in 1883, local farmers renewed calls for water rights and access to the Reserve for grazing. New fencing around the expanded Reserve dismayed these land-owners one of whom wrote to the Minister of Lands reporting

> by some means or another the Council have fenced it all in and
> used it for other purposes not allowing us to take our cattle to the
> creek for water, therefore we are deprived of our just right as we
> and others in the neighbourhood have no permanent water.[39]

The Shire of Newham contacted the Victoria Lands Department to point out that they had certainly fenced in the Reserve. Their fencing still left pathways open for cattle to get down to fresh water.[40] In November 1883 a group of locals wrote to the Minister for Lands again, to state that they were

> astonished the Council has said there is free access for cattle to
> the water. They deny that. For ten years the Council has let it,
> enabling tenants to prevent people from watering cattle upon it.[41]

If they were blocked from using the Reserve, then they wanted better access to creeks around it. Once beyond the Reserve, or so they complained, the cattle could not get to the wider parts of waterways. Council responded by claiming that cattle could be watered from bridges further away from Hanging Rock. Farmers objected again, since they knew that in a dry summer, cattle could not get down from the bridges to the last of the water.

Water disputes continued into the twentieth century. Reminding the department of lands that the land was reserved for both recreation and water supply in December 1884, the shire secretary noted that an eastern portion of the Reserve had always been left open to grazing stock.[42] The small lake within the Reserve was fenced off, and was linked to tanks by a windmill and supplied water 'solely for domestic use by the resident caretaker and picnickers'.[43] But in dry years, farmers were once again demanding access, so they could cart water from the lake. The shire was looking to the lands department for guidance. Department officials referred back to a gazetted provision (Clause 13, 11 December 1891 *Government Gazette* Victoria), which stated clearly that that farmers could use the unenclosed portion for watering stock. The council all the same still had the right to exclude them from the fenced section of Hanging Rock.[44]

Such disputed uses of the Rock were to continue. The Shire of Newham stock inspector routinely visited Hanging Rock. Here he checked to see if farmers from outside the district had put their animals into the Reserve. The inspector was called out to Hanging

Rock Reserve regularly at dawn in October 1914, looking for horses herded in after dark. Especially troubling was one travelling stockman. With his 75 horses he had constantly tried to get into the Reserve for grazing.[45] Such conflict seemed inevitable, since, both water use and recreational pursuits were embedded in the 1884 reservation. Well into the inter-war years, more than a dozen farmers were paying for grazing licenses in the Reserve, whilst others were agisting horses beneath the Rock.[46] And right up to the outbreak of war in 1939, the shire secretary continued writing to the department of lands and survey about confusing rules of access.

Hanging Rock may have provided water to the small farmers beneath its ramparts. It remained at the same time, a source of danger; a peak exposed in a plain, low and undulating, and from where the farmer's perennial summer enemy, bushfire, could suddenly spark. With any summer lightening flash near Hanging Rock, local farmers looked out for smoke above the pinnacles. Like so many others in rural Victoria, they suffered from frequent bushfires. These ravaged vast areas in 1851, in the 1880s, and again in several years in the early twentieth century. Hanging Rock itself could be the source of smaller but no less dangerous outbreaks. In 1900 one of the oldest residents of Hesket, Patrick Madden, had his farmland and four-roomed house destroyed by a fire, which had smouldered in the bush for days, before sudden wind blew it into an inferno.[47] In 1914, on a Sunday morning, fire had started on the northern side of Hanging Rock. The following Sunday, a fire started again, this time on the southern side of Hanging Rock. It took all afternoon for local people to bring it under control — and this in spring — before the summer heat took hold.[48] Bushfires ran through the district in 1929, destroying homesteads and threatening the small towns of Kerrie and Cherokee.[49] Only recently burnt firebreaks stopped the blaze from spreading further around Hanging Rock and into Mt Macedon.

If fires weren't enough of a threat, sometimes snowstorms and hail wreaked havoc. Racegoers recalled at least one running of the Hanging Rock Cup beneath a January dusting of snow on Hanging Rock itself. Regular winter snow fell on Mt Macedon, and sometimes blanketed the towns and farms around Hanging Rock. In 1899 and again towards the end of August 1906, snowstorms created 'deep drifts' on farmland around Hanging Rock and Macedon.[50] While these drifts meant fun for children and parents, who went out 'snowballing', snow and hail could destroy crops, and kill livestock and humans. In 1881 snowstorms destroyed fruit trees. Fallen branches, weighed down with snow, blocked local roads.[51] Tyndal Dewsbery Thornton was out in that storm, wandering around Hesket and Hanging Rock. 'Well connected' in England, he had recently come into a large some of money, much of which he proceeded to drink away at the Hanging Rock Hotel and in Hesket hotels. With snow falling thickly, he set off after dark from one Hesket pub. Falling down in snow, Tyndal warmed himself with swigs of whisky, before dropping into a deep sleep. The next morning his lifeless body was dug out from deep snow 'with the whisky bottle, three parts empty and (standing) in a perpendicular position alongside him'.[52]

FROM POTATOES TO POLITICS

Ongoing struggles over water certainly recurred every now and then around Hanging Rock. But compared to more remote farming districts, this was a place with good rains and very rich soils. 'This is a prosperous district, unaffected by drought, and always favoured with cool breezes' remarked one climber as he gazed over farmland from the summit of Hanging Rock.[53] Cut off to the south by the mass of Mt Macedon, the farms around Hanging Rock were able to survive for far longer than 'cockies' in other localities near to Melbourne. With farms purchased from the 1850s, and then expanded through selection and Closer Settlement Schemes, local farming families could look to a relatively secure livelihood by the time of World War 1 and even into the 1930s. There is a sense though, that by the time of World War II, farming on remnants of nineteenth-century blocks was becoming increasingly difficult. Horse breeding had been a staple of the area in the nineteenth century with farmers breeding horses for the rich trade in remounts to the British army in India, or as farm and city work animals.[54] Larger landowners took up the chancy but occasionally

Hanging Rock.
Nr Woodend 54 Miles N. from Melbourne

Hanging Rock. Near Woodend 54 Miles N. from Melbourne.
Album of Victorian views. c.1870s. Photograph by Charles Nettleton.

lucrative business of thoroughbred breeding, and imported English stallions as a basis for local bloodlines.[55] Champion work-horses such as that imported to Hesket, Purebred Suffolk Punch colt, Sir Randler, owned by R.W. Bowen, and descended from the great English horse, Rendelsham Cupbearer, were the basis for a specialised but declining trade.[56] For with more trucks available after World War 1, interest in such fine workhorses fell away.

Some farmers milked small dairy herds, although cattle raising for dairy and beef was more likely to produce a profit on larger farms, or on irrigated blocks to the north of the state. Farmers grew fruit and faced obstacles not shared by fruit growers around the more recently irrigated Sunraysia. At the same time, the district was renowned for its rich soils, generally reliable water and closeness to the markets and docks of Melbourne. By the early twentieth century, many knowledgeable observers thought that the Rochford district had some of the best soil in the state. Local farmers produced good quality oats on small lots.

Children wrote happily about life in this green, stable, self-contained little world. The farming landscape of the early twentieth century was described by one girl who grew up at Rochford. Ivy McKinly told of her journey through the district for an Easter holiday in the Cobaw Ranges at her grandmother's dairy farm. On Good Friday in 1917 she and her father drove a cart across dusty roads around Hanging Rock, to a farm with only twelve cows and a farmhouse where 'the rooms are low but cosy'.[57] Ivy went exploring along the nearby creek. Here Ivy's grandmother had planted New Zealand ferns, flax plants and poplars, with blackberries entwined around the trunks. Her aunts visited, and they went down on the Wednesday after Easter to a social evening at the Cobaw State School. School holidays were a time for other children to explore local picnic spots, especially Hanging Rock. To Ida Grady, who had grown up in Kerrie, her little farming hamlet was a wonderful spot where 'everything is so green'. Her family farm was much like others in the surrounds of Hanging Rock, and Ida delighted in the family's 'strawberries and cherries', though her favourite fruits

were 'mulberries'. Ida and her brother collected locally for farmers struggling in the dry Mallee, and thought Kerrie, a 'very pretty place', a cut above the sunburnt north of the state. On a clear day they even had views to the ships in Hobson's Bay.[58] A few years earlier, Fred Carroll had written from Kerrie remarking on the nice scenery with 'fern trees and musk' growing along creeks. For Fred, Hanging Rock was a favourite place in summer, but winters he recalled as cold, with snowfalls frequent.[59] One daughter of Hesket farmers recollected that Hanging Rock in the early twentieth century had none of the threatening associations played on in film and novel. In fact it was the Camel's Hump which frightened local children, rather than Hanging Rock. As she recalled:

> our property faced across from Hanging Rock, and as a child I played and explored in the caves nearly every weekend with other local children. We used a buggy light with candles and ropes. The Rock never held any terrors for us although we learned its history from the old timers, plus many other folk tales and stories of the district.[60]

Local children found one other volcanic outcrop far more disturbing. Camel's Hump remained in her memory, 'a dismal gloomy place supposedly haunted by bushrangers'.[61]

The parents of these young people combined a range of small farming activities, from diary cattle through to sending fruit, especially pears, to Melbourne processors. In the nineteenth century, oats were a staple crop for farmers around Hanging Rock. For others, growing and then harvesting chicory paid better than either grain or potatoes.[62] During the nineteenth century another incipient industry was tried in and around Hanging Rock. Wattle-bark 'strippers' moved through the districts in gangs, some of them composed mainly of Chinese men.[63]

Farmers tried and succeeded with a range of other experimental products. Even so, the district remained best known as a source of one staple of nineteenth and twentieth century diets, the humble potato. In 1905 the entire district could report heavy yields of potatoes, and the annual Romsey Agricultural Show became a showpiece for potato displays. At Hesket, J.H. Cook was digging ten tons to the acre. He had also pioneered his own variant, 'Cook's Favourite', with the prize tubers weighing up to five pounds.[64] Richard Adams, when he was not defending Hanging Rock Reserve from gamblers and racegoers, planted potatoes beneath the walls of the Rock. Adams, as in so many of his other activities, struck out independently when it came to potatoes. As an admiring Melbourne journalist remarked in 1886

> Not far from Hanging Rock . . . is the garden of Mr Richard Adams whose speciality is the growing of fancy varieties of potatoes for seed. . . Mr Adams does not confine himself to the sorts commonly grown for market, but rather gives particular attention to varieties which are less plentiful. Among those Adams's Excelsior is a potato which, although it did not get its deserts when first introduced by Mr Adams, is in good demand now.[65]

Away from major roads and railways, and with the Rock at its centre, the rich agricultural arc of farms typically escaped notice in Melbourne. A survey of farming at Kerrie in 1927 pointed out that the small township, though only a few miles from Romsey, was not very well known. The twenty farmers around Kerrie had been successful enough to put up solid homes and outbuildings. They were also able to contribute money for a new public hall.[66] By the inter-war years, potato growing emerged as their most lucrative activity especially when supported by dairying and pig-breeding. Because all of these small farms were committed to rotation cropping, Kerrie produce could always fetch the highest prices at the Melbourne markets. Well-known amongst progressive local farmers was L.C. Eaton, who came to Kerrie early in the twentieth century, with no experience in farming at all. He had divided his two hundred acres into fourteen fields, although half of his land remained forested. With the rest devoted to growing potatoes, as well as breeding fowls (White Leghorn and Black Orphington). Eaton's farm was held up as a model for struggling growers in other corners of the state.[67]

'Grey Gables' was likewise lauded as a typical profitable small farm of the Newham district, one owned by J.W. Clarke and worked on a share system by C.A. McKinnon. With little more than one hundred acres to work with, McKinnon succeeded with potatoes as his main crop. He milked a dozen Ayreshire cows and raised a few pigs. From this farm he exported Border Leicester lambs and kept thirty to forty acres under hay. For McKinnon, Newham was a good farming district, spared the extremes of land further north, even though it had longer and colder winters. He wondered though about the future of the district, since 'good land' was becoming 'too dear'.[68] Nigel Helliear's Lumeah farm at Newham was similarly promoted, this time as a model dairying operation. 'What impresses the visitor to "Lumeah" (wrote one agricultural reporter) is the thoroughness with which everything has been done and in connection with the dairying one is struck with recognition given to sanitation'.[69] Farmer Helliear already had experience with the new-fangled milking machines, most of which were despised by neighbouring dairy farmers. But Helliear was convinced that with initial difficulties ironed out, he would be able mechanise his entire operation within a few years.

Potato growers were also quick to adapt to new technologies. The Healey family farm at Newham experimented with a novel 'Lee Potato Digger' in 1915.[70] On Richard Johnstone's farm, the family took a chance with an experimental potato digger. The machine could dig nearly five acres a day and could keep six pickers busy the entire time.[71] Of course, even successful local farmers struggled through dry years. They could find survival elusive in times of low prices. But between the wars, Newham and other localities around the Rock were typically seen as benign places, where 'small holdings [could] succeed . . . on potatoes, milk and fat lambs'.[72]

In contrast to such go-ahead farmers, the drifters and battlers who turned up for fruit picking, or potato harvests, lived very hard lives. One such was Margaret Hall who died from drink in 1890. Margaret had lived in Kyneton. When her husband passed away she had taken to the road and lived from casual farm work. She eventually turned up at Anne Hotham's Mountain Home Hotel in Hesket in late autumn 1890. Alternating between minding a couple of local children and digging potatoes on nearby farms, Margaret passed her evenings drinking beer, some of which she cadged from bar regulars. Often she could be seen chasing her free beers down with a few nobblers of brandy. One morning, Margaret was found dead in her room in the hotel. As a witness at her inquest noted, Margaret Hall was known as a woman of 'dissipated habits'. In fact she already had a conviction for vagrancy.[73] There are also indications that some of the later arrivals around Hanging Rock were never able to catch up with the progress of long-established farms. One farmer, who had taken up land at Hesket under Closer Settlement rules in the 1890s, struggled to make ends meet for years. Always behind in payments to the lands department, he had tried to make a living from potatoes. In 1892 he failed to meet rent payments and told the department, 'the few spuds I had this year I had them in a piece of wet ground and they all rotted on me and left me without any for sale'.[74] His family was living in an abandoned school building, so he asked if he could exchange his holding for another Closer Settlement block. The request seemed to fall on deaf ears, and he fell behind in payments again in 1907. That year his entire family came down with influenza and he had trouble with his fencing. Things grew worse in the following year when he once again owed the state money. The struggling potato grower explained his renewed predicament:

> I had to bury my mother and doctor expenses left me without one pound in the house. Dear gentlemen I hope yous [sic] will overlook this and give me a while longer as I think it will be a bad winter and we can't let our four little ones starve.[75]

There were many hard winters to come in Hesket. But in most years, farmers and their families survived. Around the state, these areas were readily acknowledged as comparatively rich. As a general rule, their lands were well managed by technologically adept farmers. They were also the birthplace of unique movements in farming politics. In 1879 farmers from across Victoria had met to discuss forming a farmers' union. They wanted a state-funded immigration scheme

for agricultural labourers, reduced tariffs on farm equipment, and special freight rates on railways for agricultural products.[76] Newham farmers met as a Farmers Union in Brydon's Hotel.[77] In the decade that followed they agitated for new railways, more state support for export, and, as we might expect, improved roads and water supply. But Newham farmers seemed to be often at odds with the Victorian Farmers Union, and after several conflict-ridden meetings across 1880, the Newham group drifted apart. A Farmers Union was revived in the twentieth century, and this time the leaders of the statewide movement were drawn from Newham and neighbouring hamlets. The political voice of Australian farming in the twentieth century, the Country Party, was first heard in public halls and public houses beneath Hanging Rock. Anyone familiar with long battles over water at Hanging Rock would have recognised the leaders of this union. In fact the reborn Farmers Union was a direct descendant of the struggles over Hanging Rock water. On 5 June 1914 the 'first public meeting under the auspices of the recently inaugurated Victoria Farmers Union' was held in Newham.[78] The Kerrie-Hesket branch of the Farmers' Union was composed entirely of potato growers. In 1917 they demanded that tariffs had to be removed from the bags needed for their trade.[79] Richard Adams and other local identities behind the Newham group, had striven to retain a non-political character. This soon proved impossible. By 1917 the union had become the Country Party. By 1920 this voice for the rural voter held the balance of power in the Victorian parliament.[80]

TOWN LIFE AROUND HANGING ROCK

When Alma Whan of Hesket, aged ten, wrote to the *Farmers Advocate* in 1922, she described her township as a place with 'a church, a school, a post-office and telephone, and an hotel'. Yet, limited as her urban surroundings may have been, Alma pictured her home of Hesket as a 'pretty place' nonetheless.[81] Outsiders obviously agreed. She reported that the small hamlet of Hesket always attracted visitors keen on bushwalks, shooting expeditions, or simply climbing Hanging Rock. Newham farmers opened their Methodist chapel in 1860 and the foundation stone of the Presbyterian church was laid in

CLEARING TIMBER, MOUNT MACEDON.

Clearing timber, Mount Macedon. Wood engraving.
Illustrated Australian News. 15 March, 1880.
State Library of Victoria

1868.[82] Quiet little hamlets such as Hesket or Kerrie or Newham had a busier air on Sundays, with farming families at church or getting together in evenings for social events. Sometimes they hosted political meetings such as those run by the Farmers Union. Whilst these farmers ultimately won recognition for their political shrewdness and adventurous techniques in agriculture and stock-rearing, the same success never visited local towns. Farmers were able to get together to build churches and public halls. But decline and disappearance was always a real prospect for all of these little places. They struggled to get colonial governments to approve schools for local farm children. They had to battle to cling onto their postal services and got little response to their calls for better police protection. In 1876 residents of Hesket had petitioned the Shire of Newham to write to the Chief Commissioner of Police, demanding protection and a permanent police station at Hesket. The town they claimed had three hotels, which were largely unsupervised. With seasonal cropping workforces and timber mills attracting drifters from the city, they felt constantly threatened.

> The population is not very large but it includes some of the rowdiest characters in the district and the peaceable portions of the community are kept in a constant state of disquiet and even alarm. There are three public houses and we are assured that the scenes that occur almost nightly at one or other of them are disgraceful to a civilised community. The nearest police station is at Woodend some six miles distant'.[83]

The odd sensational local crime seemed to justify their collective fears. Councillors did agree to write requesting a police station, surmising, accurately as it turned out, that they would get no response.

If calls for police presence fell on deaf ears, locals were more successful in demanding schools for their children. These were at first crude buildings so that in the twentieth century, they were one by one closed. Committed local networks allowed a few to flourish. The Newham Primary School opened in 1860 with 66 children, in a weatherboard building with a shingle roof.[84] A new and more

solid school replaced this in 1913. The new Hesket school, known until 1879 as the 'American Steam Saw Mill School' opened about the same time.[85] Newham and Hesket schools have survived the fading of their small townships, as centres of local communities, supported by farming families, and a new wave of settlers from the city. Nearby schools proved less resilient. The school at Kerrie (no. 1290) opened in 1874 as the 'Railway Steam Sawmills School'. A pre-fabricated building, it did service as school, post office, church and Sunday School.[86] Red cedar and Douglas fir trees were planted in the schoolyard as a war memorial. This school survived threats from bushfires and declining numbers of children on nearby farms. Kerrie primary school continued with its educational mission for more than one hundred years. Eventually, it could not overcome the cost-cutting enthusiasms of neoliberal bureaucrats, and their political masters in the late twentieth century. The school closed in 1994, although its civic role was in part revived. The building was converted into a community centre.[87]

If the buildings of towns were either burnt in fires, changed their function or simply weathered away through disuse, the sporting clubs often survived, retaining as they did, an enduring association with Hanging Rock. When Macedon players visited Hesket for a football match in 1892 they had to play on a 'furrowed field' rather than an oval. 'The ground was greasy and a sleety rain helped to make the players very miserable' concluded one report.[88] It grew too dark to play the last quarter and the Macedon players trudged home without scoring. Footballers in Hesket had formed a club by the start of the twentieth century, and set about finding a better place to play. Hesket also became the driving force in a new local football league, the Riddell and District League, which was expanded to the Romsey and District League in 1917. Soon afterwards, Hesket was able to play home games on a recognisable oval in Hanging Rock Reserve. Hesket tennis players also used the Rock's courts each weekend from 1937. During World War I, the township sustained a 'Hesket Bohemians Cricket Club', and then in 1936 Hesket joined the Gisborne-Lancefield Cricket Association, playing matches at Hanging Rock.[89]

Hanging Rock from Boxshall Family Farm, c.1870 - c.1900.
Item MM 140637. Unknown photographer.

Museums Victoria

Boxshall Family Farm, Newham, Victoria, c.1870 - c.1900.
Item MM 140639. Unknown photographer.

Museums Victoria

Claims to Leases of Crown Land. Argus, 29 September, 1848.
State Library of Victoria

DEATH OF AN OLD COLONIST.

[FROM OUR OWN CORRESPONDENT.]

WOODEND, WEDNESDA

One of the oldest inhabitants of Victoria, Mr. Edward Dryden, died at his residence, Newham, on Sunday last, after a very short illness. Mr. Dryden was born in the village of Newham, near Newcastle, Northumberland, England, in 1808, and in 1836 he arrived in Tasmania. On the 1st of January, 1837, he landed in Melbourne. After a few days he travelled up to this district with some sheep and cattle, and first camped on the banks of a rivulet, now known as the Garden Hut Creek, but shortly afterwards shifted to the site of his late residence, and took up the surrounding country as a run and called it, after his native village, the Newham station, and the parish and shire were afterwards given the same name. In 1843 he married Miss Anne Robertson, sister to the late Mr. Francis Robertson, M.L.C., and leaves a family of six children. Mr. Dryden was highly respected by all who knew him for his upright, honorable conduct during his long residence in this district, which, if he had lived till next New Year's day, would have extended over fifty years. He had reached the ripe age of 78 years. The remains were interred in the Woodend Cemetery this afternoon. the funeral being largely attended.

Death Of An Old Colonist. Melbourne Leader, 1 May, 1886.
State Library of Victoria

Farmers Union of Victoria, Delegates at the First Conference, October, 1879. Newham.
State Library of Victoria

Familiar figures from the local towns were also stalwarts of Hanging Rock racedays. Jack Keating, the driving force in the racing club over many years, was born in Tasmania in 1831 and came to Victoria to mine at Fryers Creek. He, like so many other local diggers, set off for the Otago rushes in New Zealand, where, instead of digging for gold, he ran a shop as a butcher, and then as a baker.[90] Once back in Victoria, he started a carrying business for which he built up a team of over one hundred bullocks. He also ran the Newham Hotel. Patrick Francis Meagher, another familiar figure on Hanging Rock racedays (he was Clerk of the Course) was born in Tipperary in Ireland. Meagher worked for a time in the Bank of Melbourne before he too set off to dig for gold. He then tried his hand running a hotel before joining the police force. As well as working on racedays, Meagher established a reputation as a sharp breeder of horses, racing thoroughbreds included.

Not all of the local farmers, storekeepers or church builders were as keen on racedays and gambling at Hanging Rock. Eli Jones, for example, was the man who had defied threats from a shellalagh-wielding 'lessee' in a skirmish over Hanging Rock's water. Eli died in 1916, and was recalled as a man who knew the area 'before the axe had cleared the forest'. He was the last survivor of the first wave of farmers in Newham and Hanging Rock.[91] After digging for gold in both Mt Alexander and in New Zealand, Eli and his father settled near Hanging Rock. He married the daughter of Richard Adams, a figure prominent in almost every phase of the Rock's nineteenth century and early twentieth century history (and a stalwart of the Farmers Union). Like Adams, Eli was one of the founders of the Zion Baptist Chapel built near Hanging Rock in 1869. It was from this congregation that there emerged many of the opponents of the race club.[92] Patrons of social and political life could then be found in a range of local associations, not all of them in constant harmony. But beyond disputes over gambling, water or hotel rowdiness, these farmers shared an interest in progressive agricultural practices and in trying to keep local social networks alive. Looking back over their nomadic young lives, when they tried digging around Castlemaine, voyages to Otago and back, and attempts to run hotels or haulage businesses, their small farms beneath Hanging Rock no doubt established a sense of security and connection, to both neighbours and environment. There is a sense that they struggled to keep local networks alive after World War II. By then, like Eli Jones, the first band of farmers had passed on, and many of their children had moved north to larger holdings, or else headed for the city. Expanded car-ownership after 1945 may have eventually worked wonders for the tourist trade at Hanging Rock. At the same time, cars and trucks ensured the death of most of the functions of the small towns around the Reserve. But the land at the foot of the Rock remains a rich farming region. New 'settlers' have revived local social networks, and, as with the Kerrie Primary School, found a new life for old buildings. Country Fire Authority Brigades and Landcare groups fill some of the community-building roles once dependent on schools and churches. As old pursuits in growing potatoes or oats have declined, new artisanal enterprises, in vineyards for example, now flourish. Hanging Rock can still be pictured as the centrepiece of a rich, integrated agricultural and cultural life in the 21st century.

Cow yard after milking at Braemar Guest House, Woodend. c.1890 – 1919. Unknown photographer.
State Library of Victoria

Woodend

48¾ Miles N E of Melbourne, and
1840 feet above sea level, chief town
of the Shire, with good Library Institute &c

UNDER RUGGED ROCKS RESTING.
near Hanging Rock. Woodend.

Farming and fruit district, &
within easy distance of The
Hanging Rock, and The Camels
Hump

Boxshalls farm, Newham, Victoria c.1890. Creator: Stevenson &
McNicoll Studio.
Museums Victoria

The Newham Creamery. Newham, Victoria. c.1895.
Item MM 8592. Unknown photographer.
Museums Victoria

Teachers and pupils outside Rochford State School No. 540. Rochford, Victoria. c.1895.
Item MM 6328. Creator. J. P. Lind Studio.
Museums Victoria

Winning potatoes and cup at Romsey Potato Show Competition. Romsey, Victoria. c.1925. Unknown photographer.

The Romsey and Lancefield Districts Historical Society

Romsey Potato Show Competition Cup won outright by T.A.Parks June 1921. Photograph by Matthew Nickson.

The Romsey and Lancefield Districts Historical Society

Timber cutters, Kerrie. c.1925. Unknown photographer.
The Romsey and Lancefield Districts Historical Society

Endnotes

1 See *Census for the Commonwealth of Australia*, 1911, Table: Population of towns above 1000.

2 Charles Hotson Ebden, *Australian Dictionary of Biography*, National Centre of Biography, Australian National University, http://adb.anu.edu.au/biography/ebden-charles-hotson-2018 (viewed online, March 2017).

3 An Edward Dryden is listed as arriving in Tasmania on 20 August 1836 aged 28 on board the ship Amelia Thompson, Archives of Tasmania Names Index, 1468471, Series CS01/1/872, file number 18447). However the only Edward Dryden listed as departing for Port Phillip was on 26 October 1842, aboard the 'Scout' from Launceston and headed for Port Phillip, Archives of Tasmania, name index, 544402, Series POL459/1/2 p. 24. Perhaps he had returned to collect stock for his new run. Thomas Dryden is recorded as departing for Port Phillip on 27 January 1837 aboard the John Dunscombe (these details can be accessed on-line via The Archives of Tasmania Name Index at https://talis.ent.sirsidynix.net.au/client/en_AU/names/) It is Thomas Dryden's name that appears as the leaseholder near to Hanging Rock in the 1850s.

4 'Death of an old colonist', *South Bourke and Mornington Journal*, 5 May 1886.

5 J.O.Randell, *Pastoral Settlement in Northern Victoria*, 2 vols, vol. 2. The Campaspe District, Chandos Publishing, Burwood Victoria, 1982: 6; and R.V. Billis and A.S. Kenyon, *Pastoral Pioneers of Victoria*, McMillan, Melbourne, 1932.

6 Randell, *Pastoral Settlement in Northern Victoria*: 7.

7 Port Phillip, *NSW Government Gazette*, no. 55, 9 September 1840: 863-64

8 'Claims to Leases of Crown Land', *Port Phillip and Morning Advertiser*, 4 October 1848: 4

9 *NSW Government Gazette*, 21October 1848: 1515

10 ' The Land Bill', *Argus*, 21 September 1857: 5.

11 Crown Lands, *Crown Land Licences*, 1851, *Parliament of Victoria Legislative Council* 1856, John Ferries Victoria Government Printer, Melbourne, 1856: 5.

12 Return of Stations, Western Port District, *Occupants of Crown Lands*, Victoria 1853, *Return to Legislative Council*, Victoria Parliament Printing, Melbourne 1853: 24

13 Crown Lands, *Crown Land Licences*, 1851, *Parliament of Victoria Legislative Council* 1856, John Ferries Victoria Government Printer, Melbourne, 1856: 37.

14 Crown Lands, *Crown Land Licences*, 1851: 55.

15 'Death of an old colonist', *South Bourke and Mornington Journal*, 5 May 1886.

16 'Death of an old colonist', *South Bourke and Mornington Journal*, 5 May 1886.

17 See below ch. 5.

18 Edward Dryden Probate, 32/281 VPRS 28/P0002 Unit 202, PROV.

19 See the discussion in Victoria Department of Agriculture, *Minutes of the Proceedings taken at a Conference on Horse Breeding*, 7 September 1900, Melbourne, 1900, State Library of Victoria Agricultural Pamphlets.

20 'Advertisement', *Mount Alexander Mail*, 8 September 1865: 3.

21 'Mount Macedon', *Argus*, 27 April 1849: 4.

22 *Victoria Government Gazette*, 15 September 1868 p. 741 and Argus, 8 October 1881: 8.

23 Edward Dryden, Probate File, PROV.

24 *Table Talk*, 6 August 1886: 4.

25 The deserted house appears on websites devoted to the Paranormal. See for example The Paranormal Guide, http://www.theparanormalguide.com/blog/garth-homestead-misery-and-death (viewed on line, February 2017).

26 Hanging Rock File, Gisborne and Mt Macedon Districts Historical Society. See too Gisborne and Mount Macedon Districts Historical Society Inc, *Pictorial Hanging Rock, A journey Through Time*, Gisborne and Mount Macedon Districts Historical Society Inc., Keysborough Vic.,2012: 8

27 Hanging Rock File, Gisborne and Mt Macedon Districts Historical Society.

28 *McIvor Times and Rodney Advertiser*, 2 May 1878: 2, *Kyneton Guardian*, 9 September 1915: 3.

29 T. Schmidt to G.C. Darbyshire. 7 June 1890, 191/18342, Survey Correspondence, Railway Department, VPRO.

30 Minutes, 29 November 1873, Minute Book, Shire of Newham, 1873-78, 0143225 p0001/000002, PROV.

31 Peter S Knights, authorised by John R Parker Surveyor General, 'Rivers and Their Impact on Cadastral Boundaries', typescript, Victoria, October 1996, no page numbers.

32 Knights, 'Rivers and Their Impact on Cadastral Boundaries'.

33 Victoria, Legislative Assembly, *Hansard* 8 September 1886, Mr. Quick, question to Nimmo.

34 Shire Council to Commissioner of Lands Bailiff, 23 August 1871, Gisborne and Mt Macedon Districts Historical Society. In the initial proposal for the Reserve its value as a quarry was raised and colonial land officials as well as local residents had to resist a push to have Hanging Rock declared a water, recreation and quarrying reserve.

35 Minutes, Newham Minute Book, 30 January 1875.

36 Minutes, Newham Minute Book, 30 September 1875

37 Letter typescript, Hanging Rock file, Gisborne and Mt Macedon Districts H.S.

38 Kyneton *Guardian*, 31 May 1876: 3.

39 Letter to Minister of Lands 29 October 1883, Gisborne and Mt Macedon Districts H.S.

40 Letter to Minister of Lands , November 1883, Gisborne and Mt Macedon Districts H.S.

41 Letter, Residents to Lands Department, 1883, Gisborne and Mt Macedon and Districts H.S.

42 Shire Secretary, Woodend, 23 April 1938 to Secretary Lands and Survey, Hanging Rock Box, Gisborne and Mt Macedon Districts Historical Society.

43 Letter to Lands, 23 April 1938. Hanging Rock Box , Gisborne and Mt Macedon Districts Historical Society.

44 Letter. Lands Department to Secretary Shire of Newham and Woodend, 28 November 1938, Gisborne and Mt Macedon Districts Historical Society.

45 'Reports', *Kyneton Guardian*. 31 October 1914: 4.

[46] Shire of Newham, Cash Book.

[47] *Age*, 2 March 1900: 6.

[48] *Kyneton Guardian*, 31 October 1914: 4.

[49] *Age*, 9 February 1929: 20.

[50] 'Phenomenal Snow Storm', *Age*, 29 August 1906: 7.

[51] *Australasian*, 26 October 1881: 2.

[52] *Australasian*, 26 October 1881: 2.

[53] 'At Hanging Rock', *Australasian*, 10 January 1903: 36.

[54] See generally, A.T. Yarwood, Walers, *Australian Horses Abroad*, Melbourne University Press, Carlton, 1989.

[55] Patrick Meagher of Hesket/Newham for example was thought to be a sharp buyer of imported bloodstock.

[56] On connections between the Australian equine industry and India and South Africa see generally, Samuel Griffiths, *A Rolling Stone Gathers No Moss*, Angus and Robertson, Sydney, 1933.

[57] 'Holidays at Cobaw Ranges', *Weekly Times*. 9 June 1917: 37

[58] *Weekly Times*, 17 January 1903: 8.

[59] 'Nearly twenty-four years', *Weekly Times*, 17 October 1903: 8.

[60] Betty Jean Barned, *My side of the mountain, a history of Hesket, Cherokee and Kerrie*, Lowden, Kilmore, Vic., 1983: 124

[61] Barned, *My side of the mountain*: 124. The legends about Hanging Rock as a bushrangers' lair may have originated in 1879, when armed robbers stuck up a bank in Lancefield. Initially feared as an attack by Ned Kelly and his gang, who were imagined as holed up on Hanging Rock, the crime was sheeted home to two hapless drifters, who had apparently met up in a Melbourne pub, and after their raid, headed off to Bendigo.

[62] *Mount Alexander Mail*, 23 October 1875: 2.

[63] Parliament of Victoria, *Report from the Wattle Bark Board of Inquiry 1878, Victoria Parliamentary Papers*, 1878: 36.

[64] 'Heavy potato crop', *Argus*, 23 May 1905: 6.

[65] 'Potato and fruit growing at Newham', *Leader*, 14 August 1880: 13.

[66] 'Mixed farming at Kerrie', *Australasian*, 9 July 1927: 8.

[67] 'Mixed farming at Kerrie', *Australasian*, 9 July 1927: 8.

[68] Mentor, 'Settler succeeds on smallholding in Newham', *Weekly Times*, 25 April 1931: 37

[69] 'Visit to a Newham Farm', *Woodend Star*, 17 March 1917: 2.

ce Woodend', *Woodend Star*, 1 May 1915: 2.

[71] 'A potato digger trial', *Wagga Wagga Advertiser*, 2 May 1895: 4.

[72] Mentor, 'Settler succeeds on smallholding in Newham', *Weekly Times*, 25 April 1931: 37.

[73] Margaret Hall, Hesket, Inquest Deposition Files, 1 June 1890, VPRS 24/P0000/565, PROV.

[74] R.W.G. Bourke to Lands Department, 5 August 1892, Lands Department Correspondence, Series 05357/P0000/003775 7659/5 10, PROV.

[75] Bourke to Lands Department, 28 April 1908, PROV.

[76] ' The Victorian Farmers' Union', *Weekly Times*, 11 October 1879: 22.

[77] 'Newham Farmers Union', *Kyneton Guardian*, 17 September 1879: 2.

[78] 'Farmers Union', *Romsey Examiner*, 12 June 1914: 2.

[79] Farmers Advocate, I June 1917: 4.

[80] *A brief history of the National Country Party of Australia*, National Country Party, Canberra, 1979 and Ulrich Ellis, *A History of the Australian Country Party*, Melbourne University Press, Melbourne, 1963.

[81] ' Honey Bags from the Queen Bees's Storehouse', *Farmers Advocate*, 27 July 1922: 12

[82] C, McKenzie, *Looking Back Newham Primary School Centenary*, McKenzie, Newham, Vic., 1977: 32-33.

[83] 'The Brough Smyth Inquiry', *Kyneton Guardian*, 3 May 1876: 3.

[84] McKenzie *Looking Back Newham Primary School Centenary*.

[85] Barned *My side of the mountain*: 54.

[86] Heritage Branch Victoria, Victoria Heritage Data base, Former Kerrie Primary School, 1290, Entry H1631, registered 1982.

[87] Heritage Branch Victoria, Former Kerrie Primary School.

[88] *Sunbury News*, 23 July 1892: 3.

[89] 'Football', *Argus*, 12 October 1936: 6.

[90] McKenzie, *Looking Back Newham Primary*: 32-33

[91] 'Mr Eli Jones' Death', *Kyneton Guardian*, 1 June 1916: 2.

[92] 'Mr Eli Jones' Death', *Kyneton Guardian*, 1 June 1916: 2.

View of Course, showing Hanging Rock. Hanging Rock Races (Woodend). 2 January, 1905.
Punch, 5 January, 1905.
State Library of Victoria

Little Flemington

'Where in this universe is the racecourse that can equal this, with its hundred and one beauties of rural simplicity? Is it not far more impressive than Ascot with its wealth of aristocrats; far lovelier than Longchamps with its giddy throng; more enchanting even than our well-beloved Flemington with its brilliancy on a most festive day? Which of these can compare with this little remote racecourse with its modest structures and simple white rails nestling contentedly amid the slopes and hills that rise majestically to guard it'.

'A Day at Hanging Rock Races', Table Talk, 7 January 1915: 7

Daniel Lyons's Osprey jumped out alongside six other beginning horses, in the Trial Stakes at Hanging Rock's 'little remote racecourse', on the first day of the year, 1893. Under the shadow of the majestic Rock, the racing novices galloped off, along a track threading through gum trees. Although this was his first trip around Hanging Rock's tight little track, Daniel had been riding racehorses for five years. And despite being kicked by another horse in a false start, he was convinced he could handle Osprey, since he was, after all, apprenticed to the owner and trainer, and knew the horse well enough. So he angled his mount, probably a little too confidently, into a sharp turn. Osprey stumbled and fell. Daniel Lyons was crushed under the horse's weight. He died in Kyneton hospital four days later.[1]

Enchanting, majestic, and contented, the 'little remote racecourse' may well have been. But Hanging Rock had its share of raceday tragedies. A coronial inquest blamed Daniel's fall, not on his inexperience as a jockey (he was only twenty years old), but instead, on the poor condition of the Hanging Rock racetrack. 'I do not consider the course a safe one and would not send another horse to run there unless it was altered' stated the owner of Osprey, John Williams of Riddell's Creek.[2] The turns were too sharp, the track 'uneven up and down hills all the way', he explained. Jockeys at the inquest agreed with Williams. Alexander McRae was riding Fire Brigade in the same race, when he too was brought down by Osprey's fall. When he rolled clear he saw the two horses galloping ahead, and Lyons on the ground. McRae also considered the turn was too sharp and the track slippery. He had seen a good number of bad falls at Hanging Rock over the years although, at the same time, he had to admit that dangers lurked on many country tracks.[3] Sam McDougall had come up from Ascot Vale to ride that day. He recollected that Daniel seemed to lack a good jockey's patience, and was far too anxious about saving ground on the turn. All the same he went on:

> I have been riding for thirteen years. I do not think the course a safe one to race upon in its present condition. The running ground is terribly rough and the course has several sharp dangerous turns in addition to the one where Lyons fell. Last 2nd January was the

first time I rode over it and I would not come up again to ride upon it in its present condition.[4]

The Hanging Rock track, as McRae and others knew, posed no unique dangers, since racetrack falls were commonplace across the rough 1890s Victorian thoroughbred scene. If it were not for such a tragedy as Daniel's death, an isolated racetrack like Hanging Rock, hosting only one meeting each year, would barely have registered in the rising public criticism of horse racing in the 1890s. By then, with the easy pickings of the boomtime 1880s vanished, shady betting coups, corrupt and aggressive jockeys, and unscrupulous trainers and owners were muddying the reputation of the 'Sport of Kings'. A death at New Year had brought thoroughbred racing's difficulties home to Hanging Rock itself.

'On the flat, at the base of the rock, a bush racecourse is laid out, and around the booths and judge's box the people congregate, standing on the gentle slope that edges away to the base of the overhanging mass of stone' was one romanticised and commonplace account of the annual Hanging Rock raceday.[5] Hanging Rock, despite falls, warnings off, financial crises and attacks from anti-gambling forces, clung on to this picnic atmosphere through to the 21st century. Fascinating to thousands as a day out in the bush, and as a spectacular carnival for the New Year, the races drew masses of spectators throughout their twentieth-century heyday. But a horse's fall and jockey's death were entangled in antagonisms that would dog Hanging Rock races for decades. Anti-gambling crusaders in the early twentieth century used racetrack deaths as propaganda, to close down bookmakers and racing itself. The state of the track raised queries about the place of horseracing in a public reserve. In defending their cherished raceday, successive race clubs at Hanging Rock struggled to maintain Hanging Rock's amateurish, casual atmosphere, whilst at the same time responding to demands for safety, and for limits to gambling and drinking. These challenges, in keeping up a bush picnic style, and at the same time meeting professional standards, whilst also holding off the critics of horseracing, have continued to this day.

ROUGH BUSH RACING

Races have been run at Hanging Rock since the 1860s. At first these were rough and ready affairs with little prize money, no official controls, and races usually run between picnickers' horses. Such helter-skelter challenges had grown out of the general carnivalesque conjured up at the base of the Rock on New Year's Day. One nostalgic reflection turned to the 'local hack races . . . among the timber and [in which] VRC [Victoria Racing Club] rules are lightly regarded'.[6] By 1879 these rough contests were given a semblance of order, with a race restricted to the progeny of William Peters' favourite stallion, Peter Finn.[7] Horse races also alternated with contests like filling potato sacks. So little had the sports day been commercialised, that rights to raceday publicans' booths sold for only £5 each in the 1880s, whereas by the end of World War I, they fetched £200. These pioneering New Year's Day contests were held at the western base of the Rock, before a new track was laid out to the east after 1884. With meetings coinciding with the New Year's Day holiday excursions, loosely organised local groups conducted the races. Their contests shared few if any direct links to the wider thoroughbred racing world of Victoria. Only the most dedicated, or desperate professional trainer, and certainly no celebrity jockey, would bother with a trip out of Melbourne, to compete at Hanging Rock.

An organised and structured raceday programme for horseracing at Hanging Rock only emerged in the 1880s. Across that wild decade, Melbourne's boomtime real estate market gave rise to a flashy, moneyed class, parvenus eager to buy thoroughbreds, and so join the pastoral elite in the Flemington grandstands. Whilst racing clubs at provincial towns such as Bendigo or Ballarat could attract these new owners, smaller clubs struggled, and relied on often meagre local support. 'Hanging Rock Sports', in other words, a program with races for both horses and humans, were advertised for New Year's Day 1880.[8] The Hanging Rock Cup was to be run at weight-for-age and over a trip 'twice around the course and a distance'.[9] Fittingly, Edward Dryden's Commodore was hailed the winner. By 1883, the races were more formalised, although they remained proudly local,

and were organised by the 'Hanging Rock Sports Club'. Local J.P., P.F. Meagher, acted as raceday Judge, W. Peters as Starter and E. Bowen as Clerk of the Course for the day. Seven sovereigns were on offer for the winner of a Maiden Plate (for horses that had never won a race valued at more than £5). None too sure of the measurements of the Hanging Rock track, the club listed its Maiden Plate as a race of 'about one and a half miles'.[10] The winnings for the Hanging Rock Cup were twelve sovereigns and the race was run over the same distance as the Melbourne Cup, two miles, with the horses running twice around the Hanging Rock course. Unlike the winner of the Melbourne Cup, first past the post at Hanging Rock was to be put up for sale immediately after the race, with bids commencing at £50. In 1883 Daylight, a four-year-old, won, carrying nine stone four pounds to victory, before moving on to a new owner.[11]

PROFESSIONALISING RACING

With Hanging Rock Reserve extended in 1884, racing enthusiasts reorganised their racing under the auspices of the Hanging Rock Racing Club, set up in August 1885, and replacing the short-lived Hanging Rock Amateur Turf Club. Over the following decade they tried to attract more trainers and thoroughbreds from the city, with only limited success. Hanging Rock had to compete against rival New Year's bush meetings, especially that run at Lal Lal, between Ballarat and Geelong. Special trains ran from Ballarat, Melbourne and Geelong, to the little station at Lal Lal on racedays. Near to the township, the local waterfalls were every bit as spectacular as Hanging Rock, and besides, the Lal Lal Cup was run for prize money of sixty sovereigns, a sum that the Hanging Rock club struggled to match.[12]

By 1890, much of the early rough and tumble aura had faded, as Hanging Rock, along with other country race clubs, was brought firmly under the control of the VRC. The Victorian parliament had made the Victoria Racing Club the controlling body for all racing in the 1890s, in response to both the fascination with racing in the 1880s, and fears about race-fixing scandals.[13] Even though thoroughbred racing remained an enormously popular spectacle, betting controversies,

The Committee. Hanging Rock Races (Woodend). 2 January, 1905.
Punch, 5 January, 1905.
State Library of Victoria

View from Hanging Rock. Hanging Rock Races (Woodend) 2 January, 1905.
Punch, 5 January, 1905.
State Library of Victoria

and a more confident anti-gambling movement, forced new controls on clubs. No sooner had the Hanging Rock Cup begun to attract wide interest, then the Hanging Rock Racing Club found its right to run races at Hanging Rock challenged locally, and, more ominously, in Victoria's parliament.

In 1896 the Club responded to the demands of the VRC, and thought about shaping a new course. Not that this brought the injuries and danger of racing at Hanging Rock to an immediate end. On New Year's Day 1896, with the Kyneton Brass Band playing before the race, Mawika started in the handicap hurdle, only to fall at the first fence. Then, in the pony race worth £5 to the winner, Mysta started, and immediately bolted off the course, ran her rider into a tree, and broke the jockey's arm! For years the club had been warned about fallen timbers alongside the track, which caused havoc for some jockeys. Even the Hanging Rock Cup, now reduced to one mile in length, could only attract three starters.[14]

From this point onwards the club launched into a strenuous campaign to meet the increasingly stringent demands of the VRC. The committee drew up plans for modernised stables, stewards' rooms, and members' enclosure. Despite all of their work, fears of falls, like that of Osprey and Daniel Lyons, overshadowed racedays, so that reshaping the track could be put off no longer. The club at first proposed extending their racing circuit to seven furlongs and prepared the ground for new rooms, stabling and spectator facilities. At the same time, in answering the demands of the VRC, Hanging Rock Racing Club fell out with its neighbours. A decade-long struggle began, over the anomalous siting of a racing club, that had grown sporadically, and almost by accident, and which was somehow running meetings within the bounds of a popular picnic resort.

PUNTERS, PICNICS AND ANTI-GAMBLING

In 1899 the club started work on redesigning its dangerous track. Many small country clubs besides Hanging Rock were forced to upgrade tracks, and exercise greater control over bookmakers,

jockeys, trainers and horses at the end of the nineteenth century. This challenge was made more acute at Hanging Rock, because the track sat at the centre of a natural space, one which was simultaneously winning new interest from pioneer nature lovers and 'ramblers', or bushwalkers. This conflict, between Hanging Rock as a site for peaceful recreation in a natural environment, and the raucous, energetic spectacle of bush horseracing, sharpened as the new century dawned. All the while, the club was still seeking to control entry to the Reserve, and to rebuild facilities in line with the demands of the VRC. Beyond charging for all vehicles entering on New Year's Day, the racing club now proposed a charge of sixpence on each and every pedestrian racegoer, bushwalker, or any other holiday visitor to what was a public reserve. For the most part with the backing of Newham councillors, the club approached the Minister of Lands, seeking legal changes so as to begin charging. As a start to refashioning Hanging Rock, the club also wanted to extend the course, with the new track more evenly graded, so as to avoid any further catastrophes such as that which befell Osprey and his young rider. With the VRC still insisting on improvements at bush tracks, the Hanging Rock club worked to upgrade the track, and construct secure fencing between 1898 and 1911, at a cost of £500, a vast sum for a small race club.[15] In the end, this proved money well spent. With races now run on New Year's Day and at Easter, the Hanging Rock Racing Club recorded a profit on the New Year's Day races of £167 and then £37 at Easter.[16] Even so, the track still did not meet the standards set by the VRC. Hanging Rock Racing Club meanwhile had found itself caught up in Victoria-wide controversies about gambling, drinking and racing.

As a means of dampening criticism from nature enthusiasts, the club had promised to make 'improvements' to the Reserve. One racegoer's dream, of converting the Rock into a gigantic grandstand was never entertained in any serious manner.[17] Instead, as we have seen in an earlier chapter, the improvements included widespread tree plantings over several years. Immediately lovers of the bush responded. 'No improvement is necessary to enhance the natural beauties of the Rock' charged one neighbour, dismayed that racing people in Woodend were entitled to a greater say in the future of the Rock than local residents. 'A racetrack can never be anything but a disfigurement' in any Australian natural setting, charged one irate 'rambler'.[18]

There was always more to this dispute than fears about private control of a public reserve. Hanging Rock became a symbol in the wider Victorian war against gambling, drinking and rowdy recreations in general. The difficulties of the racing club were compounded by social geography. As well as the racing club occupying space at the foot of Hanging Rock, so too did the Zion Baptist Chapel. Two of the strongest voices in the congregation were Richard Adams and Eli Jones, widely respected as pioneer farmers in the district, and either on council, as was Adams, or a constant thorn in council's side, as was Jones. These two could always be found in the thick of any tussle over the future of Hanging Rock Reserve. Jones had fought with council over water rights at Hanging Rock. Now, he and Adams, along with others in their small congregation, whilst they may have tolerated horse racing, were outraged by any attempt to bring in bigger crowds, or allow bookmakers to take bets beneath their cherished Hanging Rock.

As the club continued to push for new track and stables, more booths for publicans, and expanded entry for bookmakers, the grounds of the opposition shifted from Hanging Rock itself, to the Temperance Hall in Kyneton. The jockeys, trainers and punters, and of course their horses, who raced once or twice a year at Hanging Rock, now found themselves embroiled in a nasty feud, which was to last for years. The more successful was the club in attracting New Year's Day crowds, the more anti-gamblers in nearby towns demanded that the track be closed down, or at least moved out of the Reserve at Hanging Rock. The VRC itself had complicated matters. It refused to license the course beyond New Year's Day 1906, and was pushing the club to buy land adjacent to the Reserve, for a new privately owned (proprietary) track. If they were not prepared to move, then the VRC wanted Hanging Rock's six and a half furlong course extended to seven furlongs. As they had already expended £500, the club now faced the uphill battle involved in funding works that could end up costing £2000 or £3000.

They could only fund this project by charging one shilling entry on five days a year.[19] But it was up to the minister of lands rather than the VRC itself, to grant the club five racing days each year.

The disputes over Hanging Rock came at a time of enormous controversy in horseracing and reduction in the sorts of 'al fresco' drinking and gambling that had underpinned the meeting's growing popularity. A Royal Commission into the Victoria Police, 1905-6, exposed the popularity of illegal gambling as well as the potential for police corruption in the spread of totalisators through Melbourne's inner suburbs. John Wren's name came up over and over again, as the genius behind the most lucrative of off-course totes, in working-class Collingwood. When the Methodist preacher and anti-gambling firebrand, W. H. Judkins, campaigned against betting and beer 'with as much subtlety as a sledgehammer', according to the biographer of John Wren, Melbourne racing writer High Buggy, even small clubs like Hanging Rock could barely escape censure.[20] The extension of the track and control over entry to a public reserve, initially a dispute over recreational land, was now intensified through moral campaigning. The club it seemed had launched a program of works at exactly the wrong time.

THE RACING CONTROVERSY

With the 1905 races run in front of a crowd of more than ten thousand avid spectators, and marginally interested picnickers, the club garnered a tidy profit. Racing enthusiasts and anti-gamblers alike, then turned to the Kyneton Temperance Hall.[21] The Reverend Charles Tregear presided over the packed hall and announced that the intention of the meeting was to launch a vehement protest against any concessions being granted to horseracing at Hanging Rock. Tregear had become a familiar figure across the old goldfields towns of Victoria. He was admired, and reviled, as a 'born showman', one who illustrated his frequent lectures with lantern-slides, while speaking on topics ranging from the immoralities of gamblers to the glories of the British Empire. On the stage in the Temperance Hall in Kyneton, he put his repertoire of charismatic skills to good use, before handing over the meeting to councillor David James of Newham. James thanked the good folk of Kyneton for their support in resisting the expansion of the racing club's foothold on the Hanging Rock Reserve. A 'lady from Woodend' denounced the club's entry charge of sixpence as 'iniquitous', and Mr. W. Kerr proposed that all rights of the club be withdrawn and 'racing abolished from the reserve on New Year's Day and every day'.

Others insisted that the club should just move any meetings to Woodend, only six miles away, and that the state ought to wrest control of the Reserve from the local council, appoint a permanent caretaker with his own cottage at the Reserve, and so keep racing with its attendant evils out of the picnic spot. Only then could Hanging Rock be returned to its 'natural beauty'. The immediate response of the shire was to seek a legal opinion on its right to charge admission to the public reserve.[22] Councillors sought answers on the legality of increasingly lucrative revenue derived from selling off publicans' booths. The shire's underwriting of hire costs for mounted police to control the raceday throng also seemed questionable.

Reflecting on the conflict from afar, the *Australasian* noted that 'Hanging Rock is not too romantic a spot now on the rare race days: but the swings, the booths, and the trestle-bars serve their use for an hour and then vanish, leaving little trace behind them'.[23] The dispute it seemed to outsiders, stemmed from the fact that the racing club had wanted to 'make the al fresco race meetings held at this holiday resort more like the regular thing and to this end is ready to spend money and turn some 50 acres of the reserve into a fenced and properly-equipped course'.[24] Sniped at by local clergymen, and with the anti-gambling forces in Kyneton latching onto the race club's rights as a test of local morality, the council reassembled for a special meeting on 28 July 1905. Ten councillors of the fifteen agreed that no further concessions be given to the racing club on land reserved for public recreation at Hanging Rock.[25]

Rapidly, what had begun as a petty local dispute, reached the

Victorian government. And events on Cup Day 1905, though they turned a profit, did not do much for the club's standing. The Cup in 1905 was won by J. Smerdon's Strathleen, but only after one rival fell, and another slipped badly. In an earlier race, the owner, trainer and jockey of Soprano, along with Soprano herself, were all disqualified.[26] Some months after this destabilising day for Hanging Rock racing, and in the depths of the freezing winter of 1905, the Minister for Lands, and Warrnambool farmer, Jack Murray, decided to visit Hanging Rock himself. He battled through snowdrifts around Macedon and in parts of the Hanging Rock Reserve, only to then be confronted by a 'stormy meeting' when he eventually arrived in Kyneton.[27] Dr Duncan, the shire president, was met with 'hoots and cheers' as he tried to introduce Murray. The crowd then 'indulged in truculent satire', several speakers almost came to blows, and councillor McKenzie labelled Mr. J.A. Donald an anarchist. The legendary Rev. Charles Tregear reappeared, to assert that the racing club would force picnickers to decamp to the eastern side of the Reserve, where there was no water. The local branch of the ANA (Australian Natives Association) announced their opposition to the racing club. Murray, who thought that he was coming to Kyneton to hear reasoned debate, chided the crowd for 'having behaved in such a disgraceful manner'.[28] When Mr McDonald, a VRC stipendiary steward, rose to speak, pandemonium broke out, so that he struggled to be heard. Had anyone listened, they might have understood the dilemma facing Murray. McDonald stated that he had been in the district for 34 years and had opposed the first races on the Reserve in the 1880s. Although a racing man, he reminded the crowd that 'he came from a country where the people had had more experience in the value of preserving their heritage and knew how their commons had been encroached upon and taken away'.

Hanging Rock Racing Club no doubt expected that Murray would not be swayed by such reflections.[29] An owner of racehorses and trotters himself, Murray took on some radical political stands, opposing the war in South Africa, demanding state support for Aboriginal people, and pushing plans to electrify the state's railways.[30] Jack Murray, who was a few years later to become Premier of Victoria, quickly realised that a bunfight in a Temperance Hall could turn his mission into a political disaster. He summed up proceedings, and set off back to Melbourne. But not before noting that if there was no gambling or drinking at the races, then very few of the 14,000 spectators at the Hanging Rock races would bother to turn up, and spend money in the district. All the same, racing people did not really appreciate natural beauty he mused, and so had no need to hold races beneath the glorious rock. The best that could be done he concluded, was to leave things as they were.[31] The club could race on five days but not expand their track or buildings.

MODERNISED RACING

The status quo desired by Jack Murray was not quite as it seemed, since the club was winning some sort of patronage in higher circles. The state governor attended the New Year's races the following year, to be escorted around the track by local parliamentarian, Fitzgerald.[32] Undaunted, the stalwarts of the anti-racing campaign continued their struggle. M. J. Donald, so prominent in the earlier gatherings, wrote to the *Argus* in 1907, asserting that Murray's earlier neutrality had been a massive defeat for the racing club. 'This club will never rest satisfied until they get complete possession of the reserve for racing purposes' warned Donald.[33] As swiftly as possible, chief secretary, Alexander Peacock, cut short further debate, deciding more or less in the club's favour. Peacock rejected requests for five days racing, limiting the club to New Year and Easter. At the same time he refused to meet with the delegation opposed to racing on the Reserve. Instead he proposed that since racing had been held at Hanging Rock for more or less forty years, the club was certainly entitled to continue with its meetings.[34]

This appeared as a major victory for racing at Hanging Rock. Peacock had made clear that the Reserve was for popular pastimes enjoyed by the masses, and not a place for the private contemplation of nature. The club still had to secure improvements, and now faced anti-racing forces who presented a new argument: Hanging Rock was an inferior course and ought to be closed for that reason alone. One racing fan responded:

If the Hanging Rock course is an inferior racecourse . . . who have we to thank for it remaining so? Not the club who was ready to spend thousands on it if their rights were guaranteed and who have spent hundreds on it clearing away useless timber, enabling one to have uninterrupted views across the course. Orderliness of that kind does not meet with your correspondent's approval; he wants nothing short of the picturesque. Why should a few faddists be listened to when they wish to mar the pleasures of fourteen or fifteen thousand who attend their favorite sports meeting.[35]

Clearly, notions of orderliness, useless timber and disdain for the sensitivities of 'faddists', differentiated the racetrack punters from the new and growing networks of bushwalkers, naturalists, and lovers of the picturesque. A racetrack with publican's booths, children's carnival games, and betting was bound to attract the ire of defenders of public spaces, anti-gamblers and nature lovers. Hanging Rock proved no exception. A growing number of visitors to Hanging Rock were now more often fascinated by flora and fauna, than by crowds and noise at a race meeting. Geological expeditions, reflecting the reach of Lyell's theories, attracted several. Amateur geologists and walkers by-passed the hurly-burly of races, and sideshows offering them the chance to don boxing gloves. Other crude attractions on racedays included cash for trying to ride an unbroken colt, or throwing down Aunt Sallies named 'Judkins' in dishonour of the anti-gambling crusader of the moment.[36] None of these were calculated to appeal to ascetic bushwalkers.

Still the club prospered. For racing's supporters were not as ignorant of natural beauty as Murray, and indeed the more truculent 'faddists' supposed. Even the observer who had mused about turning the Rock into a grandstand soon realised that this was taking improvement a little too far and took a step backwards, observing that clearing the Rock of trees would constitute 'cruel vandalism'. After all, he wrote, 'the natural beauty of the dark green growth around the base of the great rock outcrop is one of its principal charms'.

Inhaling Pure Mountain Ozone. Hanging Rock Races 1-1-12.
1912. Unknown photographer.

Woodend and District Heritage Society

Race tickets. New Years Day, January, 1913.
Photograph by Matthew Nickson.

Kyneton & Hanging Rock Racing Club

HANGING ROCK RESERVE.
New Year's Day, 1913.
ADMIT ONE. 6D....
PLEASE DESTROY
No 8099 J.J. Miller, Melb.

HANGING ROCK RESERVE.
New Year's Day, 1913.
ADMIT ONE. 6D....
PLEASE DESTROY
No 8098 J.J. Miller, Melb.

Hanging Rock Racing Club.

£230 in STAKES.

£230 in STAKES.

NEW YEAR'S DAY, WEDNESDAY, JANUARY 1, 1913.

To be held on the famous Hanging Rock Reserve on an Entirely New and Up-to-date Racing Track, laid out at a cost of over £2000, with running rail full length of course, which is now well grassed.

PRESIDENT Mr J Harley ; VICE-PRESIDENTS, Messrs Jas Kenny and Thos Spain ; STEWARDS, Messrs J. Harley, J W Keating, M J O'Connor, D W Birrell, W Donovan, P. Kenny, J Hemphill ; JUDGE, Mr J. Harley ; HANDICAPPER, Mr A Vowles.

PROGRAMME : First Race 1.30.

HANDICAP MAIDEN PLATE of 10 sovs. For Maiden Horses ; Five Furlongs. Entry, 10s.

FLYING HANDICAP of 50 sovs. Five Furlongs. Second horse to receive 5 sovs from the stake. Nom., 15s; accept , 20s.

HANGING ROCK CUP OF 100 SOVS.

Second horse to receive 10 sovs and the third horse 5 sovs from the stake. [A Handicap.] One Mile. Nom., 20s ; accept., 30s.

TRIAL HANDICAP OF 15 sovs. For horses that have never received a stake to the value of 20 sovs on the flat ; Six Furlongs. Nom., 10s ; Accept., 5s.

HANDICAP PONY RACE of 20 sovs. Second horse to receive 2 sovs out of stake. 14-2 a u. Height and last three performances to be sent at time of entry. Mr G Watson's or Mr Bignall's certificate accepted if produced on the course. Ponies without certificates will be measured on the course by the club's official. Five Furlongs. Nom., 10s ; accept., 10s.

ROCK PLATE (A Handicap) of 35 sovs. Second horse 5 sovs from stake. Six Furlongs. Nom., 10s., accept., 20s

☞ Nomination Fees must Accompany all Entries.

ENTRIES for all Events Close at Keating's Hotel, Woodend, or with Mr Harry Sutton, V.R.C. Buildings, Melbourne, on MONDAY, DECEMBER 16th. Entries by wire or telephone must be confirmed in writing and accompanied by all Fees, by the Following Post. **WEIGHTS** declared on or about DECEMBER 28th. **BOOKMAKER'S FEE, 21/.**

PENALTIES Winner of any Handicap Flat Race after the declaration of weights to carry 7 lbs penalty. Two or more such races, 10 lbs penalty. V.R.C. Stipendiary Steward will attend.

V.R.C. RULES strictly adhered to. OWNERS & TRAINERS are reminded of the NEW RULES now in force.

SPECIAL TRAIN

From Melbourne to Woodend [conveying horses and passengers] leaving Spencer street at 8 o'clock on morning of Races. **EXCURSION FARES** from all parts.

Booths, etc., will be Sold by Auction at Keating's Hotel, Woodend, on MONDAY, DECEMBER 9th, at 3.30 p.m

J. C. KEATING, Secretary, Keating's Hotel, Woodend.

'Phone 14, Woodend.

Kyneton Turf Club Races, December 18.

Despite recurrent threats, racing continued to attract crowds, and an improving quality of racehorse. In 1906, the Cup prize money matched that at Lal Lal a decade earlier, and stood at sixty sovereigns. Even then, and despite increased prize money, the race distance was vague and published times certainly wrong. Staple won the 1906 Cup in what was timed at one minute 45 seconds — a time comparable to winners of high quality Flemington races over the same distance! By 1907 the Cup was worth eighty sovereigns. Keating's Hotel, Woodend took entries under the guidance of Jack Keating. City owners could enter their horses at Kirk's Horse Bazaar in Bourke St. That year, a crowd of over ten thousand arrived by train, buggies, charabancs and on horseback, to watch Grandmaster win the Cup, with only seven stone four pounds and in a minute and 46 seconds.[37]

In 1908 a new gate taking record was set at £111 pounds.[38] Then, in 1909, the state governor made a return visit to the races, where he sipped on billy tea brewed over a bush fire in the forest in January's heat. Councillor Manson, in welcoming the vice-regal party, remarked that there had been some objections to the club using the Reserve for racing, Dismissing the charges, 'he ventured the opinion that His Excellency from what he had seen and the way in which all classes enjoyed themselves would not think it necessary to limit the use of the park to holding "Sunday School picnics". Victoria's governor, Sir Thomas Gibson-Carmichael, chose his words carefully, and offered no real endorsement of track upgrades or new buildings. Instead he mused about there being room for all at the Rock, and hoped he could see every one of Victoria's beauty spots during his stay in the state.[39]

In the following year, the club renewed its appeal for a track extension to seven furlongs. When it presented revised plans to the shire, this time, with the anti-gambling fervor dying, they were approved unanimously.[40] The new track was paid for, in the end by funds raised from members, and through the political and professional support of Byron Moore of the VRC. Carried out by a respected racetrack curator, Tuxen, the work cost £3000 and created a course, as had been demanded, of seven furlongs. The Hanging Rock track was now fenced on both sides of the track with oregon rails. It was fully grassed on the racing surface, and was sixty feet wide, so as to accommodate large fields with less danger of falls.

With the new track completed, the Hanging Rock Cup meeting could now attract twenty to thirty thousand visitors on New Year's Day. Over eight thousand attended at the Easter meeting 1910.[41] Income fell to an extent during the war years, although takings in 1918 far exceeded those of 1910, and of most nineteenth-century meetings. Lucky Bean the 'Carbine of the Bush', won the 1915 Cup, in front of another huge crowd.[42] Some spectators came from Melbourne 'dashing up in motors and provid(ing) a source of observation for the hayseeds'.[43] In 1916, as war raged on in Europe, twenty thousand turned up at the New Year's Races. The governor made a speech praising the efforts of Australian soldiers at Gallipoli. Then Lucky Bean won the cup and one hundred sovereigns for the second time. 'Lucky Bean has a liking for the Hanging Rock course' noted one local reporter, 'not only has he won the Hanging Rock Cup twice in succession but he also carried off the Easter Handicap there last year and in the previous year'.[44] Lucky Bean raced on, winning the Kyneton Cup in 1916, and the Gisborne Cup in 1917, before retiring as a ten-year-old. Crowds continued to build during the war years, no doubt swelled because so many other spectacles were curtailed, or closed altogether. Nonetheless, there was no doubting the appeal of the bush races at the rebuilt track, as gate takings demonstrate.

GATE TAKINGS HANGING ROCK RACING CLUB 1910-18[45]

1910:	£61-18-0
1911	£80-12-0
1912	£136-6-0
1913	£147-13-0
1914	£145-9-3
1915	£135-8-6
1916	£125-3-6
1917	£119-16-0
1918	£120 -1-0

Kyneton Guardian 1 August 1918: 2.

With war's end, and even with the revival of other entertainments, horseracing at Hanging Rock lost little of its appeal. Race fields were certainly smaller than before the war. But Jack Keating was convinced that crowds were more or less the same size. In the evening on New Year's Day, 1919, as the throng of punters headed home, 'the rising ribbon of dust along the roads told of the day completed, the end of another sporting picnic at Hanging Rock'.[46] Even at the end of the decade, with the Great Depression in the offing, the New Year races still attracted 'a fine crowd socially' with 'hundreds of motor car parties (at) the course which nestles at the foot of a big hill with a great rock overhanging'.[47]

RACING HEYDAY

Along with other racing clubs in the city and the bush, Hanging Rock kept on drawing crowds during the 1920s. The quality of horses seemed to improve and the punters kept rolling through the gates to be charged by the club. The Easter meeting was always less popular than New Year, even though the club tried to vary this by altering which day over the Easter holiday they ran races. Those present at the Club's annual general meeting in November 1927 heard that for the first time in fifteen years, the club was entirely out of debt. Its Easter meeting still ran at a loss of over £30 but the New Year's Day meeting returned a profit of more than £300. The club moreover was 'now

in a splendid position, the track is in first class order . . . and all the buildings and appointments are good'. The club was so confident of future success that it set aside £200 for prize money stakes for the 1928 meeting at New Year.[48] For the first time races from Flemington were broadcast on the Hanging Rock public address system on New Year's Day 1928. This 1928 meeting was described as neither a picnic nor a race meeting, It was rather an 'institution'. Thirty thousand people 'drawn from Melbourne to the Murray' saw Bylaw win the Cup.[49] The main difference from earlier meetings was that fewer travelled on the special race trains from Melbourne and Bendigo. Spectators now made the trip by car.

Attendances collapsed soon after. By the mid 1930s Hanging Rock races were but a pale reflection of the glory days only a decade earlier. The Easter Monday meeting was continuing to run up losses and the shire was approached to pay wages of ground staff. Some officials thought that the club had to rethink the subsidies it gave owners to bring horses up from Melbourne for the two meetings each year. The club considered allowing bookmakers to take bets outside the club members' reserve, and costs of running the enclosure on race days were to be pared back. The Easter meeting was eventually reduced to a pony event, with smaller and inferior horses to those at thoroughbred meetings. All of the club's problems could be resolved were it not for the 'stingy' attitude of the club committee, claimed one councillor, who proposed that all that was needed was for the club to better advertise the Easter meeting.[50]

As Victoria slowly edged out of the worst of the Depression, the club found itself a pioneer, even if a little reluctantly, in one of the major changes in the racing world; the use of totalisator machines rather than bookmakers, to tally up bets and sort out odds. The 1930s had brought a fevered hunt for new revenues by the Victorian government. Whereas NSW turned to an entertainment tax and a tax on punters' winnings, Victoria sought to experiment with new technology on the racetrack; in the interests, so the chief secretary insisted, of the state's hospitals and charities. The mechanical and later electric

The Popularity of Hanging Rock and New Year's Day is not easily Shaken!
Table Talk, 7 January, 1915.

Hanging Rock Races. 1929. Unknown photographer.
Kyneton & Hanging Rock Racing Club

totalisator was the invention of George Julius. Julius, who went on to an illustrious career as head of the CSIRO, had been born in England, grew up in Australia, and settled for a time in New Zealand where his father was appointed as Anglican Archbishop of Christchurch. Whilst his father devoted his spare time to collecting clocks, George tinkered with any sort of mechanical device, before eventually coming up with an extremely accurate mechanical voting machine, Since no Australasian government saw the need for such statistical accuracy at election time, Julius converted the mechanism to tally up bets on horse races. Despite his father's staunch opposition to gambling, he promoted the totalisator to race clubs until it was eventually taken up at Ellerslie in New Zealand in 1913 (it soon led to the end of bookmaking on all New Zealand racetracks). The Julius totalisator was used at Flemington in 1931. In its urgent hunt for new revenue, the state government was keen to have the tote used on country tracks as well. Most clubs resisted, arguing that the costs of installation and operating the machines would never be made up in bets. By 1932, however, a new portable 'Duplex' totalisator was available. In 1934, Hanging Rock became the first country race club to take bets on the 'tote'. With its rooftop board displaying dividends, six betting windows and two pay-out windows at the back, the new-fangled totalisator must have seemed an alien and modern intrusion into the bush carnival scene at Hanging Rock races. But on the day it opened at Hanging Rock the new contraption took £449 in bets, most of it in small wagers, since the big punters stuck with the hectic transactions of the betting ring and their favourite bookies.[51] From that experiment, tote betting has dominated punting, to the point where on-track bookmakers are a declining presence on all tracks.[52]

THE EMERGING NATIONAL SYMBOL

The post-war racing scene bought new amalgamations, with racing tending towards two distinct directions, both of which favoured the bush clubs and picnic meetings such as those at Hanging Rock. Town-based clubs were amalgamated and tracks eventually closed, whilst some of the very small isolated tracks survived as a special category for 'picnic meetings'. Hanging Rock of course was the classic picnic race setting. Although the Hanging Rock club finished the war with an accumulated debt, by the end of 1949 the club could show a profit of £850.[53] It had also become the stage for yet another unique moment in Australian racing history. In 1948 Pamela Knox took up the microphone at Hanging Rock, and for the first time, racegoers heard a female voice broadcasting a race call. Nineteen-year-old Pamela lived in Woodend, and like many young women in the country, she had grown up with a great love of horses. But Pamela was not quite typical of racegoers in the 1940s. She was not only unique as the first female racecaller in Australia. She went on from racecalling to study history and philosophy at the University of Melbourne. Pamela's was one of the more educated voices broadcast across Australian race tracks to that date. Pamela also ran her mother's, Lady Knox's, stud farm. She rode in point-to-point races, she went out with organised fox hunts, and as well, bred thoroughbreds. With one of the horses she had raised and trained, Kind Scout, running in the Maiden Plate, Pamela called the entire meeting in a faultless broadcast.[54]

So popular had the Cup become amongst owners and trainers, that by 1948, the 34 entries had to be divided into two divisions.[55] Crowds were over twenty thousand again by 1951, although about half the spectators watched from the picnic grounds rather than from within the racetrack itself.[56] Leading up to the 1954 meeting the club spent more than £2000 on improving the surrounds of the track.[57]

In 1954, the club felt sufficiently confident to spend more on improvements.[58] Hanging Rock gave up in its Easter meeting, transferring the races to Australia Day, which like New Year's Day, soon attracted a vast crowd. And in 1955 broadcasts of the Hanging Rock races were heard for the first time on racing radio across the state. For some unscrupulous punters this presented a new opportunity. S.P. bookmakers relied on radio broadcasts for their (illegal) wagering enterprises in public bars. They also tried to identify any unusual betting moves by ringing through to country tracks to check odds. With their money on Dunalister in the Improvers Handicap on Australia Day, unscrupulous punters had cut telephone wires to the

THE SMILE OF THE GENIAL SECRETARY

MR J. C. KEATING, ONE OF THE MOST POPULAR OF RACING
OFFICIALS

There is no more popular racing official in Victoria than Mr Jack Keating, who manages the famous Hanging Rock and Woodend meetings. A photographer who went to Woodend races last week spent a lot of time trying to get a snapshot of him, and finally he was heard to remark, "What sort of a man is this secretary? He never walks, and a fellow has to run to catch him." The fact is Mr Keating is a great hustler and worker generally, but even so, he goes about his duties with a radiant smile. He is every bit as good-natured as the photograph suggests— hence his great popularity.

The Smile Of the Genial Secretary. The Weekly Times, 8 December, 1917.
State Library of Victoria

Hanging Rock course, so that bookmakers could not ring and track odds. The gamblers managed to get away with thousands of pounds from the Melbourne S.P.s, but need not have taken the risk of cutting telephone wires; bookies claimed that they were not expecting any off-course betting on Hanging Rock, and so would not have bothered ringing through to the course anyway.

Despite an horrendous four-horse collision in the Hanging Rock Cup of 1957, the club could look positively to the future.[59] Crowds were growing and city owners and prominent trainers were happy to send horses to Hanging Rock events. But then, racing's own future seemed increasingly uncertain. Post-war racing acquired a more shady reputation as radio broadcasts and then television kept fans at home, and spawned a massive market in illegal bookmaking. In preparation for a new totalisator for off-course gambling, the Victorian government closed several country tracks in 1960-61, many of them across the old goldfields of central Victoria. Hanging Rock survived, as did Kyneton, but clubs at Kilmore and nearby towns were amalgamated. Eventually Hanging Rock and Kyneton merged in 2009.[60] By then the once maligned picnic races occupied a central role in the sport. The respected racing journalist Jack Pollard had written of the Hanging Rock races in 1988, that

> Asked to take their pick of the most enjoyable picnics in Victoria most connoisseurs of the field would take Hanging Rock, scene of only two meetings a year, but only a two-hour drive from Melbourne. This is a course where fences do not run straight, tubs of ice are needed to produce cool drinks, and patrons lean towards thongs and shorts.[61]

Transitions in the racing world have somehow come to favour small isolated picnic meetings like those at Hanging Rock. The reflection on which this chapter opened, had turned to compare Hanging Rock to the great racetracks of the world; Flemington, Ascot and Longchamps. To and from these tracks, Australian and European owners and trainers now shuttle horses for rich meetings like the Ascot Gold Cup or the Melbourne Cup. Jockeys ride in Hong Kong. Then a week

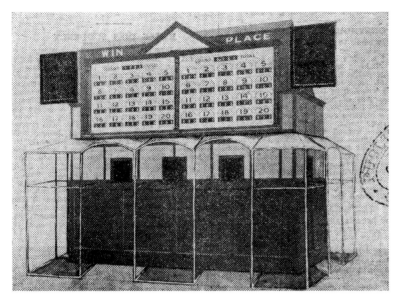

The Duplex mobile totalisator first used at Hanging Rock, January 1, 1934. *Herald and Weekly Times*, 30 December, 1933.

State Library Victoria

later they might be lining up for the richest races in Europe or North America. The contrast between the bush picnics and the major race days could not be more stark. Silver Shark won the Hanging Rock Cup in 1989, 1990 and again in 1991. Instead of travelling to the international races at Flemington and Caulfield, the local star headed off to northern Australia, winning the Darwin Cup in 1991, the Cairns Cup in 1992, and then the Alice Springs Cup in 1993. It does seem that the enormous money lavished on global breeding and racing enterprises, and on promoting events such as the Melbourne Spring Carnival to a global audience, have only strengthened the appeal of the very different bush meetings, amongst them, Hanging Rock. The Hanging Rock Cup has survived the protestations of anti-gamblers and nature lovers. It has flourished in spite of the broader decline of raceday crowds and the racing authorities' emphasis on major globalised carnivals. The Hanging Rock race days have remained true to that older spirit of Australian horse racing summarised in the

twentieth century by one observer as, 'ostensibly a race meeting. . It [the Hanging Rock raceday] is in reality a gigantic picnic. City and country meet . . .the racetrack encloses a miniature forest . . . the extended wooded slopes of the hill are thronged with groups of merry-makers'.[62]

It is this distinctive setting, of a small track at the foot of a massive rockface, that has sustained Hanging Rock races into the 21st century. Not though without further crises. In 2007, drought forced the Cup meeting to be transferred to Kyneton.[63] In 2011 the entire Australia Day meeting was called off, when kangaroos invaded the track. After trying to start the first event three times, the starter gave up. Trainer Mick Sell, who had Oskaiben Prince in the 1800 metres Maiden, muttered to journalists that the calling-off was ' a kick in the bum', but then mused that it could not be helped.[64] One Hanging Rock club spokesman reflected on some of the traditional character of crowds at Hanging Rock racedays, when he pointed out that 'most of them (spectators) hung round, sitting on the lawns having a beer and a chat. I'm not sure half of them are aware we've even called it off'.[65]

In 2012 the Australia Day meeting was again abandoned, after a pot hole was discovered on the course. Hanging Rock races were too important for these failures warned one observer, journalist Matt Stewart. The track needed more upgrades and drainage systems had to be renewed. Writing in the *Herald Sun*, Stewart pointed out that 'the Rock is precious; racing's most beautiful shop window . . . an ampitheatre of picnic rugs in the shadow of a tourist icon'. Nonetheless it was an icon under threat.[66] Legendary racecaller Jack Styring lost the chance to call his last Hanging Rock Cup before retiring, when kangaroos closed down the 2011 meeting. Jack Styring is eulogised as the legendary voice of bush racing, inventor of such bon mots as, 'they came out of the contraption like scalded cats' (to capture the essence of a distinctively fast exit of horses from the starting gates). Not one to be defeated by errant kangaroos, Jack did resurface from retirement, to call his final Cup in 2014. The Cup winner, Al Wafi, strode in by three lengths. Kangaroos again bounded across the track before the start of the last race. According to one of the more definitive accounts of Jack Styring's race call, by Peter Flynn, Jack 'seems to have forsaken humour in order to retain accuracy ... I wish that Jack would not worry too much about accuracy and pepper his calls with the sayings and vernacular that have made him a legend'.[67] Perhaps, finally, the demands of orderliness, system, and modernisation have triumphed over the carnivalesque of race days at Hanging Rock. ✷

On The Road. Hanging Rock Races, Held On January 1. The Australasian.
11 January, 1913.
State Library of Victoria

6—Argus, Fri, Jan 2/48

Girl describes races at Hanging Rock

Miss Pamela Knox, 19-year-old Woodend resident and well-known competitor in gymkhana and hunt club events, yesterday described the Hanging Rock races over the course amplifying system. She is probably the first woman to fill this role.

In the six events she covered she did not call a wrong horse. Her comment was clear and concise, and she received many congratulations for her performance.

Miss Knox had another interest in the Hanging Rock meeting. Her horse Kind Scout was an acceptor in the second division of the Maiden Plate, but he finished out of a place.

Girl describes races at Hanging Rock. The Argus, 2 January, 1948.
State Library of Victoria

New Year's Day Meeting 1947, Hanging Rock.
Photograph by "The Argus".

New Year's Day Meeting 1947, Hanging Rock. Photograph by the *Argus.*
Kyneton & Hanging Rock Racing Club

Hanging Rock Races. 1968. Photograph by News Ltd / Newspix

Hanging Rock Races. 1975.
Photograph by News Ltd / Newspix

	26	Interest.	B/S	30 · 20.
1975 Jan.	3.	New Years Day Receipts.	B/S	1654 46.
	8.	Picnic Fees & Bookings.	293	58 00.
	28.	Australia Day Receipts.	B/S	540 · 60.
Feb.	17	Picnic Fees & Bookings.	294 295.	193 00.
	27	" " " "	296	81 00.

1976 Jan.	29	Interest.	B/S	− 43 11
	14.	Picnic Fees & Bookings.	1223 1224	− 207 00
	6.	New Years Day Receipts.	B/S.	4621 00
	19.	Picnic Fees & Bookings.	1225	82 00
	28.	Aust. Day Receipts.	B/S	2447 10
Feb.	13.	Picnic Fees & Bookings.	1226 1228	148 00

Impact of the film *Picnic at Hanging Rock* shown on race
attendances in 1976 compared with the same race meetings in
1975. *Hanging Rock Committee of Management Cash Book,
Dec. 1903 – Sept. 1982.*

Macedon Ranges Shire Council

Silver Shark, winner of the Hanging Rock Cup with strapper. 1989.
Silver Shark won the 1989, 1990 & 1991 Hanging Rock Cups.
Unknown photographer.

Kyneton & Hanging Rock Racing Club

Now And Zen ridden by John Allen wins the Hanging Rock Cup, Australia Day, 2017.
Photograph by Brendan McCarthy / Racing Photos

Endnotes

1 Coronial Inquest, Daniel Lyons, Kyneton, 13 January 1893, no. 189346, Coronial Reports, Public Record Office of Victoria.

2 John Williams of Riddell's Creek. evidence, Coronial Inquest, Daniel Lyons, PROV.

3 Alexander McCrae of Cobaw, evidence Coronial Inquest, Daniel Lyons, Kyneton, 13 January 1893, PROV.

4 Samuel McDougall (Ascot Vale) evidence Coronial Inquest, Daniel Lyons, Kyneton, 13 January 1893, PROV.

5 *Port Melbourne Standard*, 23 January 1892: 2.

6 Winning Post, 'Hanging Rock Course', *Weekly Times* 7 April 1917: 16.

7 Country Racing Victoria Media Release, research by Robyne Blee, 7 December 2005, Kyneton and Hanging Rock Racing Club papers, Kyneton.

8 *Kyneton Guardian*, 13 December 1879: 3.

9 *Kyneton Guardian*, 13 December 1879:3.

10 *Victoria Racing Calendar,* 1882.

11 *VRC 1883*, p. 248.

12 'Lal Lal Falls Races', *The Australasian*, 7 January 1893: 16.

13 John Pacini, *A Century Galloped By: The First Hundred Years of the Victoria Racing Club*, VRC, Melbourne, 1988.

14 *Argus*, 2 January 1896, p.3.

15 *Australasian*, 1 September 1909.

16 *Australasian*, 5 November 1904.

17 ' Hanging Rock Races and Picnic', *Weekly Times*, 7 January 1905: 18.

18 *Argus*, 13 July 1899,3.

19 'Hanging Rock Reserve', *Age* 31 July 1905: 9.

20 Hugh Buggy, *The Real John Wren*, Widescope edition, Melbourne, 1977, p. 64.

21 'Racing Club Concessions', *Argus* 21 July 1905: 6

22 *Argus*, 22 July 1905: 6.

23 *Australasian*, 22 July 1905: 37.

24 *Australasian*, 22 July 1905: 37.

25 *Argus*, 28 July 1905.

26 'Hanging Rock Races', *Age*, 4 January 1905: 8.

27 *Australasian*, 5 August 1905: 9.

28 *Argus*, 31 July 1905: 6.

29 Andrew Moore, 'Murray, John Eric (Jack) (1907–1983)', Australian Dictionary of Biography, National Centre of Biography, Australian National University, http://adb.anu.edu.au/biography/murray-john-eric-jack-15098/text26297 , published first in hardcopy 2012, (viewed online, 14 May 2016).

30 His death was connected to horses also. Murray's pony bolted along the main street of his home town of Warrnambool. Jack Murray was thrown from his trap and later died.

31 '*Sunbury News*, 19 August 1905: 3.

32 *Argus*, 2 January 1906: 7.

33 *Argus*, 28 March 1907: 4.

34 *Argus*, 4 September 1909: 7.

35 'True Sportsman', *Argus*,12 July : 4.

36 *Argus* 2 January 1908: 5

37 *VRC*, 1907: 203.

38 *Sunbury News* 11 January 1908: 2.

39 'Governor's visit', *Australasian* 9 January 1909: 26.

40 'New Track Approved Of', *Age*, 1 December 1910: 8.

41 'A picnic race meeting', *Australasian*, 2 April 1910: 46.

42 'Hanging Rock Races', *Geelong Advertiser,* 2 February 1915: 7.

43 'A day at the races', *Table Talk,* 7 January 1915: 7.

44 Hanging Rock Races, A popular meeting', *Rochester Express*, 4 January 1916: 3.

45 *Kyneton Guardian* 1 August 1918: 2.

46 'A Sporting Picnic', *Age,* 2 January 1919: 5.

47 'Best picnic races', *Western Mail*, 10 January 1929: 34.

48 *Age*, 12 November 1927: 15.

49 *Age* 3 January 1928: 7.

50 'On the Rocks', *Kilmore Free Press*, 28 March 1935: 4.

51 'Topical Racing Notes', *Adelaide News*, 8 January 1934: 2.

52 *Age*, 8 March 1934.

53 *Argus*, 2 September 1949: 8.

54 *Age*, 2 January 1948

55 *Argus*, 23 December 1947: 20

56 *Age*, 2 January 1951: 10.

57 'Hanging Rock Improvements', *The Age*, 10 December 1954: 12.

58 *The Age*, 10 December 1954: 12.

59 'Four Riders Hurt in Crash', *The Age*, 2 January 1957: 14.

[60] See generally Robert White, *Courses for Horses, the story of Victorian and Riverina Racecourses*, Hawthorn 1965. See too Racing.com> https://www.racing.com/news/2009-07-14/kyneton-and-hanging-rock-clubs-merge (viewed July 2017).

[61] Jack Pollard, *A Racegoer's Companion to the Australian Turf: Australian Horseracing*, Angus and Robertson Melbourne, 1988: 420.

[62] 'At the Rock', *Argus*, 2 January 1908: 5.

[63] 'Drought forces relocation', *ABC Regional News*, 25 January 2007.

[64] *Herald Sun*, 27 January 2011.

[65] *Herald Sun*, 27 January 2011.

[66] Matt Stewart, 'Hanging Rock: a gem in need of a polish', *Herald Sun*, 3 January 2012: 54.

[67] Peter Flynn, 'Racing: Mad Dog Morgan, Lord Lucan, Jack Styring...It's a Great Cast at Hanging Rock', *Footy Almanac*, 30 October 2014, http://www.footyalmanac.com.au/racing-mad-dog-morgan-lord-lucan-jack-styring-its-a-great-cast-at-hanging-rock/ , (viewed online July 2016).

Hanging Rock - view from top. 1902. Group of buildings at the crossroads is the Hanging Rock Hotel.
Photograph by Mark James Daniel.

Carnival Times

'To be sold by public auction . . .
That very valuable freehold property
Well-known as
HANGING ROCK HOTEL
That very valuable hotel, which has become a very popular and favourite place
of resort for tourists, pleasure-seekers, and invalids from all parts of the colony'

'Public Auctions', Australasian, 6 April 1878: 15

In 1914 the Victoria Licensing Court sat in Woodend — to deliver sentence on an institution of almost fifty years — the Hanging Rock Hotel. When auctioned off in 1878, the brick and timber hotel had eight rooms, stabling for travellers' horses, an orchard, and a lease over 110 acres of prime pasture within which stood 'the celebrated Hanging Rock'.[1] Anyone buying the hotel would have the right to charge admission to this land on holidays, the most valuable of which were at New Year and Easter. Bidders were assured that gate takings at picnic events, especially racedays, would more than cover any lease payments. No one at the auction doubted Shepherdson, the auctioneer, when he asserted that the Hanging Rock Hotel would produce 'a sure fortune' for any 'energetic and enterprising' publican. Sadly, several subsequent publicans proved neither sufficiently energetic nor consistently enterprising. Once a hub for much of the social life around Hanging Rock, the pub degenerated into a hidden drinking haunt. So, when in 1914, the Licensing Reduction Board made an offer of more than £240 in exchange for the license, the Hanging Rock Hotel served its last drinks.[2] The pub lived on in name only, because the Newham Hotel was renamed Hanging Rock. But it too gave up the struggle, and despite a last ditch attempt to transfer the license from Hilda Brennan to Arthur Cassell, the Hanging Rock Hotel was again slated for closure in 1928.[3] And so, the summer carnivals each New Year's Day at Hanging Rock vanished. The crowds at Hanging Rock for the first day of each year now headed to the racetrack, rather than to a publican's picnic grounds.

The Hanging Rock Hotel had opened its doors in 1866. Almost immediately it started playing host to local festivities. Rural life, from sales of farms and livestock, services fees for stud thoroughbreds brought to the pub stables, to meetings of clubs, electoral campaign lectures, and wedding celebrations, were all held at the Hanging Rock Hotel. All too often though, in building up a tourist trade fixed on only a few days each year, hoteliers forgot their roles in these local networks. This widening gap, between the place of the Hanging Rock Hotel in both an expanding tourist trade, and in shrinking social networks, was reflected in the pub's decline. A similar unease was for a longtime visible in rivalries amongst the eclectic mass of visitors to Hanging Rock itself. As the nineteenth century progressed, the Rock played host to racetrack punters, drunken New Year revellers, annual reunions of bush families, genteel excursionists from Melbourne or Macedon guesthouses, Hesket and Newham sporting clubs, nature lovers, bushwalkers and car travellers. And not to forget of course the neighbouring farmers, who saw in the Hanging Rock Reserve, little more than good grazing land with reliable water. The changing status of Hanging Rock in the tourism industry has been carefully plotted.[4] Thorough as such accounts may well be, isolating the tourist industry inevitably leaves the many conflicts over the uses of Hanging Rock to one side. For Hanging Rock has been a place of rivalries over ownership, use, and reconstruction. Unsurprisingly, some of this tension has survived, and is even being exaggerated in the 21st century. The story of this confusing social and recreational life begins with the liquor booths, sideshows, musicians and acrobats, all of them employed by licensees of the Hanging Rock and nearby hotels, and brought up to the Reserve to entertain New Year's Day picnickers.

CARNIVALS

Last drinks at the Hanging Rock Hotel drew one phase in holiday-making at Hanging Rock to an end. For the slow death of the hotel coincided with the years across which cinemas, radio, and motor cars radically revised leisure time.[5] Many years before this, the first Hanging Rock get-togethers of the 1860s had been casual events, meetings of families and friends with a very local flavour. Onetime gold miners from Mt Alexander and Bendigo had been prominent amongst the first small-scale farmers of the district. New Year at Hanging Rock gave them a chance to celebrate progress, or catch up with old mining mates. Soon afterwards, bands and visitors from Woodend started arriving at the Rock on New Year's Day. Within a few years, publicans had seized on the festivities and began to sell drinks. The volunteer brass band from Woodend now had to compete with 'Upson's Christy Minstrels', a troupe paid for by the licensee of the Garden Hut Hotel. These popular minstrels were brought up from Melbourne for the sole purpose of drawing picnickers into the Garden Hut Hotel's liquor booths at Hanging Rock.

Successive licensees of the Hanging Rock, and other local hotels, quickly established themselves as patrons to all-encompassing, spectacular, outdoor gatherings around the Rock, to the extent that these speedily overshadowed casual family get-togethers. Hoteliers in the years after the gold rush in Victoria set great store on such festival events. Christmas, New Year and any other public holiday meant that hoteliers across the colony set up stalls on open ground, near to their bars and lounges. They underwrote sports like quoits, foot racing, and occasionally, as at Hanging Rock, horse races. Sharp impresarios amongst the colony's licensed victuallers paid for circus entertainments, from sideshow alleys to jugglers and contortionists. Hanging Rock proved no exception to these ventures. And few publicans could turn to such a unique symbol of wild outdoor enjoyment as the Rock itself. By the time of the 1878 auction, Hanging Rock could be announced as 'the most popular place of resort for holiday-makers in the colony'.[6]

These festival days were, for much of the later nineteenth century, restricted to Boxing Day, New Year's Day, and eventually, though on a lesser scale, Easter Monday, and even Good Friday. For a time they were organised (more or less) into Tradesmen's Picnics, held for the first time on Boxing Day, 1864.[7] A Woodend brass band left for the Rock at 9 a.m. sharp, and those who followed could enjoy lemonade and ginger beer, or play quoits beneath the rock walls. Evidently, the day passed off well for local tradesmen and families, as one local journalist went on to report that

> The merry strains of the Volunteer Band soon after 8 o'clock in the morning sounded the note of preparation and the conveyances and equestrians soon began to gather . . . close upon a hundred [conveyances] were counted on the grounds ... cricket, quoits, swings and last though not least, good old English kiss-in-the ring were resorted to, and not for many a day has the quaint old rock resounded to such merry echoes and joyous peels of laughter as it did on Boxing Day.[8]

That Boxing Day in 1864, as the account went on, resembled 'more

the busy hum of a town than the quiet of a sylvan retreat', and it was this congested, urban spectacle rather than the 'quaint old rock', which drew crowds for day-long excursions to Hanging Rock.[9] By 1866, the numbers attending these festive picnics had fallen away a little, with less than one hundred counted when the picnic was moved to New Year's Day. But then, these smaller crowds gave hoteliers the opening they needed. Hanging Rock Hotel was the first to capitalise on the New Year picnic. The pub made sure that thirsty picnickers had a broader choice than that between lemonade and ginger beer. Robert King, who had taken over as licensee at Garden Hut, and William Adams of the Hanging Rock Hotel, the first promoter of recreation at the Rock, both applied for licenses for liquor booths between Christmas and New Year, 1868.[10] Residents in Woodend, Newham and other small hamlets around the Rock had petitioned the Victoria Board of Land and Works to protect the Rock and surrounds as a recreation reserve in 1867.[11] Adams though, managed to win both ways. He sold the hotel, and at the same time held onto his own rights to liquor booths on the Rock. [12] By the time the board set aside 96 acres as a 'site for public recreation' in May 1870, Adams was firmly in control of the carnival events, clinging to his right to set up publican's booths within the Reserve on every Christmas and New Year. [13]

With Adams and other publicans now in command, the 1869 festival broadened its offerings, as one picnicker recalled:

> As usual this beautiful spot attracted a very large number of holiday makers. The neighbouring publicans had got up a full programme of sports, amongst which the driving of a pair of geese, harnessed to a tub across a small lake in the vicinity attracted most attention. There were also foot races, jumping in sacks . . . and other amusements of a kindred character, by no means forgetting some music quite good enough to tempt those anxious for a dance to disport themselves at will.[14]

By 1870, King, Adams and fellow publicans were excelling themselves, dragging out their spectacle beyond Christmas and into Easter Holidays. In 1871, with the Recreation Reserve declared, Easter entertainments were expanded even further. As well as the time-honoured kiss-in-a ring, or the equally entertaining geese and tub herding, liquor licensees, now including several from Woodend as well as Newham and Hanging Rock, compiled an elaborate and spectacular program of events. R.W. King, noting that world-famous entertainers had recently visited Melbourne, was determined that 'his country friends shall not be forgotten'.[15] So he had ensured the return performance of the now famous Upson Troupe whose 'Comicalities of Wit, and Humour, [would] amuse, cheer and delight all who visit at Hanging Rock reserve on Good Friday and Easter Monday'. Visitors could ease into both long days with a spot of pigeon shooting, 'duck-in the-hole', Aunt Sally, or for those not sharp enough to hit a pigeon, 'Fowl Shooting'. On Easter Monday, 'gentlemen' were expected to bring their own guns. The best 'Scotch Piper in the Colony' would also be on hand to entertain. So enthralling was this extravaganza, that Robert Walsh King and William Adams succeeded in having their booth licenses extended.

When allotments were put up for sale around the 'far-famed' Hanging Rock in 1876, the area was described as 'a favourite resort for thousands from all parts of the colonies'. Mass tourism was seen, even at that early stage, as a forerunner to property booms, and advertisers went on to remind potential bidders that 'land in this locality must rapidly increase in value from the demand that will arise for building sites'.[16] Hanging Rock, at the centre of potential building booms, along with its annual New Year outings, could now turn even greater profits for publicans and sideshow operators. The Rock, no longer just a place for annual family reunions, was speedily transforming into a lucrative business opportunity in more ways than one.

The Christian sanctities of Christmas and Easter appeared to hold almost no sway over Hanging Rock's shooters, drinkers and dancers. With the Reserve set aside and booths sold off, and with the Hanging Rock Hotel no longer holding exclusive rights, new rivalries drove wilder scenes. The crush at liquor booths regularly shocked more sedate visitors looking for a day within a 'sylvan retreat'. For Adams

and King were now attracting holiday-makers from far beyond the local district. Successful events in 1870 and 1871 were themselves surpassed by holiday crowds in the following year. Over Christmas and New Year 1872, 'the number who visited Hanging Rock was never so many by hundreds on any previous holiday within memory of the most inveterate frequenter of that romantic spot', claimed one observer.[17] These years, however, seemed the high-water mark of the publicans' unseasonal saturnalias. In 1876, William Claringbold took over the license of the Hanging Rock Hotel.[18] Claringbold took a less strenuous approach to holiday festivities and his restrained advertisements reflected a desire for wedding parties and temperance societies, rather than shooters and drinkers. His music was now going to be 'select', with dinner and accommodation provided at the hotel, rather than by way of liquor booths. He had though, seen the money to be made from sideshow spectacles. And so, by the end of the decade, even though he was getting out of the Hanging Rock Hotel, he kept on applying for booths on the Reserve. At the same time he supplied drinks and food to crowds at race meetings, which, by the later 1880s, had begun to overshadow the picnic festivities themselves.[19]

EXCURSIONISTS

Perhaps Adams and King had been too successful in advertising their spectacular holiday events. For whilst Claringbold turned to temperance societies and school excursionists, Melburnians had latched onto the uniqueness of Hanging Rock. City folk heading up to Hanging Rock from Melbourne (or down from Bendigo/Sandhurst) were not particularly tempted by shooting galleries and drinking booths. Instead, more of them looked forward to a picturesque outing with forests, quiet glades and spectacular views. Lyell's geology, so important in changing scientific accounts of Hanging Rock, also stimulated a new form of tourism. On summer weekends, excursionists headed to any rock outcrop near Melbourne, where they tried to analyse and date boulders and pinnacles. Even when the fairground festivities were in full swing, many visitors chose to climb up Hanging Rock, before making their way to the calm of Macedon. They might then have travelled on, to Kyneton or Woodend, for an overnight stay, before heading back to the city by train. Such was one excursion accounted for elaborately in 1871. For this group, sideshow alley, and even the tub-pulling geese, held few charms. Instead, the party set out to explore the natural wonders of Hanging Rock and Mt Macedon. After taking the train to Macedon, and walking up to the plateau to survey the landscape, they returned by way of the Camel's Hump. Only then did they venture on to Hanging Rock.[20] After taking compass bearings, the friends set off to complete a comfortable stretch of walking downhill. Once at the foot of the Rock they swiftly passed through the holiday-makers at the publicans' booths, before heading up the rock walls. Here they could follow a path which

> winds up the hill up the grassy slope at the foot, up between two towering rock walls, beneath an enormous boulder which lies jammed between them forming the cyclopean gateway of the fortress up the tree-covered slope, which is found again, within the outer ramparts until it is finally lost amidst various rock masses which crown the top of the hill.[21]

Seduced by the Rock, they returned the next day. The drive back home by dray took them to Woodend, and the writer concluded that even if holiday-makers were stuck with 'prejudices against Australian scenery', they would do well to ignore the beaches at Brighton or Mordialloc. They might even overlook the ferneries of Ferntree Gully in the Dandenongs, and instead head north, to Hanging Rock, for 'at least as place of picnic resort there is none to rival this one'.[22]

Such advice notwithstanding, bayside beaches continued to attract many more holiday-makers than Hanging Rock, especially over hot summers. But during the 1880s, and reflecting publicity surrounding the plans for a public reserve, Hanging Rock drew in more and more city folk. As the hardiest visitors to Macedon ventured across country, to explore the strange monolith of Hanging Rock, this landmark became a site for more frequent and reflective excursions, even if these were tacked on to a New Year or Christmas picnic. By 1880 Hanging Rock was being promoted as an easy day trip from Melbourne, from where excursionists were advised to 'go up by the morning train

[and] you can, if you please, spend six hours at the picnic ground and be back at Spencer Street at a quarter to 8 in the evening'.[23] Not convinced of this, one group reported on their trip, for which they had set off to Hanging Rock on Christmas Eve, 1880. They took the train to Kyneton, where they stayed a few nights before setting out for the Rock. They spent the day climbing up and down Hanging Rock, rather than cavorting around liquor booths and sideshows, and set off back for Kyneton at five in the evening.[24]

Advertisement. Auction of Hanging Rock Hotel.
The Bendigo Advertiser, February 24, 1900.
State Library of Victoria

135

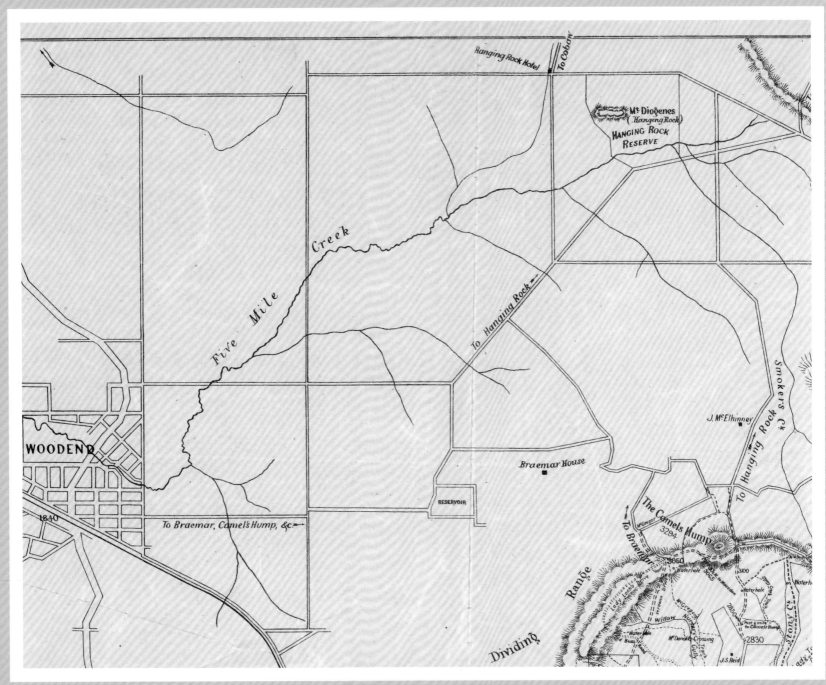

Section of *Tourist map, Mt. Macedon & district*. Department of Crown Lands and Survey. 1908.
State Library of Victoria

A NEW RECREATIONAL SPACE

The original 96 acres of public land at the foot of Hanging Rock had been temporarily reserved by Order-in-Council on 31 May 1870.[25] From the 1870s onwards, a campaign to buy back private land, and to have a much larger site declared a public reserve, grew in strength. Residents in around Hanging Rock were not alone in making these demands for recreation spaces. A system of recreation reserves in all Victoria municipalities had been a vision close to the heart of Governor La Trobe. Taking up his advice, town councils had set aside land for public recreation. Often these were, like Hanging Rock, popular beauty spots, or well-known picnic places. Others were pegged out around important water sources. Not all were guaranteed survival because, throughout the 1870s, the demands of mining companies, alongside the increasing pace of land selection, threatened many such reserves. Municipal councils sold off land at the edges of reserves as values rose. Some reserves emerged as ornamental gardens whilst others were given over to sporting clubs. Increasingly, a broadening popular desire for bush rambles, including ascents to high points seeking out panoramic views, took hold amongst visitors to the surviving reserves. It is not surprising then, to find a delegation of councillors from Newham, Romsey, Kyneton and neighbouring districts seeking out parliamentarians, to propose that Hanging Rock be included in a new, expanded public reserve. In May 1873, the Presidents of the Shires of Newham, Kyneton and Romsey were presented to the President of the Lands Board by John Care Riddell, Member of the Legislative Council Victoria, and a survivor of the squatting era around Gisborne. The presidential delegation noted that in the 'early days' of the colony, land that included the Rock itself, was sold off for a few pounds per acre. [26] William Adams subsequently sold most of his land, hotel included, to William Anderson. He did though, hold onto the Rock itself. As a result the unique Hanging Rock was now in the hands of an ex-publican, who had control of the site, and charged visitors to attend the festivities there each summer. As well as pocketing the entrance fee, complained the presidential troupe, Adams was also making money supplying food, drink and entertainments. Riddell proposed that the government could buy the land back for £600 and then, pay

off the debt by selling off the adjoining Crown land of 96 acres, cutting the area up for small allotments, to be sold off from £8 to £10 per acre. The President of the Lands Board agreed that selling Hanging Rock had been a terrible mistake. He also told them that he was averse to 'the present owner making a profit out of the government', in other words he wanted the buy-back to be as close as possible to the price Adams originally paid. [27] This haggling over price dragged the purchase out for more than a decade, complicated by another change of ownership. William Adams, swamped by mortgage debt, sold out once more, to William Anderson, in September 1876. Anderson continued to commercialise his expanded holding, reconstructing fences and closing off entranceways. Apparently, he was also sharp enough to hold onto water rights to the Reserve dam until the end of the nineteenth century.[28]

Negotiations with both Adams and his successor did not go well. With the area to be purchased reduced, the former publican wanted nearly double the valuation put on the site by the district surveyor.[29] Anderson also wanted to be compensated for 'improvements' he had made to the site.[30] All the while, the popularity of the Rock increased, with visitors from other colonies now included in the picnic parties headed there. Throughout the 1870s, popular magazines carrying the image of this unique place around the continent. In 1877, the *Australasian Sketcher* for example, asserted that 'of all the places of holiday resort for pic-nic purposes open to the choice of the leisure-seeker, there is none at once more interesting, picturesque, popular and readily accessible than the Hanging Rock'.[31] And yet, despite these fine qualities, visits to the Rock itself depended on the whims of, and payment to, the owner of private land. As the *Sketcher* explained,

It is humiliating to add that a place so well suited to serve as a holiday resort to thousands of people and thus to be a great public benefit to the community, was sold by the stupid, short-sighted policy of the Government some years ago . . . few can visit the spot without a feeling of indignation at the imbecility of the Government which for something less than £100 permitted the alienation of what ought to have been reserved as public property for public recreation and amusement.[32]

When the Hanging Rock Hotel was put up for sale in the following year, 1878, demands for a Hanging Rock buy-back grew louder still. Unfortunately, as the *Australasian* charged in 1879, 'our practice here has been to sell everything which anybody would buy'.[33] This abject failure of the state in securing recreational land was typified in the fate of Hanging Rock, 'the resort in holiday times of thousands of visitors', which for several years, the shire council and colonial Lands Office had been negotiating to buy back at of course 'an enhanced price'.[34]

Newham councillors redoubled efforts to persuade the colonial land authority to purchase the Rock in 1883. Early in 1884, S.T. Staughton, the long-standing conservative member for West Bourke, had approached the minister for lands (and his one-time rival for a legislative assembly seat) Alfred Deakin, to suggest that the colony could repurchase the Rock. Deakin insisted that he needed to visit the site before he could give a decision, a trip that caused some consternation amongst interested locals, since it was suspected that Staughton had confused the area already in public hands, with the site

east. Processions of children bound for picnics, groups of parents and others looking after the comfort of the little ones, lent variety to the scene, and everything told a tale of prosperity, and well-doing, which augured well for the year which had just commenced. By twelve o'clock, the town was almost entirely deserted.

THE HANGING ROCK.

Notwithstanding the numerous attractions elsewhere, this favourite resort was as well attended by excursionists as ever. Numbers from Melbourne, Castlemaine, Lancefield, and even more distant localities were present, making up an assemblage of at least three thousand persons. When these were scattered over the picturesque upheaval of rugged rock, a scene was presented which we believe could hardly be equalled in any other locality in Victoria. A great variety of amusements had been provided—horse racing, foot racing, quoits, cricket, and the like, and into these every one seemed to enter heartily. There were also dancing booths, which were a great attraction to the young of both sexes. It is pleasant to record that although there were unusual facilities for obtaining refreshments, not a single drunken person was to be seen upon the ground.

THE SUNDAY SCHOOL UNION PICNIC.

The Kyneton Sunday School Union held their annual picnic on New Year's Day, in Mr Menzies' paddock. The schools in connexion with the Wesleyan, Baptist, and Presbyterian

The Hanging Rock. The Kyneton Guardian, 4 January, 1873.
Kyneton Historical Society

SPORTS. SPORTS. SPORTS.

WHERE are you going to spend Christmas Day? At the HANGING ROCK RESERVE, as at King's Booth there is sure to be plenty of Music and Dancing.

WHERE are you going to on Boxing Day? To the HANGING ROCK RESERVE, as the Doctor ordered Father to take us all to hear the UPSON'S CHRISTY MINSTRELS at King's Booth, and says it will be better than all his medicine.

WHERE are you going on New Year's Day? To the HANGING ROCK RESERVE, as Everybody and two or three other people are going to hear the Christy Minstrels, at King's Booth.

CONCERT AND BALL EVERY EVENING

At the Assembly Hall, adjoining the Garden Hut Hotel.

Advertisement. *Sports, Sports, Sports.*
The Kyneton Guardian, 18 December, 1869.
Kyneton Historical Society

of the Rock to be added to it.[35] Staughton, for his part, told the council that any new plans for a deputation to the minister would be pointless. Councillor Glover insisted that the minister be written to immediately, and invited to visit, since the best way to impress the value of the Rock on him was a visit in fine weather.[36] Deakin's trip, as it turned out, was shaped almost entirely by discussions about funding new bridgeworks rather than any public reserve.

Just as these discussions unfolded, changes were underway at the hotel itself. The license had passed through several hands since 1866. By 1880 it appeared that an R.P.Hall was the licensee. This Mrs Hall had already faced court, on what would be the first of several legal actions over the decade that followed. Mrs Rosetta Phillys Hall was charged in 1882 with selling alcohol without a license. Although Rosetta was listed as 'the keeper' of the Hanging Rock Hotel, it appeared her husband was the actual licensee, even though he didn't seem to be living with his wife in the hotel. Woodend justices of the peace ordered Rosetta to pay a fine of £25 pounds, as well as costs of £2/10/-. The justices further ordered bailiffs to confiscate all the liquor in the Hanging Rock Hotel. Hall fought back, seeking to have the penalties set aside.[37] Two years later and Rosetta Hall was back in court, charged with passing valueless cheques.[38] The time did seem ripe for the hotel, once a respectable establishment for ramblers and wedding parties, to lose any proprietary rights around or over Hanging Rock.

It was left to the minister for lands, Albert Tucker to take up the cause for an expanded reserve. Tucker represented the densely packed inner suburb of Fitzroy and it was perhaps his experience with crowded working-class lanes and back streets, which convinced him of the value of public recreational space. Tucker joined Deakin on his trip north, arrived at Woodend station in the morning, and was driven out to Hanging Rock, which he at once committed to buy on behalf of the people of Victoria for £20 per acre.[39] After a meal at Woodend's Commercial Hotel, Deakin and Tucker took the last train back to Melbourne, and local councillors celebrated their victory in having

successfully returned Hanging Rock to public hands. Albert Tucker, a strong proponent of public welfare and community organisations, arranged the purchase of the Reserve in October 1884. Tucker repurchased 72 acres to link to the 96 acres already in public hands.[40] Now joined together, the two areas, according to one enthusiast, 'may fairly be described as one of the most beautiful and picturesque public reserves in the colony'.[41] Visitors could now climb to the top on any day of the year to explore ledges and caves. The government ought to be congratulated on regaining this 'fine property' thought one journalist, a place, 'which, it is to be hoped, will never again pass from the hands of the people'.[42]

Not all Victorians rejoiced with 'the people'. No sooner had the new Reserve been declared than councillors faced rumblings from local farmers whose cattle were removed from open space beneath the Rock. Observers from more distant parts of Victoria were contemptuous of the purchase of this odd landmark. Commenting on the visit by Tucker and Deakin, one scribe in Kerang, in north-western Victoria, complained that the government was about to waste money on a 'curio . . . a sort of natural waxworks'. Hanging Rock, asserted this observer from afar, was 'the most useless bit of property within the four corners of Victoria'.[43]

Many thousands disagreed. Over the following decade they flocked to the new Reserve. By the end of the 1880s the Rock was bringing in a diverse range of visitors, each of whom found something unique in this newly-purchased expanse. As news of the expanded Reserve spread, many more determined 'ramblers', made it across country, and then up to the Summit of Hanging Rock. The joys of the cross-country trip, commencing at Macedon, and ending at Woodend, or perhaps even Kilmore or Lancefield, caught on quickly. And more often than not, 'The Hanging Rock' occupied the focal point of a long excursion. In this new Reserve, visitors could climb, explore, survey an immense landscape, boil billies over campfires, and socialise under gum trees. In an expanded Reserve there would be space for climbers, picnickers and horseracing fans. The Rock would become a public asset, valued and understood, and Melburnians, locals and inter-colonial visitors could all delight in walking through a natural environment, with less time wasted at publicans' booths or the varied vulgarities of the sideshow crowd.

Now safeguarded in a public reserve rather than sitting as an obstacle in farmland, the majesty of the Rock seemed amplified. Hanging Rock was 'one of the most remarkable natural formations in Victoria' announced the *Australian Town and Country Journal* from Sydney.[44] For this writer, it was the rock formations rather than any picnic festivities that attracted interest, with the 'gigantic tors stand (ing) out in solitary grandeur, bearing a striking resemblance to Druidical monuments and in a few instances requiring no great force of the imagination to conjure up colossal statues of grotesque designs'.[45] Such 'Druidical' Stonehenge similarities struck other observers too. In the 1880s, Victorian Spiritualists had decided that this was a place attuned to their psyches, and gathered beneath the Rock's pinnacles.[46]

MOTORING RUNS AND MORE

Trains from Melbourne to Woodend or Macedon, followed by a trip in horse-drawn dray, had brought a widening circle of visitors to the new public reserve at Hanging Rock. In 1900, the Hanging Rock Hotel, now doubled in size to sixteen rooms, along with its adjacent thirty acre garden, sold once again. The license for holiday liquor booths was sold to T. Hogan of Bendigo for £80.[47] Their value was already on the decline. As visitors came to marvel at the picturesque, the majestic and the romantic form of Hanging Rock itself, New Year carnivals for local families faded away. Ascetic adventures to the Summit now drew in visitors from afar. The *Williamstown Chronicle* in January 1896 urged residents of the seaside suburb to forego their beach over summer, and instead head to the ranges around Woodend. Williamstown holiday-makers were advised that the ascent of the Rock was 'easy' and the view from the top 'beautiful'.[48] Edwardian club outings included all sorts of groups from suburban Melbourne. In 1908 for instance, the Prahran Rifle Club set out for the Rock on the 6.45 a.m. train to Woodend. They spent an hour 'clambering through

the many narrow and difficult passages with which the Rock is so amply provided'.[49] The hares and rabbits of the Reserve distracted some club members, fascinated by the ease with which they could mow down unsuspecting animals. They then turned to a shooting contest with local rifle club members. Even a conference of the YWCA, held in Kyneton in 1914, abandoned their bible analysis and 'mission classes', so they could set off to Hanging Rock.[50] And both racegoers and picnickers at the Rock were together discovering new ways of travelling. Automobiles brought relatively genteel visitors to the race meetings, elevating the 'fine crowd socially', or so thought one observer.[51] As the twentieth century unfolded, the novel contraption of the motor car allowed differing bands of excursionists to enjoy, not just the racetrack, but an expanded Hanging Rock Reserve.

Motoring enthusiasts could now follow point-by-point instructions for driving to Hanging Rock.[52] One set of widely studied 'Wheel Notes' announced that

> perhaps the most popular run for the day is to Macedon and Woodend. I dare say taken all year round more cars traverse this, the Mount Alexander Road, than any other highway leading out of the city . . . [from Macedon] the track is on easy grades, gradually falling until the railway line . . . if time permits a run further . . . could be made to Hanging Rock (Mount Diogenes) six miles from Woodend. [53]

Adventuring auto enthusiasts took in the network of roads around Hanging Rock, often circling through the district from the Woodend station turn-off. They bumped along dirt tracks before returning to Melbourne after a long day. The highlight of many of these tours remained always that strange rock formation of Hanging Rock.

Hanging Rock had also piqued the interest of 'bicyclists', whose constant presence meant that residents of Woodend didn't even turn heads as these mobile curiosities passed by. Pedalling frantically, clad in strange outfits, and perched atop flimsy machines, they rode off towards Hanging Rock.[54] The speed, daring, and freedom of bicycles

THE *Herald* of last night reports :—A deputation from the shire councils of Newham, Kyneton, and Romsey, introduced by Messrs Riddell and King, M.L.A.'s, waited upon the hon the Commissioner this morning, at the Crown Lands Office, to endeavor to persuade the Government to purchase the ground on which the Hanging Rock now stands. The rock had passed into the hands of a publican, who had bought it for L550, and demanded a small toll for admission to his property. It was a favorite resort of many people from all the country round, and the people in the neighborhood thought it ought not to be in private hands. It had been sold in the early days. Only the rock was wanted, and such ground surrounding it as would give access to it. The ground round it was valued at from L8 to L10 per acre, but the rock itself was useless. Mr Casey remarked that the present owner had evidently possessed himself of a white elephant, in that the rock was of no earthly use to him; but if he thought he was going to take advantage of his possession to put a fancy price upon the property, he would find his mistake in applying to the Government for it. Mr Casey promised thatl if the gentlemen would ascertain what moderate amount the present owner would sell the property at, he would bring the matter before his colleagues, and let their decision be known. The Honorable Commissioner remarked that the land ought never to have been sold

The Herald of last night reports: The Kyneton Guardian, 7 May, 1873.

Kyneton Historical Society

HANGING ROCK HOTEL, NEWHAM.

WM. CLARINGBOLD

BEGS to inform excursionists visiting the Hanging Rock that they will find every accommodation at the Hotel. Dinners, Pic-nic and Wedding Parties, Temperance Societies, and Schools contracted with at reasonable rates.

Special Arrangements at the Rock on Christmas and New Year. Select Music for Dancing and other amusements. Dinner provided in the Hotel and Booth at the Rock during the Holidays.

A Coach leaves Woodend twice daily for the Rock, returning in time for the Melbourne and Sandhurst trains, extra accommodation during the holidays.

HANGING ROCK SPORTS
ON
NEW YEAR'S DAY, 1879.

STEWARDS:—

Mr Savage	Mr Birney
„ Keating	„ Stokes

Mr Collins.

Judge—Mr W. Peters.
Starter—Mr P. F. Meagher.
Clerk of the Course—Mr M. Bowen.
Treasurer—Mr C. J. Row.
Weigher—Mr J. J. Stammers.

PROGRAMME.

MAIDEN FOOT RACE OF 100 YARDS.
To start at 12.45 p.m.
First prize, £1 ; second, 10s. Entry, 1s. For boys under 14 years.
MAIDEN PLATE. To start at 1 p.m.
Of 8 sovs. For all horses that have never won an advertised race exceeding £5. Distance about one mile and a half. Weight for age. Entry 10s.
RUNNING LONG JUMP. To start at 1.30 p.m.
First prize, 15s ; second, 5s. Entry 1s.
DISTRICT FOOT RACE. To start at 2 p.m.
For boys from 14 to 17 years of age residing in Newhamshire. First prize, 20s ; second, 10s. Entry 2s.
HANGING ROCK HANDICAP.
To start at 2.15 p.m.

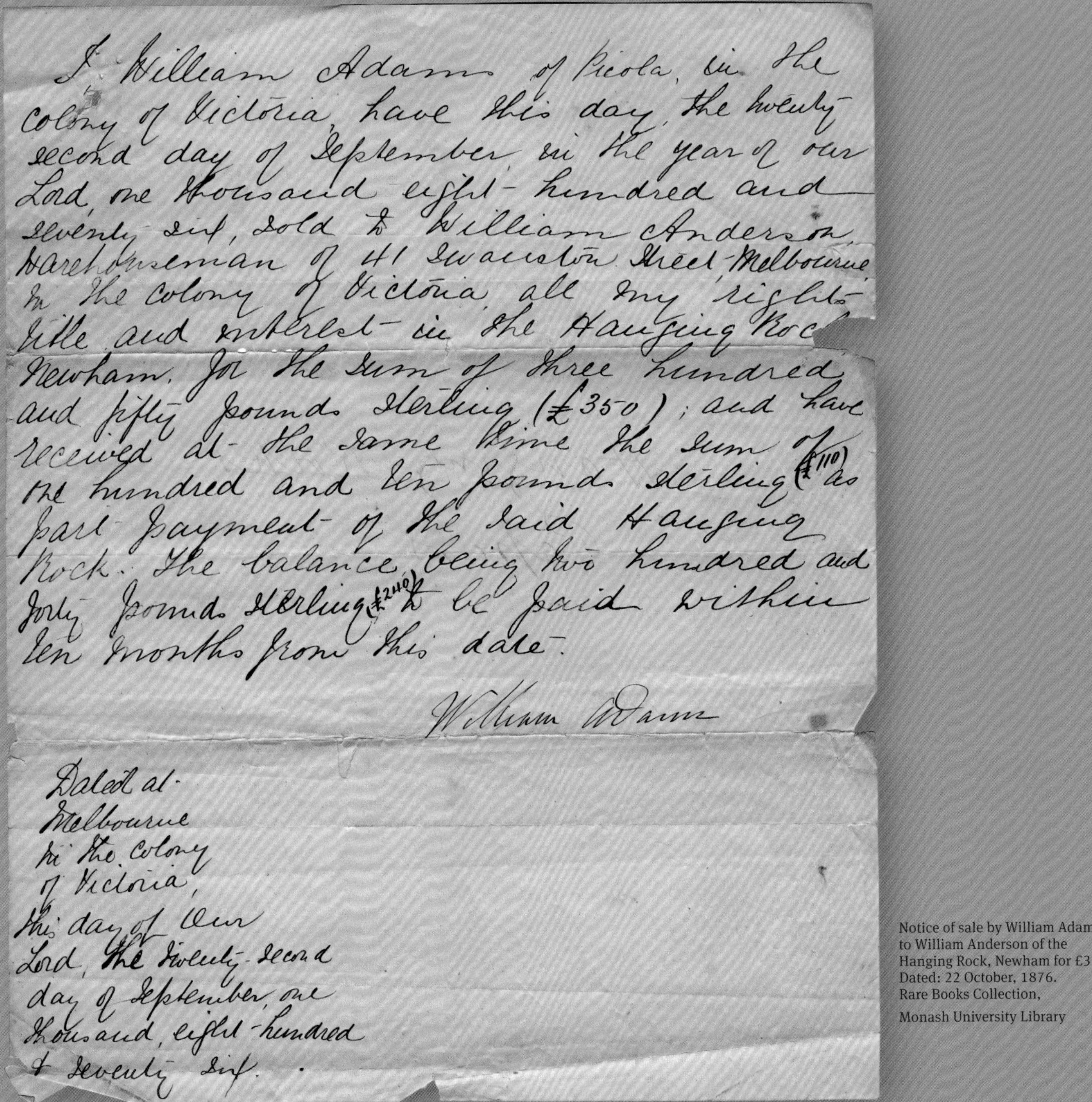

I William Adams of Picola in the colony of Victoria, have this day, the twenty-second day of September in the year of our Lord, one thousand eight-hundred and seventy six, sold to William Anderson, Warehouseman of 41 Swanston Street Melbourne in the colony of Victoria, all my rights title and interest in the Hanging Rock Newham. for the sum of three hundred and fifty pounds sterling (£350); and have received at the same time the sum of one hundred and ten pounds sterling (£110) as part payment of the said Hanging Rock. The balance being two hundred and forty pounds sterling (£240) to be paid within ten months from this date.

William Adams

Dated at
Melbourne
in the colony
of Victoria,
this day of Our
Lord, the twenty-second
day of September, one
thousand, eight-hundred
& seventy six.

Notice of sale by William Adams to William Anderson of the Hanging Rock, Newham for £350
Dated: 22 October, 1876.
Rare Books Collection,
Monash University Library

Purchase of the Hanging-Rock Reserve.

The purchase of the well-known and attractive recreation ground, known as the Hanging Rock, Mount Macedon, was completed last week, by Mr. Tucker, the Minister of Lands. The land purchased comprises about 72 acres, a short distance from Woodend, in the parish of Newham, and adjoins a piece of comparatively level ground of about 100 acres still in the possession of the Crown. The two areas, will, therefore, form one reserve of 172 acres, which may fairly be described as one of the most beautiful and picturesque public reserves in the colony. Mr. Tucker gave instructions yesterday for its permanent reservation and dedication to the free use of the public from henceforward. The value of the recreation ground now secured may be estimated when it is taken into consideration that, although a charge was made for admission by the proprietor, frequently from 5000 to 10,000 people have visited it on holidays, and that it is also visited by tourists from all parts of the colony. The strange feature is, of course, the immense and almost numberless rocks, many of them hundreds of tons in weight, that stand together in all sorts of fantastic shapes and positions, but so that paths between them and over them lead to the very top of the highest, which may be reached by foot or on horseback, from whence a splendid panoramic view is obtained of the country for miles around. Clear icy cold rills and springs of water on the hottest day flow and emerge from between the crevices whilst underfoot the ground reverberates like a drum, showing the existence of caves, which will probably be now opened up and explored. The Government may be congratulated upon regaining this fine property, which, it is to be hoped, will never again pass from the hands of the people.—*Age.*

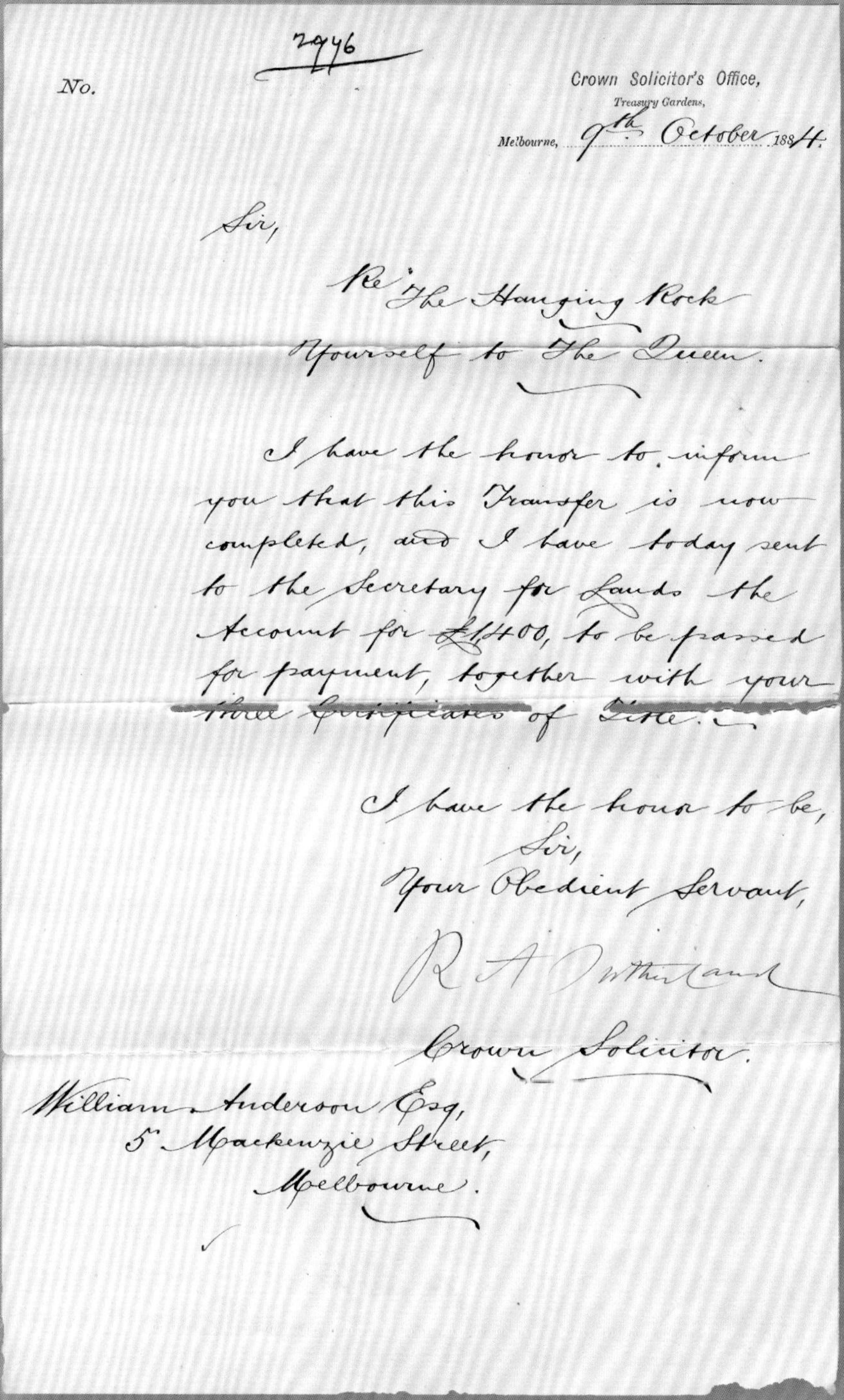

No. 2946

Crown Solicitor's Office,
Treasury Gardens,
Melbourne, 9th October 1884.

Sir,

Re The Hanging Rock
Yourself to The Queen.

I have the honor to inform you that this Transfer is now completed, and I have today sent to the Secretary for Lands the Account for £1400, to be passed for payment, together with your three Certificates of Title.

I have the honor to be,
Sir,
Your Obedient Servant,
R. A. Sutherland
Crown Solicitor.

William Anderson Esq,
5 Mackenzie Street,
Melbourne.

Letter from Crown Solicitor to William Anderson regarding purchase of Hanging Rock by the Victorian Government for £1,400. Dated: 9 October, 1884. Rare Books Collection, Monash University Library fascinated Edwardian Melbourne, so that Hanging Rock drew more and more excursionists from amongst adventurous two-wheeled men and women. In January 1907 twelve members of Melbourne's 'Inter-Club Cycling Association' accompanied by two 'Sociables' set off an 9.00 a.m. for Hanging Rock by way of Essendon and Diggers' Rest. By 12.30 the group had reached Gisborne. After lunch at Gisborne's Victoria Hotel they mounted bikes once more, and pedalled for Hanging Rock, reaching Thorburn's Hanging Rock Hotel in time for tea. After a night at the pub, the intrepid cyclists took a quick spin to the base of Hanging Rock. Leaving their machines below, the party climbed to 'MacDonald's Lookout' from where they could make out Woodend to the south-west, the Jim Jim Ranges to the north-west and in the distance, the Cobaw Ranges. Taking up the bikes once more, they cycled on to Riddell's Creek, and the train back to Melbourne. The bicycling adventurers got home at 11.30 that night. Afterwards, they thoroughly recommended a trip to Hanging Rock to any energetic club members.[55]

But it was the motor car that really expanded the range of twentieth-century visitors to Hanging Rock. Cars opened up the Macedon Ranges to suburban families and brought farmers from further north down to Hanging Rock. So one young girl, Jessie Laurie, from near Rushworth, summarised her picnic to Hanging Rock and the trip by car:

> Dear Aunt Connie . . . I will tell you about a picnic we had at the Hanging Rock it is about 75 miles from our place so we had to start early in the morning in a motor car . . . we got there at one o'clock and we had our picnic and then we went and climbed the mountains. These were the first big rocks I had seen. We then had to leave for home and got back after dark.[56]

Cars remained a luxury item for most Melburnians. Even so, those with these new machines delighted in the freedom they brought for country trips.[57] The 'most popular run' for drivers wanting to get out of Melbourne remained that between Macedon and Woodend.[58] Motoring through the bush often meant a more distant perspective on the Rock. Compared to train travellers, the automobile passengers often showed

far less enthusiasm for actually getting down from their seats and climbing up the Rock. So one set of instructions in 1917 talked not so much about the Rock itself, or the view from the Summit, but the perspective from the road to the Rock.

> Mount Diogenes is a great outcrop, and might more appropriately be called 'Rifted Rock' as its rugged sides show huge parallel crevasses almost from top to bottom. One has a fine view of the 'Rock' on the south from the road . . . and also of the pretty enclosure at the foot.[59]

Another account outlined a journey from Macedon to Newham and then a turn to the south from where 'Mount Diogenes — better known as Hanging Rock — was soon passed'.[60] By 1928 the RACV was alerting members to the improvement in the road to Bendigo through Woodend. The 'easy run' north from Melbourne now brought many more auto excursionists into the Black Forest and on to Macedon. 'Fair to good roads' then ran through to Hanging Rock, where drivers could go into the Reserve through the gate and 'use the ground'.[61]

As car ownership spread, and loyal fans of distinct 'marques' formed clubs, car owners discovered that Hanging Rock was a fine destination for their weekend rallies.[62] In 1936 the recently formed Morris Club brought its members together for a day at Hanging Rock. Not to be outdone, inter-war motorcyclists also ventured out to Hanging Rock. By the 1930s there were races around the Rock for motorcycle clubs. Mr H.E. Ford wrote to the shire council as spokesman for the Northcote Motor Cycle Club, suggesting that the Rock could be the venue for racing.[63] By 1935 the motorcycle races were held using the racecourse grass track. This proved both fast and safe, with Reg Hay managing to reach over 68 miles per hour down the straight. The program included a side-car race, followed by a two-lap race, which rounded out a program of more than six events, all run under the control of the Autocycle Union of Victoria.[64]

Bus companies began to run weekend excursions to Hanging Rock. School groups would also turn to the Reserve, often for break-up

O.31.at Woodend. 1880.

O.31.at Woodend. 1880. Photograph by Victorian Railways. State Library of Victoria

picnics. As a reward for their success in basketball, the girls of St Joseph's College Kilmore ventured to the rock in 1931. Once at the Rock 'suitable games in which all joined were played until dinner time'. After climbing up and down the Rock another round of games 'were again indulged in'. The girls could not drag themselves away until seven o'clock in the evening, when the party set off back to Kilmore. So ended 'a joyous outing [that] will be long cherished by all, among the happy memories of school days'.[65] The Newham and Woodend Residents Association began to hold summer excursions and athletics carnivals at Hanging Rock.[66] Girl Guides too camped at the Rock, where instead of learning new bush skills, or climbing the wet and slippery slope, the girls shared in 'the thrill of sleeping in the jockeys' quarters and running races on the racecourse'.[67]

Car travel, cycling, school excursions, and shooting all helped to fix Hanging Rock firmly in the minds of holiday-makers in the years between the wars. But it was the heroes of Australian Rules football who really established Hanging Rock as a place worth a trip out from the city. By 1934 the Hanging Rock Reserve included a cricket pitch and an oval (eventually home to the Hesket Cricket Club in summer and the Hesket Football Club in the Mt Riddell League in the winter). Within the Reserve, a tennis court was ready for use before 1939.[68] These arenas now attracted a more famous cast of sporting heroes. Fitzroy Football Club were the first VFL club to venture up to Hanging Rock, setting off for a day-long excursion during the 1934 season. Their trip was organised by club president and Fitzroy manufacturing magnate, Ozzie Porter, whose horses raced at Hanging Rock. Ozzie put together a program of relay races, long kicking contests, and goal kicking at Hanging Rock's new oval.[69] 'South's Picnic at Hanging Rock' made headlines as the 1937 VFL season approached. The South Melbourne players set out for Hanging Rock to play a cricket match against the stars from the Footscray Football Club. Families went along too, and the club arranged a sports program for wives, girlfriends and children. The tennis courts were opened up for casual matches, and the day was to finish off with a dance, and music under the Rock's walls.[70] South Melbourne won the cricket and Syd Sherrin

donated two cricket balls, to be mounted and presented to the best players.[71] The league clubs no doubt got the idea for this outing from smaller suburban neighbours. North Fitzroy Football Club had set off for Hanging Rock in November 1898. The players spent the morning climbing Hanging Rock, and taking in the bush panorama. They then set off for a long lunch at the Haymarket Hotel, Kyneton, before finally turning out for a match against Kyneton at three in the afternoon. Needless to say, Kyneton won.[72]

MANAGING TOURISTS

Eventually, manufacturing firms saw Hanging Rock as a perfect spot for cheaply run works picnics. The pioneering industrial firm of Thompsons, with employees at Williamstown and Castlemaine, ran a sports day and picnic at the Rock in 1951. The firm hired nine buses from Melbourne, and 28 for staff at the company's Castlemaine works. In an 'old buffers' race' and a tug-of war battle, alongside serious sprints run at the base of the Rock, the 'country workers were too good for the city boys'.[73]

Hanging Rock had began to fall out of favour during the war years, so that these and other works outings probably signalled a downturn that was to last for some time. Certainly some of the old sideshow operators continued to turn up at Hanging Rock on race days. 'No one except a few diehards confined his or her attention to the racing in front of them' observed one Melbourne journalist at the 1940 Hanging Rock Cup Day. For, away from the track, just as for years past, 'to those who like to relax at darts, or try their luck at Aunt Sallies, the sideshows gave a hearty welcome'.[74] A report of the following year's race day was less enthusiastic, and it did sound as if the sideshow carnival was nearing collapse. As one visitor lamented in 1941:

> The last threads of the Aunt Sallies, hooplas that are modernised and you now shoot them with a popgun. The stall selling fancy sticks, balls on strings and other novelties is still there and there are still other sideshows but they are getting less in number.[75]

Within a few years, car travellers were heading further afield as roads and automobiles improved. The Victorian and Edwardian fascination for the picturesque and romantic no longer gripped the suburban imagination. Urban fringe recreation reserves could no longer compete with the Grampians, Lakes Entrance, or eventually, the Gold Coast.[76] In fact the rise of the Gold Coast after 1945, driven by adventurous hoteliers, builders and impresarios like Eddie Kornhauser and Stanley Korman, resembles in many ways the manner in which Adams and other publicans shaped the first years of tourism to Hanging Rock.[77]

New excursionists turned up, taking the place of motorists and cyclists after the war. Melbourne University students had formed a pioneer rock climbing club in 1947 and a few years later discovered the challenges of Hanging Rock. Successor to the university group, the Victorian Climbing Club, produced a guide to Hanging Rock in 1957.[78] Early ventures were not all that inspiring. Climbing leaders later recollected of Hanging Rock that 'miraculously no one has died there yet, but that is due more to good luck than good management'. Climbers had faced 'some monumental plummets' off the rock walls. Even so, 'beginners continue to come in droves to risk life and limb on the unprotected easier climbs under the supervision of inept instructors'.[79] Club members set off for Hanging Rock in April 1965 for one training course, only to find that the Rock was shrouded in 'perpetual drizzle and wind all day'. Novice climbers from Monash University along with 'appalling organisation', meant that there were not enough ropes for the climb and:

> Groups of shivering beginners were forced to stand around for literally hours waiting their turn, only to fall off climbs which in the conditions prevailing were unsuited to their stage of development. A poor introduction to climbing.[80]

Rock climbers returned to Hanging Rock, and later in the year identified a series of challenging climbs. 'The Hearse' was a short climb along a route 'done entirely by bolts' and starting at the tourist track below an overhanging rock.[81] 'Morgue Wall' took climbers up a line of 27 bolts 'to a very steep bulge with loose rock and poor bolts'. Veering right on a rock wall, climbers were warned to look out for a wet mossy groove and then use hand-holds. They could abseil down forty feet from wet slabs at the peak, or walk back down the tourist track.[82] It took climbers nine hours in the middle of winter to complete the trip. Climbers developed other routes up the face of Hanging Rock, although their real interests lay in the Grampians and Mt Arapiles in particular. Bushwalkers too, were slow to embrace Hanging Rock, preferring the purity of wilderness in the Australian Alps. It was not then, until the later 1970s, and a revived interested in environmental protection, bushwalking and knowledge of Victorian nature, that a new generation of visitors rediscovered Hanging Rock.

Restructured with new management systems in 1976, the Rock continued to bring in crowds for race days and to casual picnics. Hanging Rock, by then a hybrid landscape, struggled to attract tourists hoping for neat and manicured picnic surrounds. Neither was the Reserve sufficiently untamed to attract anyone seeking a day in the wild. Local groups did, however, build on an older interest in motoring excursions. The Mount Macedon and District Motor Club organised runs to Hanging Rock from the 1980s. The club's annual 'classic car' picnic and display will be held once more in February 2018. As we shall see in later chapters, the global success of the film *Picnic at Hanging Rock* introduced a whole new mass of potential tourists to the Reserve. The 2018 television series will no doubt draw in another new band of visitors. But in trying to follow in the footsteps of the movie's fictional Miranda, or simply picnicking beneath the Rock, these waves of visitors expose some of the complex pressures on the Rock and the Reserve.

When seen from the viewpoint of tourism theory, Hanging Rock has followed a familiar trajectory.[83] Once set alongside other recreation and scenic reserves in Victoria, Lal Lal Falls or Buchan Caves for example, Hanging Rock can be seen to progress through several stages, from its initial 'pre-tourism' through its elevation and enshrinement, to its social reproduction as seen in film and novel of *Picnic at Hanging Rock*.[84] All the same, Hanging Rock's varied, often conflicted roles, as a carnival place, sports ground, ramblers' panorama, sylvan retreat, climbers' challenge and gambling arena, point to a series of crises, declines and resurrections. Any direct progressive account of Hanging Rock, from the viewpoint of the tourist industry and its commentators, explains one central aspect of the place. Hanging Rock, though, was never simply a tourist resort. For publicans like Adams and King it was an extension of their day-to-day business. For farmers, a social centre for a few days each year, and a resource for grass and water each summer. For footballers or tennis and cricket players, it remains a performance space. Racegoers treat the Rock as a carnival setting. It has filled a need for nearby townsfolk, whose small hamlets could support few places for public events.

Over time, sideshows, drinking, dancing and gambling around the publicans' booths at Hanging Rock picnic races, were gradually divorced from family picnics, such as that enjoyed by Jessie from Waranga. In the early twentieth century, the first adventurous car or motor-cycle excursionists put Hanging Rock on the maps of round trips from Melbourne. The Reserve catered reasonably well for most of these events. Even so, by the later decades of the twentieth century, rival demands had begun to tell. Balancing commercial claims on the Rock with the social get-togethers, which had lasted from the 1860s, has proved complex enough. By the end of the later twentieth century these claims on the Rock would be confronted by new demands for a return to a more natural and unmodernised Hanging Rock. Decades later, these tensions remain unresolved. ❋

Start of Girl's Egg and Spoon Race.
Woodend and Newham Residents Entertain Visitors
at Hanging Rock Sports.
The Weekly Times, 22 February, 1930.

State Library of Victoria

NEWHAM—Site for Public Recreation.—Ninety-six acres two roods two perches, county of Dalhousie, parish of Newham, being allotment 7a of section 2: Commencing at the north-east angle of allotment 6; bounded thence by that allotment and and allotment 12c bearing south 44 chains 10 links; thence by a road bearing N. 78° 19′ E. twenty-three chains sixty-three links; thence by allotments 7e and 7b bearing north thirty-nine chains thirty-two links; and thence by a road bearing west twenty-three chains fourteen links to the point of commencement.—(69.T.16526.)

JOHN A. MacPHERSON,
Commissioner of Crown Lands and Survey.

Lands and Survey Office,
Melbourne.

Government Gazette, Victoria. No.38,
3 June, 1870.
State Library of Victoria

The following Notice was gazetted 1° on 24 October, pursuant to to Order of 20 October 1884.

NEWHAM—Site for Public Recreation and for affording Access to Water about to be permanently reserved.—One hundred and sixty-seven acres three roods twenty-three perches, county of Dalhousie, parish of Newham, comprising allotment 7ᵃ and parts of allotments 6 and 12ᵉ of section 2: Commencing at the south-west angle of allotment 7E; bounded thence by a road bearing S. 78° 19′ W. twenty-four chains nineteen links; thence by lines bearing respectively N. 61° 40′ W. eleven chains fifty-one links, N. 0° 47′ W. eight chains sixty-two links, N. 38° 7′ W. three chains forty-nine links, N. 51° 10′ W. four chains thirty links, N. 36° 18′ W. four chains fifteen links, N. 21° 53′ W. nine chains ninety-five links, and north twelve chains thirteen links; thence by a road bearing east forty-five chains fifty-three links; and thence by allotment 7B and allotment 7E aforesaid bearing south thirty-nine chains thirty-two links to the point of commencement.—(N.59(³)) (84.L.20467.)

A. L. TUCKER,
Commissioner of Crown Lands and Survey.

Lands and Survey Office,
Melbourne.

Government Gazette, Victoria. No.125,
24 October, 1884.
State Library of Victoria

LAND PERMANENTLY RESERVED FROM SALE.

IN pursuance of the provisions of *The Land Act 1869* (33 Vict. No. 360, § 6 and 8), the Governor in Council has reserved from sale, *permanently*, the land hereinafter referred to, viz. :—

Reserved by Order of 25 November 1884.

NEWHAM—Site for Public Recreation and for affording Access to Water. See *Gazette* of 24 October 1884.

A. L. TUCKER,
Commissioner of Crown Lands and Survey.

Lands and Survey Office,
Melbourne.

Government Gazette, Victoria. No.136,
28 November, 1884.
State Library of Victoria

Picnic Group At Hanging Rock, Woodend. Annual meeting of delegates of the Ancient Order of Foresters held at Kyneton. Herald and Weekly Times, 3 February, 1906.

State Library of Victoria

View of motor paddock, Hanging Rock Races. Punch, 4 January, 1912.
State Library of Victoria

Wild West Show. Picnic Races: New Year's Day Meeting At Hanging Rock, Victoria.
The Australasian, 9 January, 1904.
State Library of Victoria

MacDonald's Lookout, Hanging Rock. Bronzewing Cyclist's club members.
Table Talk, 7 February, 1907.

State Library of Victoria

Endnotes

[1] 'Public Auctions', *Australasian*, 6 April 1878:15

[2] Daylesford *Advocate*, 1 August 1914.

[3] 'A Licensee's Difficulty', *Age*, 8 May 1928:11, and 'Hotels to Close' *Argus*, 12 July 1928: 9.

[4] Ian D Clark, ed., *An Historical Geography of Tourism in Victoria: Case Studies*, De Gruyter, Berlin, 2014.

[5] On the history of hotels around Hanging Rock generally see the careful chronologies in Jannyse Williams, *Time gentlemen please: Hotels of Woodend and surrounding district*, Woodend and District Historical Society, Woodend, 2013.

[6] *Australasian*, 6 April 1876:15.

[7] *Kyneton Guardian*, 22 December 1864.

[8] *Kyneton Guardian*, 29 December 1864.

[9] *Kyneton Guardian*, 29 December 1864

[10] *Kyneton Guardian*, 3 April 1869.

[11] Typescript correspondence summaries, Hanging Rock Box, Gisborne and Mount Macedon Districts Historical Society Collection, Gisborne.

[12] *Kyneton Guardian*, 23 October 1868.

[13] Typescript correspondence summaries, Hanging Rock Box, Gisborne and Mt Macedon Districts HS, Gisborne.

[14] *Kyneton Guardian*, 29 December 1869.

[15] *Kyneton Guardian*, 6 April 1870.

[16] *Kyneton Guardian*, 10 June 1876: 3.

[17] *Kyneton Guardian*, 3 January 1872.

[18] *Kyneton Guardian*, 21 June 1876.

[19] Coles Hotel Index, State Library of Victoria.

[20] 'How we spent Christmas and Boxing Day', *Argus*, 28 December 1871: 6.

[21] 'How We spent Christmas and Boxing Day', *Argus*, 28 December 1871: 8.

[22] 'How We spent Christmas and Boxing Day', *Argus*, 28 December 1871: 8.

[23] 'The tourist, easy trips from Melbourne', *Australasian*, 10 January 1880: 6.

[24] 'A Trip to the Hanging Rock', *Mercury and Weekly Courier*, 3 January 1880: 3

[25] 'Typewritten notes', Hanging Rock Box, Gisborne and Mt Macedon Districts HS Collection, Gisborne, *Victoria Government Gazette*, 3 June 1870.

[26] *Argus*, 4 May 1869: 5.

[27] 'News of the Day', *Age*, 7 May 1873: 3.

[28] Letters, Adams, Anderson, Victorian government, Bill of Sale, Hanging Rock Archive, Monash University Library.

[29] *Argus*, 11 March 1873.

[30] 'Typescript Summary, 'Notes of Correspondence July 1873', Hanging Rock Box, Gisborne and Mount Macedon Districts Historical Society.

[31] 'The Hanging Rock', *Australasian Sketcher*, 17 February 1877.

[32] 'The Hanging Rock', *Australasian Sketcher*, 17 February 1877.

[33] *Australasian*, 5 April 1879: 17.

[34] *Australasian*, 5 April 1879: 17.

[35] 'Typescript Notes' Gisborne and Mt Macedon Districts H.S., extracts from *Kyneton Guardian*, 29 March 1884.

[36] 'Typescript Notes', Gisborne and Mt Macedon Districts H.S.; *Kyneton Guardian*, 3 May 1884.

[37] 'Supreme Court', *The Australasian*, 21 June 1882: 23.

[38] 'South Melbourne Police Court', *Port Melbourne Standard*, 1 November 1884: 3.

[39] 'Ministerial visit to Kyneton and Woodend', *Argus* 30 May 1884: 3.

[40] Mount Alexander *Mail*, 13 October 1884: 2.

[41] Mount Alexander *Mail*, 13 October 1884: 2.

[42] Mount Alexander *Mail*, 13 October 1884: 2.

[43] Kerang *Times*, 3 May 1884: 2.

[44] 'Pleasure Resorts of Victoria', *Australian Town and Country Journal Sydney*, 25 May 1889: 26-33.

[45] 'Pleasure Resorts of Victoria', *Australian Town and Country Journal Sydney*, 25 May 1889: 26-33.

[46] 'Spiritualists Picnic', *Age*, 16 November 1874: 2.

[47] *Argus*, 10 December 1901.

[48] 'In and about Woodend', Williamstown *Chronicle*, 25 January 1896: 3.

[49] 'Prahran Team at Woodend', *Prahran Telegraph*, 23 May 1908: 3.

[50] 'YWCA Conference', *Kyneton Guardian*, 24 January 1914: 2.

[51] 'Best picnic races', *Western Mail*, 10 January 1929: 34.

[52] RACV *Touring Guide*, RACV, Melbourne, n.d.

[53] 'Wheel Notes', *Australasian*, 6 September 1913: 27.

[54] 'In and about Woodend', Williamstown *Chronicle*, 25 January 1896: 3.

[55] Table Talk, 7 February 1907: 32

[56] Jessie Laurie , (nine and six months years old from Waranga Basin) to 'Aunt Connie Column, *Weekly Times*, 9 February 1924: 28

[57] Graeme Davison, 'Motor Cars', *e-Melbourne Encyclopedia of Melbourne*, http://www.emelbourne.net.au/biogs/EM01017b.htm .(viewed November 2016).

[58] 'Wheel Notes', *Australasian*, 6 September 1913: 27.

[59] 'A motorist on circuit', *Kyneton Guardian*, 30 October 1917: 4.

[60] Broadbent, 'Motoring around Mount Macedon', *Argus* 9 July 1919: 6.

[61] 'Motoring safety at night', *Argus* 7 February 1928: 3.

[62] Morris rally', *Argus*, 1 December 1936.

[63] 'Motor Cycle Racing at Hanging Rock', 4 April 1935, *Kilmore Free Press:* 4.

[64] 'Motor-cycle races at Hanging Rock', *Argus*, 6 November 1935: 5.

[65] 'Convent picnic', *Kilmore Free Press*, 19 November 1931:1.

[66] *Weekly Times*, 22 February 1930: 36.

[67] 'Girl Guides Camp', *Argus*, 25 January 1934: 1.

[68] *Argus*, 3 September 1936

[69] 'Fitzroy Club Picnic', *Argus*, 28 May 1934:13.

[70] 'South's Picnic at Hanging Rock', *Emerald Hill Record*, 20 February 1937: 4.

[71] 'South's Picnic at Hanging Rock', *Emerald Hill Record,* 27 February 1937: 4

[72] 'North Fitzroy v Kyneton', *Fitzroy City Press*, 10 November 1898: 3.

[73] 'Thompson's Picnic', *Williamstown Chronicle*, 30 November 1951.

[74] 'Hanging Rock Racing Parties', *Argus*, 3 January 1940: 8.

[75] 'Races of Old', *Australasian*, 11 Januarly1941: 2.

[76] On tourism to the Gippsland Lakes see Coral Dow, 'In search of the picturesque', *Tourism Culture & Communication*, no 2, 1999: 111-22. For the Grampians see Stawell Times, *Stawell and the Grampians visitors guide and directory*, Stawell Times News, Stawell, 1970.

[77] On the role of Melbourne hoteliers and contractors in the rise of Surfers Paradise and the Gold Coast as tourist resorts see M.A. Jones, *A sunny place for shady people: The real Gold Coast story*, George Allen & Unwin, Sydney, 1986.

[78] G. Shaw, ed., 'The V.C.C. Rock Climbing guide to Victoria', typescript, 1962.

[79] Chris Baxter, *V.C.C. Rock Climbing Guide, Central Victoria*, VCC, Melbourne, 1974.

[80] Victorian Climbing Club, 'VCC newsletter' *Argus*, April 1965: 3.

[81] Victorian Climbing Club, 'VCC newsletter' *Argus*, July,1965: 4.

[82] Victorian Climbing Club, 'VCC newsletter' *Argus*, August 1965 :2

[83] Clark, ed., *An Historical Geography of Tourism in Victoria*.

[84] Clark, *An Historical Geography of Tourism in Victoria*.

Picnic at Hanging Rock.
Jacket design: Alison Forbes.
F. W. Cheshire Publishing Pty. Ltd. 1967.

Photograph by Matthew Nickson

Vanishing Heights

[Extract from a Melbourne Newspaper 14 February 1913]
'It was thought at the time that the missing persons had attempted to climb the dangerous rock escarpments near the summit, where they presumably met their deaths; but whether by accident, suicide or straight out murder has never been established, since their bodies were never recovered ... thus the College Mystery like that of the celebrated case of the Marie Celeste, seems likely to remain forever unsolved'.

Joan Lindsay, Picnic at Hanging Rock,

First published Cheshire 1967, Penguin edition, 2008: 1888-99

In the afternoon of 14 February 1900, four schoolgirls set out to reach the Summit of Hanging Rock. Three vanish. One of their teachers also climbs Hanging Rock. She too disappears. What happens to these vanished souls, all from the pretentious rather than prestigious Appleyard College, remains the enduring mystery of Joan Lindsay's novel, *Picnic at Hanging Rock*.[1] It is a mystery revisited in Peter Weir's film of the same name. Lindsay, in the oft-quoted introduction to her tale, suggests that any differences between the facts and the fiction of Hanging Rock hardly matter.[2] And yet, this evasion of historical truths only partly explains why her 'College Mystery' continues to fascinate us. As it has turned out, the story has become far more than an intriguing fictional, or perhaps true, crime story. A tale of disappearance, suicide, warped chronology and faulty memory, it relies on Lindsay's recasting of that popular picnic spot, Hanging Rock, as a macabre, vanishing point. Almost half a century after the novel was first published, and more than a 150 years after the first photographs of Hanging Rock were taken, by Richard Daintree, Lindsay's image, of Hanging Rock as a supernatural monolith, both threatening and alluring, still fascinates readers of all ages. Once Peter Weir re-imagined the novel's setting in his 1975 film, Hanging Rock was recast as a global icon. The Hanging Rock Reserve now attracts film and fiction fans from around the globe.

Joan Lindsay's novel has become a modern Australian classic. This is not entirely due to her confounding of fact with fiction. Since they first fascinated readers, the exact identities of schoolgirls disappearing at Hanging Rock have never been publicly confirmed. After almost five decades of relentless sleuthing, fans of *Picnic at Hanging Rock* have been unable to agree on any accurate date for real disappearances. No investigator has been able to bring to light any hidden police inquiry into presumed deaths at Hanging Rock in 1900.[3] To mask her fiction, Joan Lindsay presents what seem credible police statements in the text, and closes the novel with an interview that she has apparently discovered in a 1913 Melbourne newspaper.[4] Suggestive as these hints have proven to be, Joan Lindsay's success, in entangling the real and imagined, depends in part, on Hanging Rock itself. Since readers first

encountered Miranda, Marion, Irma, and their mathematics teacher, Greta McCraw, the strange outcrop, Hanging Rock, has remained a place of imagination. It lives on as far more than a geological oddity, a racetrack, or day-trippers' recreation spot. And yet, Joan Lindsay's novel is only one in a long succession of images constructed about Hanging Rock. For beyond the unresolved events of February 1900, it is the unfolding of the Rock's visual imagery, both realist and romantic, factual and fictional, which brings enduring life to the novel. This perhaps is the most intriguing of the novel's many mysteries. How did Joan Lindsay manage to convince readers that the wild Hanging Rock imagined by artists in the 1870s, had survived to threaten and confuse school excursionists in 1900? For by then, as we know, the wild country of Hanging Rock had been restrained through a modernised racecourse, graded pathways towards the Summit, avenues of imported trees, and the celebrations of thousands of New Year visitors. The hold which the novel continues to exert might be best explained by returning to the visual imagery that Joan Lindsay exploited so cleverly.

CAMERAS, ENGRAVINGS AND THE ROCK

Just what images of Hanging Rock did Joan Lindsay revisit, refashion, and embellish? She certainly converted Hanging Rock into a melodramatic locale. In her novel, a party of excited schoolgirls sets out with teachers in tow for Hanging Rock, and a St Valentine's Day picnic in the year 1900. Three girls and one teacher don't return. Only one of these girls is discovered. She has no memory of their vanishing. A fourth girl (Edith, the school 'dunce', or so we are told) who watched her friends climb the Rock, is found dead in Melbourne, a decade later. Another Appleyard College student, the school's youngest in fact, either suicides or is murdered in the school itself. If she is a murder victim, then the College headmistress becomes the prime suspect. Two lesser characters in the book perish in an hotel fire. The school too, Appleyard College, burns to the ground. Despite all of these tragedies, which, when taken together, make up an absurd catalogue of death and destruction, the novel's appeal eventually depends on Lindsay's skill in bringing new life to older visual images. In many ways she has resurrected the 'weird and spectral' Hanging Rock, which so unnerved the climbers with whose journey this history began.[5] Reviewers have now devoted countless words to accurately locating *Picnic at Hanging Rock* within an Australian literary canon. But where does the novel fit in Hanging Rock's constantly changing visual imagery? To appreciate the legacy of Lindsay's novel for Hanging Rock itself, her writing needs to be placed within a visual rather than a literary context — Hanging Rock as seen by photographers and artists. This story begins long before the twentieth-century publication of a novel about disappearing schoolgirls. And in fact, their vanishing is probably the least intriguing mystery in this longer history.

Generally welcomed by critics and the public, the novel's enduring popularity rests in part on a blending of history with fantasy, but more consistently it relies on Lindsay's clever reworking of Hanging Rock's malevolence, a characteristic invented by journalists and magazine illustrators in the nineteenth century. The novelist's Rock reiterates and then constricts older portraits of Hanging Rock as a forbidding place. In these, the Rock is wild nature, capable of both resisting and overpowering modernity. The images to which Lindsay returns, seen in engravings, newspaper sketches, a few photographs and landscape painting, typically depict Hanging Rock as a brooding edifice, towering above picnickers or racegoers, or both, in the Reserve below. One journalist put this succinctly, in reflecting on a photograph of Hanging Rock in 1895. He noted that Hanging Rock's, 'great altitude is brought out by comparison with the figure of the gentleman standing at its foot and by the surrounding trees'.[6] Sometimes writers could contrast Hanging Rock, and its Australian asymmetry, to the order and neatness of summer homes at nearby Mt Macedon, a trope crucial to the success of the novel. Most of the time though, both writers and visual artists are hinting at something more than the landscapes we can immediately perceive.

The first photographs of Hanging Rock were, though, more objective than later sketches.[7] Alfred Selwyn, in recruiting his team of surveyors in the 1850s, turned to a young man recently arrived from England,

Richard Daintree. Daintree had dropped out of both Christ College Cambridge, and from his geology degree. He then tried, and failed, to make his fortune on Victoria's gold fields. The one-time University of Cambridge student finally turned to his friend, Selwyn, for work as an assistant surveyor on the Geological Survey of Victoria.[8] Returning to England to study mining technology, he instead discovered the new art of photography. Working again in Victoria, and once more on the Geological Survey, he photographed Hanging Rock. Often framing the Rock between eucalypts, Daintree was both recording the place as an aid to his survey work, and hinting at a potentially deeper meaning. For photography proved a medium both useful to science and to romantic story telling. Captured on wet plate negatives and developed by Daintree, Hanging Rock seemed to mimic Stonehenge, to be ancient in a European sense, and to be composed of shapes that concealed power and threat.

Carting clumsy and heavy photographic equipment through the bush, Daintree at first set up at a distance from Hanging Rock. Tall trees frame the Summit, which is central to his photographs, and seen in the middle distance through scattered trees. The Rock appears from this distance to be little different from peaks elsewhere in the central highlands of Victoria. Its outline might be uneven, but it is pictured rising in a symmetrical cone, to a defined point.[9] As Daintree moved his camera stand closer to the base of the Rock, wave-like elevations of rock columns fill the image. Their looming presence hints at the unknown. These photographs though, remain, in the final analysis, fixed on a geological object.[10] There are only minor hints of mystery suggested in the strange formations of the rock walls.

Daintree, like Selwyn himself, soon tired of Victoria and its professional disputes. He left for Queensland, where alongside perfecting his photographic techniques, and recording life in the subtropical colony, he tried farming. Eventually he found himself back in professional work, on another colonial geological survey. Succeeding him at Hanging Rock were Charles Nettleton and Nicholas Caire, both pioneering figures in Australia's photographic history.

Drydens Rock, north side. c.1858. Photograph by Richard Daintree. State Library of Victoria

Unlike the government employee Daintree, Nettleton and Caire both ran commercial practices. They had little choice but to meet the aesthetic expectations of suburban buyers. In doing so, they tried to document the progress of towns and farmlands in Victoria. They then sought out scenes of bush life and distinctive, especially mountainous, landscapes. Nettleton tied himself to the cumbersome wet plate technique and his attempt to make a living from portraits remained precarious. He then turned to landscape photography, as well as set-piece documentation of prominent city buildings, before eventually trying to capture the essence of places like Hanging Rock. So Charles Nettleton depicted Hanging Rock in the middle distance, without any obvious attempt at impressionistic manipulation.[11] In several of his other photographs, weird contortions of the rocks, standing apart from familiar landscapes, needed no further interpreting.[12]

Nicholas Caire, unlike Nettleton, embraced dry plate photography. Keen to explore the boundaries of this new technique he set about photographing from the high points of Victoria, amongst them Hanging Rock.[13] Hanging Rock, even with its 'Witches Hats' and pinnacles, lacked the inspiration he was eventually to find in alpine scenery, at spots like Mount Buffalo. His views of, and from Hanging Rock, were less searching, and even more conventional than those of either Nettleton or Daintree.[14]

Whereas these photographers were documenting rather than reimagining Hanging Rock, engravers and sketchers remained free to explore the Rock as metaphor rather than landform. And William Blandowski in the 1850s was the first to do so. Whilst Daintree framed the Rock as a largely unexceptional landscape element, Blandowski exaggerated the Rock's unique features. The results included some highly impressionistic portraits of Hanging Rock. In these we can see the origins of the sublime, romantic, perhaps picturesque renderings of later newspaper illustrators.[15] And in common with these illustrators, Blandowski sought to capture a sense of sombre and overwhelming mystery emanating from the Rock, qualities essential to the success of Lindsay's novel.

Mary Mackay has pointed to the fascination that unusual rock formations held for nineteenth-century Australians. In part, she traces this to the publication of Lyell's work on geology and the growth of 'rock' or 'geological' tourism, for which Hanging Rock was an obvious attraction.[16] Representations of Hanging Rock also drew on other, more aesthetic, rather than scientific tropes familiar to colonial artists. Some painters stuck to a pastoral impression of the Australian landscape, softening harsh colours and placing a cosy domesticity, of selector's house and farmyard animals, in the foreground. Others framed massive and unusual landmarks, such as Hanging Rock, within a tradition of the sublime, in which nature was awesome, perhaps threatening, but fundamentally more powerful than human beings, a difference suggested in comparative scales, especially height. Between these two perspectives, the Australian environment could be painted as 'picturesque', neatly balanced, partially domesticated, and yet all the while retaining hints of awesome, indeed threatening authority. [17] Commencing with William Blandowski's images (engraved by John Redaway in Melbourne), Hanging Rock is represented as a sublime, and sometimes picturesque shape. In Blandowski's engravings, the rock columns are gathered beneath a moon. They seem to lean forward, or expand outward. Hanging Rock becomes a unique life form. In one of these sketches, the columns tower over Aboriginal figures in the foreground. A lightening strike, as Mackay notes, causes 'the Aboriginal figure (to) reel back in horror at the spectacle; his arm raised in astonishment: the classic convention to signify he is in the presence of the sublime'.[18] In another of these engravings, European climbers, one on hands and knees, stare up at a fearsome set of serrated peaks — each one distinct — separated from each other as a forest of rock trees, rather than any corrugated wall, as in Daintree's photographs. Blandowski, according to Mackay 'illuminates a surreal scene in which unbelievable rock forms locate the sense of unease generally felt by visitors to the location'.[19]

Painters as well as photographers were drawn to Victoria's mountain peak after the middle of the nineteenth century. In their travels around this remote British possession, they generally found the most spectacular scenes in the Grampians to the west, or the Australian Alps in the north-east of Victoria. Even so, one prolific artist did paint some scenes around Hanging Rock. Henry Leonardus van den Houten had come to Victoria, like so many others in the story of Hanging Rock, to mine for gold. Failing to make his fortune on the goldfields, he turned back to the craft he had studied in his birthplace, Holland, applying Dutch landscape painting techniques to Victoria. His paintings fit generally within the pastoral tradition so that we can see them now as representing an alternative to Blandowski's sublime. The wilds of central Victoria are domesticated and softened, even appearing quite European. And yet, when he exhibited his Hanging Rock scene in Melbourne, it too was hailed as capturing some overpowering essence in the Rock. When the Victorian Academy of Arts held its fifth exhibition in 1875, van den Houten's Hanging Rock painting was deemed 'a capital interpretation'. He had captured

> the gigantic rocks … jutting up towards the sky like the remains of some great fortress and the rays of the setting sun glinting through the trees combine to produce an effect recognised by anyone who has seen this most remarkable natural beauty.[20]

Alexander Burkitt arrived in Melbourne, from London, in 1855, and had already dabbled in landscape painting in southern England. He then shared the fate of so many thousands on Victoria's gold fields, where his digging cost him more than he won through gold. So Burkitt eventually found work at the Williamstown Observatory, in 1862. Within a year he was travelling through central Victoria, painting pastoral landscapes and gold towns. Amongst his works is one panorama of Hanging Rock, towering in exaggerated height and reaching a sharply defined peak. Like Daintree, Burkitt too, decided to head north, to Ipswich in Queensland, where his family was already settled.[21]

In 1864, as Burkitt was setting off for Queensland, a more widely-recognised landscape painter, Eugene von Guérard, sketched Hanging Rock. His two surviving sketches have none of the malevolence evident in Blandowski's scenes, or in the works of engravers who were

to reimagine the Rock a few years later. Von Guérard was introduced to the visual arts through the Habsburg court in Vienna.[22] Like Blandowski, he trained in Germany, at Dusseldorf, and beforehand had studied painting in Italy. He too had tried his hand at gold mining, failed, and so returned to painting. Like Blandowski too, he was schooled in that German exploratory scholarship exemplified by the great naturalist Alexander von Humboldt. Humboldt insisted that naturalists ought to seek out a bridge between scientific recording of the natural world, and its poetic interpretation. Von Guérard did just that, and his landscapes were both scientifically accurate in the most minute details, and then, metaphorical, in suggesting an inner meaning in the natural world. His technique fused these methods, with accurate black and white sketches compiled to create his extraordinary landscapes, and, in fact, sitting beneath the paint on his canvas.[23] His Hanging Rock sketches however, never proceeded to this second stage, of a painted landscape. And even had he rendered Hanging Rock as a panoramic landscape, he would not have been able to reproduce the overpowering Rock of romance. His two sketches actually show trees blocking the Rock.[24] The perspective is from a point more or less level with the rock formations. They could be any one of a number of rock outcrops around central Victoria. There is then, nothing either unique or overpowering in this landscape.

In Lindsay's novel, the one familiar depiction of the Rock, to which her characters refer directly, is an 1875 painting by William Ford. As Marion, Miranda and Irma are searching for a pathway upwards through the sheer walls of the Rock, they try to recall where they have seen a similar landscape. Miranda remembers that her father once showed her a painting of a picnic at the Rock, in which women and men are pictured with a gap in the rock wall behind them.[25] This painting was William Ford's 'At the Hanging Rock, 1875'. And unlike the heightened and forbidding imagery of the Blandowski sketches, in Ford's painting, the Rock is not an overpowering presence at all. Instead, it is shaded by trees and obscured by an undulating foreground.

Drydens Rock near Wood End. c.1858. Photograph by Richard Daintree. State Library of Victoria

*View Of The "Hanging Rock",
Near Mount Macedon.* 1877.
Photograph by Nicholas Caire.
Anglo-Australasian Photo. Co.
State Library of Victoria

Approach To The Hanging Rock, Mount Macedon. Illustrated Australian News, 23 April, 1872.
State Library of Victoria

Ford was a popular artist in nineteenth-century Melbourne, recognised widely as a painter who sought to bring a comforting, pastoral calm to Australian bush scenes. And his Hanging Rock certainly has that quality. It is quite different to the photographs and lithographs of an enormous rock, which overwhelms humans beneath its ramparts.[26] The picnickers in Ford's Hanging Rock are scattered in small groups in the foreground, in a dappled light, at ease, and sheltered beneath trees.[27] This is not the threatening Rock as depicted by Ford's contemporaries amongst newspaper illustrators in the 1870s. Instead it is a relaxed and composed pastoral scene, the Rock softened, and the emphasis directed to scattered picnickers, especially the women and children amongst them. In other words, the painting anticipates the mood of the Appleyard College girls, as they too venture confidently up, and into, Hanging Rock. The seminal painting for Lindsay's book also had a connection to her life. William Ford died in 1884 more than a decade before she was born. But his house in St Kilda was close to where she lived and went to school.[28]

Sometime Mt Macedon resident, Fred McCubbin's scene of Hanging Rock, draws viewers into an even softer landscape. In his paintings, the Rock's outline, is not at all overpowering and the sky and views to distant plains attract the viewer.[29] McCubbin also painted 'Hauling Timber Macedon Heights' in 1911, with a smoothed and innocuous Hanging Rock in the background. In both these paintings, the artist 'revelled in the colours of the scene', enlarging the clouds, lightening and smoothing any dark or jagged edges on Hanging Rock itself.[30] Joan Lindsay's Hanging Rock emerges as far more threatening and wild than anything in the work of these two artists. The nearest parallel is in the tradition commenced by Blandowski, and which inspired newspaper illustrators in the 1870s, before being usurped by more innocuous depictions around 1900, the year, as we know, of Appleyard College's excursion.

THE MALEVOLENT ROCK

From the 1870s onwards, newspaper and magazine sketchers typically drew on the most explicitly awesome and superhuman characteristics of Hanging Rock. Perhaps in response to demands for public ownership of Hanging Rock, the 1870s illustrated magazines were including images in full-page displays of black and white sketches. Conventionally, these accompanied a written account of a picnic or day out. Such woodblock engravings, circulated through illustrated magazines, remained immensely popular in the Victorian era, largely because of their supposedly accurate reproduction of reality. In the novel, Michael encounters Miranda and the other girls in the Hanging Rock picnic ground. Joan Lindsay has him reading a copy of the *Illustrated London News*.[31] Suburban magazine subscribers could open up journals such as the *Illustrated Australian News*, and wonder at scenes from across the British Empire, or around Australia. Amongst them were often engraved excursionists at Hanging Rock.[32] Such engravings might include tranquil picnic scenes, not so different to that which Lindsay initially presents to her readers. But in the hands of a magazine illustrator, the Rock itself could be manipulated into all sorts of shapes. Typically artists chose to sketch Hanging Rock as an over-arching presence dominating the human beings below its walls. In at least one sketch, intrepid bushwalkers stand in the foreground. In others we see tiny figures with staves in hand, disappearing below the rock walls.[33] In several, the trope identified by Mackay as typifying the sublime, the arm of the dwarfed human figure thrust upwards, is employed by the artist. In one such illustration, the walkers are seen marching along a wide track grasping their wooden staves and carrying packs. Several walkers are headed towards a darkened gap in the rock wall and trudge downhill rather than upwards; forced to descend, or so it seems, into some mysterious subterraneous universe, before they can begin to climb the Rock itself.[34]

Magazine illustrators often presented Hanging Rock as a sheer wall, with undulations flattened, the ridge line narrowed and heightened. Other sketches and photographs present rock formations as eccentric jigsaws of boulders and columns, defying gravity.[35] Joan Lindsay must have imagined Hanging Rock with these exaggerations of its form in mind. She obviously knew of both Ford's and McCubbin's paintings, which, even if they did spark the initial idea for her story, ultimately proved both too tame for the deaths and destruction of her Picnic. Nor was she especially interested in images created by pioneer photographers. In her reflections on travel in the United States, she remarked that old photographs of her childhood only disillusioned her. She preferred the rich exaggeration of memory to the camera's claim on objective knowledge.[36] Not surprisingly then, it is the exaggerated Hanging Rock of nineteenth-century weekly and monthly journals to which she returns.

FAMILIAR ROCK

Joan Lindsay may have been dismissive of photography as the destroyer of private memories.[37] Nonetheless by 1900, the year of her fateful picnic, photographers were routinely scaling the heights of Hanging Rock. From between the Witches Hats they captured rural panoramas, family picnic groups, and often both. With photographic techniques making landscape reproductions commercially viable, postcard series (the Rose series in particular) grew more popular. Souvenir shots were sold to holidaymakers. Agencies like the Victorian Railways commissioned photographers to record Victoria's beauty spots, Hanging Rock included.[38] Passengers in train carriages across Victoria could now marvel at contorted rock formations, vast landscapes, and winding tracks; exotic scenes photographed just out of Melbourne, and within easy reach of Victorian Railways stations at Macedon or Woodend. Hanging Rock had become a familiar place. A whole new audience, many of whom would never have been to Hanging Rock, grew to know the scenes of picnics, rock walls and giant boulders.

In these images, observers now discovered a completely different perspective on Hanging Rock, the very opposite to the dark threat exuded from Blandowski's sketches, illustrated magazines and Lindsay's disappearances. With lighter equipment than in the days of Daintree or Nettleton, photographers were now more inclined to capture the view from the top of the Rock, with distant, flat plains extending to Hesket and Cobaw, or even as far as Heathcote.[39] In place of walkers miniaturised before the enormous rock walls,

photographers now recorded picnic parties scattered across the Summit or climbing between rocks and trees. Men and women in broad-brimmed hats were photographed surveying the countryside from between rock pillars.[40] Pathways to the rock's highest point looked broad and welcoming. Couples sat beneath pinnacles smiling at cameras. Family groups perched between the columns of the Summit gazing across a now orderly landscape of small towns, farms and distant forests. The family photographs reproduced by the local historical society display happy leisure-seekers sitting around Rock pinnacles, or framed against a panorama extended to the horizon, from atop Hanging Rock.[41] The fearsome Hanging Rock had now been tamed. Photographers took in the view from McDonnell's Lookout, or captured excursioners venturing into a narrow passageway at 'The Squeeze', or passing the rock formation at 'Berry's Head'. These sobriquets suggest to us that the Rock and its strange formations were no longer frightening. Instead, the holiday-makers' Hanging Rock was pictured as another enjoyable Victorian leisure space. One within easy reach of Melbourne, and made familiar through colloquial naming. There is little in these images to authenticate Joan Lindsay's ominous monolith of Hanging Rock, with its dark crevasses, impenetrable rock jumbles and confusing dead-ends.

AN ENIGMATIC ROCK

Joan Lindsay's *Picnic at Hanging Rock* was first published in 1967. It was a very slim volume, one made even briefer because editors had excised the final chapter, thus leaving a mystery for the reader to resolve.[42] Many thousands have tried to do just that, since Lindsay and her canny editors had left these readers a quite simple and open-ended melodramatic tale. In brief outline, her mystery is little more than a conventional tale of gothic horror, although one with which readers can never feel comfortable. Are the overblown events intended as tragedy or comedy, fact or fiction? It is through such uncertainties that *Picnic at Hanging Rock* has taken on a life of its own.

Whilst readers and critics have routinely reflected on the malevolent power of Hanging Rock, the book draws often on the lush gardens

Hanging Rocks 1864. Eugene Von Guerard. Sketchbook - in album
10.4 x 16.5 cm. Dixson Galleries,
State Library of New South Wales

composing a Europeanised landscape at nearby Macedon. The house, gardens and daily routines of 'Lake View' at Macedon, with its horses, swans and garden beds is described carefully by Lindsay.[43] Such English mountain retreats are never quite safe from an encroaching Australian forest. Nonetheless, Lindsay neatly juxtaposes orderly, gardenesque landscapes to the wilds of the Rock.[44] As Elspeth Tilley has pointed out, Appleyard College and its suffocating routines also remain critical counterpoints to the Rock itself.[45] Before readers are introduced to Hanging Rock's grandeur and harshness, Lindsay paints a lush garden, blooming in late summer at Appleyard College.[46] The college sits on an unpromising stretch of land beneath Macedon, a faux Italianate palazzo, which nobody in the entire district wanted to buy. Mrs Appleyard purchased the pile on sight, stuffing the place with Victorian furniture, in an era when that style was losing favour. Even the reader's first encounter with Hanging Rock is diminished by the sense of entitlement shared amongst children of the colonial gentry. The girls, their teachers and the college horse handlers set out for the picnic, and pass scraggy rows of eucalypts, down through a generally desolate, dusty and over-heated roadway. Hanging Rock comes upon them suddenly by way of slight turn in the road. The girls' first glance is towards a 'grey volcanic mass ... slabbed and pinnacled like a fortress'. It looms above the barren, burnt plains. The Summit has no vegetation, and 'a jagged line of rock cut across the serene blue of the sky'.[47]

The Appleyard College girls quickly take possession of the crude picnic ground. Once the girls and their teacher vanish, and an alarm has been raised, search parties move through the lower flat lands of the Reserve, where they are constantly cut and entangled in low bracken, their perspective regularly blocked by dogwood trees.[48] These images of the search are generally confused, uncomfortable and disorienting. In them, the Rock as majestic landform, so powerfully pictured by Lindsay, has disappeared. To searchers, it is simply a barren, disorderly wilderness, resisting any efforts at bringing a proto-military order to their hunt. At some places in the book, Hanging Rock reappears through dream-like sequences.[49] As if to convince

the reader of her command of a factual geography, Lindsay is very clear in informing readers about the different faces of the Rock, the south-western corner from which the girls discover a narrow entry, or the eastern face where pinnacles are slowly brought to life in each dawn light.[50] In other words then, Hanging Rock is initially a majestic and dominating point in the landscape. It subsequently becomes confusing and threatening to those who try to return the girls to order and respectability at the college. Nonetheless, Hanging Rock has the power to transport a few chosen individuals into another time and place through dreams. Readers are allowed to discover that only one character is not thwarted by any of this. She rushes out of the college, races to Hanging Rock, and scrambles up the rock walls. Mrs Appleyard is perhaps following the footsteps of the vanished girls, perhaps not. When she gets to the boulders known as 'The Monolith', headmistress Appleyard, still wearing her brown hat, leaps outward. Her body crashes off the rocks and finally, lifelessly, still with its brown hat, it is trapped by a rock pinnacle.[51]

Having disposed of the college principal, cruelly and, we might surmise, gleefully, Joan Lindsay continued on with the story of Miranda, Marion, Irma and their mathematics teacher. As is now well known, Cheshire's editors cut the final chapter so that generations of readers were able to speculate on the fate of Miranda and friends. In 1980, Yvonne Rousseau made up for the lost chapter by presenting several alternative resolutions to the mystery.[52] When finally printed and released in 1987, after Lindsay's death, the final chapter explained the disappearances, in a manner not particularly satisfying to those enchanted by the mystery.[53] In a sharp turn to a fantastic ending, the girls defy the restrictions of a modern, bourgeois education. They discover a shaft that leads into another and different, place-time.[54] As might be expected, editors at Cheshire didn't think much of this ending, so out of character with the chapters that had led up to it. The excised chapter did however make one telling point. Lindsay's original story was never intended as a murder mystery, despite her eventual resort to a fictitious newspaper extract about the girls' presumed deaths. As the excised final chapter makes explicit,

172

they were not murdered, kidnapped, nor accidentally killed. They did not die in some suicide pact. Instead, they and their teacher literally escape into Hanging Rock.

AN ENDURING IMAGERY

Picnic at Hanging Rock has puzzled readers for decades, with some sleuthing fans still convinced about the historical authenticity of the narrative. Joan Lindsay of course, had little time for what she regarded as any search for hard historical facts. As she wrote in her non-fiction account of an American trip:

> The subject called HISTORY, as taught to a good many Australian children of my generation was mainly a hideously boring recapitulation of HARD FACTS to be committed to memory for examinations and quickly forgotten.[55]

If, in the novel, Hanging Rock reflects an older visual history, one commencing with Blandowski, and extended by magazine illustrators, those hoping to discover the reality of the disappearances, turn more often to the 'hard facts' of Lindsay's own life. Her youthful experiences are, somehow, entangled in, and yet never fully consistent, with the novel. Holidays to Macedon and Hanging Rock, familiarity with artists' renditions of the Rock, and education in a girls' college were all aspects of Lindsay's life.[56] Joan Lindsay (born Joan Weigall) shared in both the establishment connections of her mother, and the more artistic milieu opened up to her through the à Beckett' ancestors of her father Thyre à Beckett'.[57] The Boyds were cousins, and her maternal grandfather had been governor of Tasmania. Through her mother's side of the family, Lindsay had visiting rights to the summer retreats of the elite at Mt Macedon.[58] Lindsay's cousin, Margaret Donaldson, has left a vivid account of these holidays, in which mothers and children settled at Macedon for summers. Fathers, from the law, business and medicine caught the train up to Macedon, and were taken to their summer homes by Cogger's Coach. Families intermingled in garden parties, quoits and other garden games as well as sharing evening dinners.[59] Differences between the author's life and the novel, can in some key aspects seem quite sharp. Lindsay's Clyde schooling,

for example, with its appeal to student imagination and scientific skills, and the repressive routines of Appleyard College, with their pretentious homage to the classics, have been succinctly distinguished by Frith.[60] In its curriculum, its teaching style and discipline, Joan Lindsay's Appleyard College, as Frith demonstrates, seems unlike Joan Weigall's Clyde. And Mrs Appleyard had very little in common with Clyde's imaginative headmistress Isabel Henderson, as Marjorie Theobold reminds us.[61] And whereas Mrs Appleyard had her hands on her school's finances, Clyde Woodend was secured through what was claimed at the time,as a unique financial arrangement, providing for 'government by a council and vested in trustees, who after a fixed dividend has been paid to the shareholders, take the profits for the benefit of the school'.[62]

Although we can find many reasons to distinguish Appleyard College from Clyde itself, Terence O'Neill did note one direct connection between the structure of the novel and the experiences of Clyde's schoolgirls. As O'Neill explains:

> There is a direct borrowing from life in the genesis of the novel … it is a … mundane, yet significant connection: a brief article in the Clyde school magazine by a Miss McCraw. The author of the article shares her uncommon surname with the mathematics teacher who disappears on the rock. Miss McCraw was a teacher at Clyde during Lindsay's time there; then when the school moved to Woodend in early 1919, Miss McCraw moved with it. Then in December 1919, she wrote an article in the *Cluthan* describing a school photographic excursion she led to Hanging Rock.[63]

As a student of the school when it was in St Kilda, the suburb in which she had grown up, Joan Lindsay had been dux of Clyde.[64] Her school's relocation, from Clyde Girls Grammar School in St Kilda to Woodend, (some years after she had left the school) seemed to signal a rejection of the flagging gentility of St Kilda itself. This 'revolutionary step', from city to the bush, was driven by Isabel Henderson, the first headmistress at Woodend.[65] At the centre of the students' new world of Macedon/Woodend stood Hanging Rock. As one of the first

At the Hanging Rock 1875. William Ford.
Oil on canvas, 79.2 x 117.5 cm.

National Gallery of Victoria, Melbourne.
Purchased, 1950 (2255-4)

Hanging Rock from Braemar House. c.1900. Braemer House became the Clyde School, Woodend, in 1919.
Unknown photographer. (possibly Nicholas Caire).

pupils enthused on behalf of her schoolmates: 'We love the hills, and the smooth green lawns, and the inimitable green mountains in the distance, and the changing beauty of Hanging Rock'.[66] The Clyde students were happy about the summer coolness of Macedon's forest, a world away from an increasingly raucous and vulgar St Kilda. Out of holiday season, the Macedon forest could seem almost a private possession. Margaret Donaldson recalled journeys through forested glades to nearby farmhouses, or Sundays spent reading and chatting in the bush, when they were supposed to be contemplating the Bible in isolation.[67] The girls waited for the first snow to fall each year.

Isabel Henderson opened her new school on 10 March 1919. Adventurous students immediately headed off to Hanging Rock, climbing to the Summit and taking in the panorama before March came to an end. Henderson and the headmistress who succeeded her, Dorothy Tucker, were just as enthusiastic about their new bush setting as were their girls. Isabel Henderson spoke eloquently about the Macedon bush whilst fending off criticisms that her girls were so rich that all owned either ponies or motor cars, and so ill-disciplined that they spent their time at Woodend trying out fashionable uniforms and playing cards. Dorothy Tucker pointed out to parents at the 1924 Speech Night that the school had moved to Woodend, not to become 'aloof', but because in a quiet setting, students would be able to discover 'our true relationship to the rest of the universe'. Although she had left the school before it moved to Woodend, Lindsay's imagination, despite her loathing of photography, was almost certainly sparked by inter-war field trips for the school's camera club.[68] Each year the club published competition-winning photographs in the school magazine, a long-lived journal at one time edited by Joan Lindsay, The *Cluthan*. They even dabbled in moving pictures before the 1930s, and a Mr Porter came regularly from Kodak to teach film development. Almost in defiance of the orderly traditions of an elite private school, one supported on council by an industrial magnate Essington Lewis, a Victorian attorney-general, Sir Edward Robinson, and newspaper barons, the Murdoch family, Clyde allowed girls to push all sorts of boundaries at Hanging Rock. On

their cherished excursions, climbing the pinnacles, exploring the Summit, and charging around the racetrack, seemed to take up more time than photography. Over the years, what had begun as a camera club field trip expanded into an annual adventure for the entire school.[69] This became 'one of Clyde's most treasured traditions, and lasted the life of the school'.[70] Clyde's august camera club transformed into coterie of students whose real role was simply to organise this annual excursion.[71] Olga Hay described these excursions as taking place in third term — between September and Christmas.[72] The entire school was invited with club members organising food and drinks for more than one hundred teachers and students. In recompense, the organisers were allowed to ride on the spring cart behind Peter the Horse, as the rest of the school walked off to Hanging Rock, and trudged back in the dark, their way lit by hurricane lamps.[73]

To most readers, distinctions between Clyde and Appleyard College, or similarities between the novel's Macedon settings and Weigall family holidays spent there, probably do not matter all that much. Lindsay's sharp, visual descriptions are enough to convince most of the reality of her story. This is not surprising, since before she turned to writing, Joan Lindsay was already an accomplished artist. She has left us exceptional landscape paintings of places along the Yarra River.[74] Her landscapes, drawing on the picturesque in nineteenth-century painting, had little of the sublime rendering, common in several depictions of Hanging Rock. They a shaped in part by an awareness of abstraction and the modern. Interest in both the picturesque and the sublime would wane across the twentieth century, as the modernist movement made gains amongst other Australian artists and their clientele.[75]

By the time of the camera club excursions at Clyde, the malevolence of Hanging Rock, so important to *Picnic at Hanging Rock*, was very much out of time. For Lindsay's sombre Rock relied on a disintegrating nineteenth century perspective. By 1900, Hanging Rock had been transformed from a mountainous menace into a fabulous vantage point, to be enjoyed rather than feared. In light of these unstable images, it seems unsurprising that the novel has sparked a number of imaginative readings; a liberation of incipient feminists; a clash between wilderness and civilisation; a post-colonial lament for settler nationalism. At least one researcher proposed that silence and soundscape, rather than the Rock and landscape, are at the core of the story's many resonances.[76] All of these have been given deeper complexity in the film and subsequent 'paratexts'.[77] The macabre and evil rock is only one part of these images. Might the story have resonated differently in the 21st century had it continued on to the excised chapter eighteen? After all, fantasy-writing, especially when set in elite and remote boarding schools, and inspired around the globe by J.K. Rowling's shifting of time and space through 'wormholes', now has a massive global reach. To Harry Potter's fans, the excised final chapter would not seem all that outlandish.

MODERNISED HANGING ROCK 1900

Unceasingly, literary sleuths have hunted for historical facts about deaths at Hanging Rock. They pour over newspapers from the start of the twentieth century, hoping to uncover empirical validation for the schoolgirls' disappearance. They seem far less consumed by a parallel between Mrs Appleyard's mad scramble, and any actual suicidal leap, or tragic fall, from Hanging Rock. But then headmistress Appleyard was never an invitee to garden parties on Macedon. Nor could she enjoy summer stays in guesthouses, so familiar to Joan Lindsay herself. Mrs Appleyard was rather, a widow, a secretive tippler, desperate to escape penury by exploiting the cultural insecurities of a colonial elite. Lindsay once recalled her mother's reflexive conservatism, and describes her as 'a firm believer in stabilised marriage, the Church of England, Debentures and the Melbourne Club'.[78] Mrs Appleyard is excluded from such certainties, whereas Lindsay's friends, and presumably the College students, move easily between Macedon and the Rock. Appleyard's mercenary culture, in contrast, with its stifling, almost desperate routines and niceties, is measured out in seconds and minutes, from which the girls manage to escape.[79] Far from being a tale of the Australian landscape repelling an historicised European culture, it is the modernity of a bourgeois Australia, symbolised by

Mrs Appleyard, which is crushed by the Rock, with all its malevolent force. Mrs Appleyard's death, both connects the novel to historical fact, and changes the tenor of Lindsay's narrative. Not surprisingly the scene of her death did not appear in the final cut of Weir's film.

The real import of the novel is encased then, not in the students' vanishing, but in the death of Mrs Appleyard, and the utter destruction of her world — through the death of students and staff, resignation of a teacher, and withdrawal of fee-paying students. Eventually, her own suicide and the school's fiery destruction, ensure that her entire world disappears. Appleyard College is, after all, as Sarah Frith has shown, not Clyde. It seems fitting then, that Mrs Appleyard's demise, is the only one of the novel's many disappearances or deaths, which is reflected, at least vaguely, in historical reality.

In Mrs Appleyard's death, alongside the fire which engulfs her school, Lindsay puts to rest the threat of a moneymaking middle class, in the year leading up to Australia's Federation. And in ridding the Macedon district of Mrs Appleyard, Lindsay, for the only time in the novel, manages to rework a real-life tragedy at Hanging Rock. Within a year of the fateful picnic, on another festive day, the New Year raceday at Hanging Rock in fact, a young carpenter named James Flight set off to climb Hanging Rock. Flight was seen on the Rock, and was seen also to fall, after what may have been an argument with a couple of shaded figures on a rock ledge. He had started his climb with his two children by his side. James Flight had sent the children running back down from the Rock to their mother, because the ground was ' too rough'.[80] By five o'clock that evening his wife, Alice, had grown anxious, and searched for James on the Rock, with no luck.[81] By then, James Flight's body had been taken to the Hanging Rock Hotel. He had fallen from Hanging Rock, although many there that day harboured suspicions that he was pushed. More curious, was the fact that Alice Flight was convinced her husband had gone up the Rock with five sovereigns in his pocket. He told her, as they left their South Yarra home, that the money was safer with him than left behind in a household drawer. When James's body was taken to the

Hanging Rock March 1919.
Clyde schoolgirls on the top of
Hanging Rock soon after the school
opened at Woodend on 10 March, 1919.
Elizabeth Weigall photo album.
Elizabeth Weigall was the cousin
of Joan Lindsay (nee Weigall).

Clyde School collection,
Geelong Grammar School Archives

Hanging Rock picnic March 1919.
Elizabeth Weigall photo album.
Elizabeth Weigall was the cousin of Joan
Lindsay (nee Weigall).

Clyde School collection,
Geelong Grammar School Archives

Hotel, there were no sovereigns in his trousers, and his pockets had been ripped open. Woodend and Macedon police testified that they could find no evidence of coins fallen from James Flight's pocket. They seemed inclined to believe that the death was an accident, one of only a handful over 150 years at Hanging Rock.[82] Nonetheless, this did not prevent newspapers pronouncing James Flight's death a mystery. 'Murder or Accident?' as the *Age* asked weeks afterwards.[83]

Joan Lindsay's novel is now familiar to readers throughout Australia and around the world. She created this classic tale by drawing on her awareness of art history, to resurrect the sublime imagery of Hanging Rock, as depicted by Blandowski more than a century earlier. She drew on family networks to select aspects in the life of Clyde and Macedon. And to compensate for the loss of her final, fantastic chapter, she hinted at murder on the Summit of Hanging Rock. In presenting Hanging Rock as a supernatural and alluring force, into which the girls and teacher escape, and which destroys any threat from a pedagogic mercenary such as Mrs Appleyard, Lindsay has to alter Hanging Rock as it was in 1900. Like many who came before her, she had little time for the modernising forces at work on the Hanging Rock Reserve. In the novel, as the school excursion enters the picnic grounds, Joan Lindsay ridicules attempts at improvement, pictured in crude fireplaces and the toilet fashioned after a Japanese temple.[84] This of course was not how picnickers at Hanging Rock saw the Reserve in 1900. There was already an easy pathway almost to the Summit. The racetrack was being modernized, and its surrounds made orderly. Regulations were being framed to ban both fires and also horses, such as those driven into the grounds by the College handlers. The Hanging Rock Hotel could still advertise in December 1900, some months after the fictional disappearances, that Hanging Rock offered 'absolutely the most enjoyable New Year's Day outing'.[85] The Rock itself could be presented as 'this stupendous mountain of rock afford(ing) Alpine climbing and magnificent and entrancing landscape views'.[86] Joan Lindsay's picnic ground would have been unrecognisable to visitors at Hanging Rock in 1900. A year later, the Rock hosted thousands of visitors celebrating the new Australian Commonwealth. And Mrs Appleyard seems a very distinctive, if unfortunately by then, deceased, symbol of this new national, rather than colonial democracy. Was Lindsay delighting in Mrs Appleyard's death as a last act of revenge? One by which an antiquated Anglophile colonial elite could rid itself of bourgeois pretenders? Such a resistance to modernity is only made credible, because Joan Lindsay has reconstructed a malevolent Rock, at the expense of the modernised Hanging Rock, home to horseracing, picnics and happy family photographs. ✳

Looking Towards Macedon from the Summit, The Hanging Rock Races.
The Leader, 12 January, 1907.
State Library of Victoria

Joan Lindsay's time. Sundial in the garden at her home Mulberry Hill. Photograph by Richard R. Andrew, c.1925 – c.1935.

Picnic at Hanging Rock.
Jacket design: Alison Forbes.
F. W. Cheshire Publishing Pty. Ltd. 1967.
Photograph by Matthew Nickson

Endnotes

1 Joan Lindsay, *Picnic at Hanging Rock*, first published Cheshire, Melbourne, 1967, Penguin edition, 2008.

2 Lindsay, *Picnic at Hanging Rock*: 6.

3 Lindsay, as noted by astute researchers, disguised the day on which St Valentine's 1900, fell.

4 See the quotation with which this chapter began. Interestingly Lindsay compares the disappearance at Hanging Rock to the mystery of the Marie (Mary) Celeste, the ship which sailed on, drifting through the Atlantic after her crew vanished in 1872. This celebrated case fascinated generations, and was subject to years of false recollection — one of the most of important of which was syndicated through the world's newspapers in the year of her fictional report, 1913. However, no such report appeared in the Melbourne press on 14 February 1913, although the Mary Celeste Mystery was much publicised later in the year.

5 See above Ch. 1.

6 'The Hanging Rock', *Weekly Times*, 5 January 1895: 21.

7 The earliest engraving seems to be from 1865, and follows the composition of Daintree's photographs.

8 G. C. Bolton, 'Daintree, Richard (1832–1878)', *Australian Dictionary of Biography*, National Centre of Biography, Australian National University, http://adb.anu.edu.au/biography/daintree-richard-3350/text5043, published first in hardcopy 1972 , (viewed online, 9 December 2016).

9 Richard Daintree, 'Hanging Rock, 1859', State Library of Victoria, Photographic Collection.

10 Richard Daintree, 'Hanging Rock 2', 1859, State Library of Victoria, Photographic Collection.

11 Charles Nettleton, 'Rocks on the top of Hanging Rock', State Library of Victoria, photographic Collection, H84.79/1, See too, Anne-Marie Willis, *Picturing Australia: a history of photography*, Angus and Robertson, North Ryde NSW, 1988.

12 Charles Nettleton, 'Hanging Rocks at Woodend, 54 miles from Melbourne', H29707, Photographic Collection, State Library of Victoria.

13 Anne and Don Pitkethly, *N.J. Caire, landscape photographer*, the authors, Rosanna, 1988.

14 J. Cato, *The Story of the Camera in Australia*, Angus and Robertson, Melbourne, 1955.

15 William Blandowski, 'Foot of Diogenes Monument', 1855 and James Redaway and Sons, 'Anneyelong looking south', 1855.

16 Mary Mackay, 'Singularity and the Sublime in Australian Landscape Representation', *Literature and Aesthetics*, vol. 8, 1998: 113-27.

17 G. Scaramellini, 'The picturesque and the sublime in nature and the landscape: Writing and iconography in the romantic voyaging in the Alps', *GeoJournal*, vol, 38, no. 1, 1996: 49-57.

18 Mackay, 'Singularity and the Sublime': 122.

19 Mackay, 'Singularity and the Sublime': 121.

20 'Victorian Academy of the Arts', *Leader,* 13 July 1875: 13.

21 W.R.F, Love, 'The Burkitt family in Queensland, 1861-1981', *Journal of the Royal Historical Society of Queensland*, vol. 11, no. 2, 1981: :117-31

22 Candice Bruce, Edward Cornstock and Frank McDonald, *Eugene von Guerard: a German Romantic in the Antipodes*, Alister Taylor, Martinborough NZ, 1982.

23 For a discussion of the technique see Michael Varcoe-Cocks. 'A Brush with Fidelity: Three works by Eugène von Guérard', National Gallery of Victoria.

24 Eugene von Guérard, sketch books, State Library of New South Wales, 1864, DLPXX17.

25 Lindsay, *Picnic at Hanging Rock*: 31.

26 Joost Daalder, 'The Brave New Feminist World of Joan Lindsay's "*Picnic at Hanging Rock*", *Gulliver*, no 23, 1988: 121-34.

27 William Ford, 'At the Hanging Rock', 1875, oil on canvas, accession number 2255-4, National Gallery of Victoria and artists' file William Ford, State Library of Victoria.

28 William Ford, Australian Art and Artist file, State Library of Victoria; Victorian Art History, http://www.avictorian.com/Ford_William.html (viewed March 2017).

29 National Gallery Australia, 'McCubbin,'"Last Impressions" 1907-17', exhibition and catalogue, http://nga.gov.au/Exhibition/MCCUBBIN/Default.cfm?IRN=190243&BioArtistIRN=15672&mystartrow=37&realstartrow=37&MNUID=3&ViewID=2 , (viewed online, December, 2016).

30 National Gallery Australia, 'McCubbin,'Last Impressions' 1907-17.

31 Lindsay, *Picnic at Hanging Rock*: 25.

32 *Illustrated Australian News*, 23 April 1872.

33 *Illustrated Australian News*, 23 April 1872.

34 *Illustrated Australian News*, 23 April 1872.

35 *Illustrated Sydney News*, 16 January 1875: 17.

36 Joan Lindsay, *Fact Soft and Hard*, Cheshire, Melbourne, 1964.

37 Joan Lindsay, *Time Without Clocks*, Cheshire, Melbourne, 1962: 4.

38 For example 'Mt Macedon from Hanging Rock', Rose Series, State Library of Victoria, no 874 Rose Series and 1930s Bulmer postcard, State Library of Victoria, Photographic Collection; Victorian Railways, 1953, view 12, 'Approaching the Saddle', State Library of Victoria Photographic Collection.

39 Victorian Railways, 'Racecourse from Hanging Rock', State Library of Victoria Photographic Collection

40 See for example *Australasian,* 12 January 1907: 1-2 and Sydney Johnson, 'Hesket from Hanging Rock', State Library of Victoria Collection; ' McDonnell's Lookout', c. 1910, State Library of Victoria, Photograph Collection.

41 Gisborne and Mount Macedon Districts Historical Society, *Pictorial Hanging Rock: A Journey through Time*: see especially photographs: 29-38.

42 Lindsay, *Picnic at Hanging Rock*.

43 One reflection on the book and film refers to an overarching structure of the 'pastoral' with its elements of contemplation, human immersion in nature, myth and aesthetic celebration as well

as hints of loss. See Victoria Bladen, 'The Rock and the Void: Pastoral and Loss in Joan Lindsay's *Picnic at Hanging Rock* and Peter Weir's film adaptation', University of Queensland library espace, https://espace.library.uq.edu.au/view/UQ:292779 , (viewed online January 2017).

44 Several of the key scenes are set in Lake View House Macedon; for example Lindsay, *Picnic at Hanging Rock*: ch 7.

45 Elspeth Tilley, 'The uses of fear: spatial politics in the Australian white-vanishing trope', paper in a special issue, *Fear in Australian Literature and Film*, Nathaniel O'Reilly and Jean-Francois Vernay, eds, Antipodes, vol. 23, no.1, June 2009: 33-41.

46 Lindsay, *Picnic at Hanging Rock*: 7.

47 Lindsay *Hanging Rock*: 18.

48 Lindsay, *Hanging Rock*: 79.

49 Lindsay *Hanging Rock*: 135.

50 Lindsay *Hanging Rock*: 128.

51 Lindsay, *Hanging Rock*: 187.

52 Yvonne Rousseau, *The Murders at Hanging Rock*, Scribe, Fitzroy Vic., 1980.

53 Terence O'Neill, 'Joan Lindsay A time for everything', *La Trobe Journal*, no. 83. May 2009: 46-48; see too, Joan Lindsay, 'Student Days', *Overland*, no.98, April 1985: 59-63.

54 Lindsay, *The Secret of Hanging Rock*, 1987

55 Joan Lindsay, *Facts Soft and Hard*, Cheshire, Melbourne,1964 : 1.

56 Terence O'Neill, 'Lindsay, Joan à Beckett (1896–1984)', *Australian Dictionary of Biography*, National Centre of Biography, Australian National University, http://adb.anu.edu.au/biography/lindsay-joan-a-beckett-14176/text25188, published first in hardcopy 2012 , (viewed online, 8 February 2017).

57 O'Neill, 'Lindsay, Joan à Beckett (1896–1984)', *Australian Dictionary of Biography*.

58 O'Neill, 'Lindsay, Joan à Beckett (1896–1984)', *Australian Dictionary of Biography*.

59 Margaret Donaldson, 'I remember well', typescript folio, Manuscripts, State Library of Victoria.

60 Sarah Frith, 'Fact and Fiction in Joan Lindsay's Picnic at Hanging Rock', Master of Education Thesis, University of Melbourne, 1990.

61 Marjorie Theobold, *Knowing Women: Origins of women's education in nineteenth-century Australia*, Cambridge University Press, Melbourne, 1996: 53-4.

62 'New public school', Melbourne *Argus*, 3 June 1921: 3.

63 O'Neill, ' Joan Lindsay: A Time for Everything': 42-61.

64 O'Neill, 'Joan Lindsay' *Australian Dictionary of Biography*.

65 'Speech Days at Schools, Clyde, Tributes to Founder', *Argus*, 16 December 1940: 2.

66 D.S., 'First Days at Clyde, Woodend', *Cluthan*, vol. 1no. 11, May 1919: 12.

67 Margaret Donaldson, 'I remember well'.

68 'Clyde Girls Grammar School Woodend', *Argus*, 24 December 1919:11 and 'Clyde Girls Grammar School, Country Life Praised', *Argus*, 17 December 1924: 26; Olga J. Hay in collaboration with M. Olive Reed, *The Chronicles of Clyde*, Brown, Prior Anderson, Melbourne, 1966: 154.

69 Melanie Guile, *Clyde School, 1910-1975*: An uncommon history, Clyde School Old Girls' Association, South Yarra, 2008.

70 Guile, *Clyde School*: 86.

71 Guile, *Clyde School*: 2, 24.

72 Hay, *Chronicles of Clyde*.

73 Hay, *Chronicles of Clyde*: 155.

74 Joan Lindsay, artists file, State Library of Victoria and Joan Lindsay, View of the Yarra, watercolour painting, c. 1925, State Library of Victoria. McCubbin taught drawing to Joan Lindsay at the National Gallery School. She and her classmates often set out to sketch along the Yarra banks. See Lindsay, 'Student Days'.

75 For one recent discussion of the chronology of the sublime, the pastoral, the picturesque and the modern see Mark Dober, 'Finding the Romantic sublime in Fred Williams' You Yangs', Melbourne Age, 12 September 2017.

76 Adam Hulbert, 'The Precarity of the Inarticulate: Two Kinds of Silences in Joan Lindsay's Picnic at Hanging Rock', *Philament Journal online*, no 22, December 2016: 27-56. http://www.philamentjournal.com/wp-content/uploads/2016/12/Philament-22-Precarity-BOOK-FINAL-1.pdf , (viewed online, March 2017).

77 Amongst the most recent writings taking the story forward is William Fuery, *Dream within a Dream*, Mobius, Wodonga Vic., 2010.

78 Lindsay, *Time Without Clocks:* Cheshire, Melbourne, 1962: 8.

79 Lindsay, *Hanging Rock*: 132.

80 'Murder or Accident', *The Age*, 17 January 1901.

81 Alice Flight testimony, James Flight Inquest, Woodend, 2 and 15 January 1901, Inquests, 190112, Public Record Office Victoria.

82 Bernard Kavanagh, Mounted Police, Macedon, testimony, at James Flight Inquest, Woodend, 2 and 15 January 1901, Inquests 190112, PROV.

83 Murder or Accident', *The Age*, 17 January 1901.

84 Lindsay, *Hanging Rock*: 20.

85 Advertisement, *Argus*, 26 December 1900.

86 Advertisement , *Age*, 26 December 1900.

Seaside Frolics. Cannes Film Festival, Cannes, France. 1976. Photograph by Keystone / Hulton Archive / Getty Images

Cinema Place

*'I read somewhere where Peter Weir was in America and he was showing it (Picnic at Hanging Rock)
to distributors and some distributor threw a cup of coffee at the screen at the end of it because he said
it's a mystery and there's no damned answer to the mystery'*

Margaret Pomerantz, Film Critic, 'At the Movies' ABCTV

http://www.abc.net.au/atthemovies/txt/s3626005.htm

185

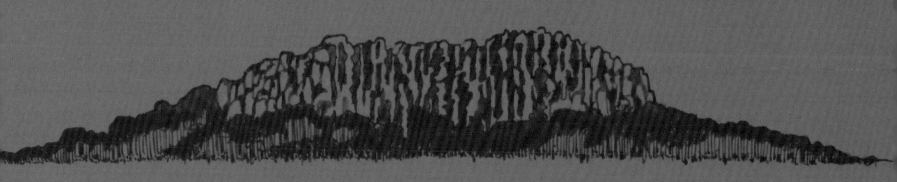

Who could have known that, in cutting the closing chapter of Joan Lindsay's novel, Cheshire's book editors would transform Hanging Rock from a picnic ground into a global icon? When screenwriter Cliff Green adapted *Picnic at Hanging Rock* to the cinema, he and subsequently director Peter Weir, resisted demands that their film resolve that 'damned mystery' of vanishing schoolgirls.[1] In leaving the mystery unresolved, they converted Joan Lindsay's melodrama into the signature movie of Australia's 'Film Renaissance'. At the same time, their film turned a rapidly expanding popular curiosity towards Hanging Rock itself.

Picnic at Hanging Rock played a crucial role in the 1970s revival of the Australian film industry. Capable of both driving U.S. film distributors to apoplexy, and beguiling European festival directors, the film version of Joan Lindsay's novel has also launched a worldwide network of fans. Some lovers of the film have been coming to Hanging Rock each 14 February, to re-enact the disappearance of Miranda and friends, or to pay homage at an outdoor showing of the movie. And as with any popular culture myth, these fans refuse to accept that the story has no factual basis. To the true fans, Miranda and friends, just like Elvis, must live on somewhere. In these obsessive returns to the St Valentine's Day vanishings, the place of the Rock itself in the film, the story of its reconstruction for the screen, and the legacy that the film-makers bestowed on the Hanging Rock Reserve, are routinely overshadowed. The doyen of Australia's film revival, Phillip Adams, once suggested that the novel and film formed 'a piece of horse-drawn science fiction pitched somewhere between the mysticism of a [E.M] Forster and the quasi-scientific speculations of an H.G. Wells'.[2] Of course the film can be viewed in this light. It can also become the wellspring in searches for human remains, and newspaper references to schoolgirls vanishing. It sometimes inspires speculation about alien abduction. At the same time, there is much more to the story of the film and, in particular, to the place of Hanging Rock's landscape within it.

MAKING A MYSTERY

In 1975, an invited audience queued in Hindley St Adelaide, waiting to get into the city's newest cinema complex. Few of these South Australian dignitaries knew what to expect from the premiere of a strange-sounding film, one shaped by a young and imaginative director, known best to a tight circle of admirers for his offbeat and comedic horror movies. In any case, many were there, not because they were intrigued by a movie set in a strange place in another state. Instead, they came for the opening of a new cinema complex, one which promised to bring a modicum of sophistication to Adelaide's eternally constrained 'nightlife'. Once seated in one of the brand-new Greater Union complex's cinemas, the invited South Australian elite were introduced to both film and cinema by the state's Premier, Don Dunstan. Perhaps not wanting to spoil the mystery of *Picnic at Hanging Rock*, Dunstan instead lauded the 'quite splendid' cinema complex as 'part of an international trend to smaller, intimate cinema theatres'.[3] No doubt anticipating an audience disgruntled by the film's lack of storyline resolution, Dunstan also by-passed plot, cast and camera crew. He barely acknowledged Peter Weir. Then too, he may simply have been unnerved by a recent restaurant evening with the film's producers and stars; during which one of the cast thoroughly enjoyed his state's signature wines, and insisted on addressing Dunstan as 'Mr President' for the rest of an entirely awkward night.[4] So, rather than dwell on a film that would soon transform Australian movie-making, the inimitable Don Dunstan emphasised the role of the South Australian Film Corporation, which had funded the film, along with the Australian Film Development Corporation, and B.E.F. Film Distributors.[5] The producers, 29-year-old twin brothers Hal and Jim McElroy, he presented as experienced operators, able to bring complex projects to the screen. He gave no such acknowledgement to the woman whose tenacity had made the film possible, Executive Producer, Patricia Lovell.

Finally, as if to forewarn the audience that the ending of *Picnic at Hanging Rock* might well disappoint all and sundry, Dunstan highlighted the complexities in the film's creation. In exchange for funding, the South Australian Film Corporation demanded that 24 of the 34-day film shoot had to take place in South Australia. So Albyn Terrace, Strathalbyn stood in for the main street of Woodend. Martindale Hall, near Clare, starred as Appleyard College; Marbury School in Stirling as Colonel Fitzhubert's Macedon mansion.[6] South Australian schoolgirls filled roles as students at Appleyard College. Staff of the SAFC took up production roles. The script consultant, line producer, and others on the crew were all South Australian. In these pioneering days of the Australian cinema's 'New Wave', any production was always difficult to fund. Hence the seminal role of Dunstan's flagship South Australian agency. 'It has come a long way in just over two and a half years and the process has confounded its critics and detractors at each move' proudly announced the premier. Only then did he belatedly invite the Hindley St audience to enjoy what was to become an Australian film classic.[7]

Enjoy the film audiences certainly did, though with a bemused rather than dissatisfied reflection on the open-ended final scenes. This reaction had been somewhat anticipated with a decision made at a production meeting in October 1974; that the film, in its setting and in its protagonists, the South Australian schoolgirls, would have to be 'visually stunning'. This was proposed as 'an "insurance policy"', against audience dissatisfaction with the story itself'.[8] Nonetheless, Patricia Lovell was dismayed by the reception of her cherished project at this premiere. In the Hindley St complex's shiny new foyer, she overheard 'more derogatory comments than praise' for the film.[9] Only when she went along to a later screening, to sit alongside a paying audience, did she realise the powerful impact her first major movie was having on Australian cinema goers. Popular magazine writers had no doubt about its quality. *Australian Women's Weekly* thought it 'one of the finest and most visually beautiful movies ever made in Australia'. Weir and Boyd's use of Patricia Lovell's period style, combined with the setting had allowed the team to shape 'a rare little spellbinder'. [10]

Lovell's project was not the first time that Hanging Rock had taken centre stage in movies. Phillip Adams had in fact made a short film, on a minimal budget, with Hanging Rock as the setting in the mid-1960s. The Rock featured some decades earlier in a locally-made bushranger epic, *Held for Ransom*. This was the work of the Victorian Amateur Cine Society, and was directed by Mr J.H. Jackson, theatrette owner in the Melbourne suburb of Sunshine. *Held for Ransom* was shown as an aid to the war effort in 1940. Sadly, the outlaw adventure struggled to attract audiences beyond the loyal and local patrons of the director's Sunshine cinema.[11] Decades later, and moving quickly after Lindsay's novel was published, an imaginative band of Melbourne school students converted the story to film. Shooting on weekends, and with costumes liberated from grandparents' wardrobes, these private school boys and girls had put together ten minutes of silent footage, before Lovell bought the rights to the novel from Joan Lindsay.[12] Tony Ingram directed the project. He didn't want to film with Super-8, the standard home movie medium of the day, and found an old World War II Bell and Howell camera in a second-hand store. He had already made a short film based on William Golding's *Lord of the Flies*, a standard of school reading lists in the 1960s. Tony and his friends from Melbourne Grammar, St Catherine's and other schools in Melbourne, set off each weekend to Hanging Rock to film, until out of the blue, Tony opened a letter from Joan Lindsay telling him she had sold the rights. That put an end to his project. The students' pioneering enterprise made way for Lovell's commercial undertaking, which soon amassed profits in Australian cinemas alone. The film certainly lived up to Hal McElroy's demand; that it would be 'visually stunning'. Indeed, so richly composed were the set pieces on the screen, that few viewers could comprehend many of the barriers Lovell faced in funding her project. Nor could audiences be expected to comprehend the camera and lighting challenges that threatened to derail the entire project. And yet, within three months of the Adelaide release, *Picnic at Hanging Rock* had already covered costs.[13] In less assured hands than those of scriptwriter Cliff Green, director Peter Weir, and director of photography Russell Boyd, this film might well have become an absolute disaster.

Also at:
142 Victoria Road,
Marrickville, NSW 2204
Phones: 51-5798, 51-8948
Garema Place,
Canberra City, ACT 2601
Phones: 4-2502,
49-1501, 49-6319
Accounts:
362 Little Bourke Street
Melbourne, 3000
Phone: 67-9532

F · W · CHESHIRE PUBLISHING PTY · LTD ·
380 Bourke Street Melbourne 3000 · Telephone 67 9271 (Ten lines)
Cables · Cheshirebooks · Melbourne

28th February, 1969.

Mr. Tony Ingram,
5 Torresdale Road,
<u>TOORAK</u>,
Vic. 3142.

Dear Mr. Ingram,

Lady Lindsay has discussed with me your letter and
your plan to make a film of her book PICNIC AT HANGING
ROCK.

I told Lady Lindsay that although the film rights of
her book are under option in London, I can see no
objection to your and your friends' plan - all of you
under fifteen - to make a film for yourselves. In
fact, I am very impressed by your enterprise and hope
that this exercise will lead you all to become, one day,
successful film-makers and revive the Australian film
industry.

It is essential, however, that your film be only
<u>privately</u> shown, otherwise a breach of copyright would
be committed.

Could you tell me what sort of camera and film-size you
have in mind? I should also very much like to hear from
you when the film has been completed.

Best wishes,

Yours sincerely,

A. Fabinyi

Letter from F. W. Cheshire Publishing Pty. Ltd.
to Tony Ingram regarding the film rights to
Picnic at Hanging Rock.
Dated: 28 February 1969.
Courtesy of Tony Ingram

Images from Tony Ingram's film.
The Day of St Valentine. 1969.
Top: Miranda (Clare Strang), Irma (Gillian Carr) and Edith,
Middle: Michael Fizhubert (Patrick Robertson-Macleod),
Bottom: Edith (Lindy Strickland),
Courtesy of Tony Ingram

Martindale Hall, Mintaro, South Australia. c.1879. State Library of South Australia (B 53693)

Patricia Lovell, much-loved in Australian television as the human face of the ABC's children's program, Mr Squiggle and Friends, had gone on to co-produce ATN7's morning show, 'Sydney Today'.[14] Her journey with Joan Lindsay's mystery commenced out of the blue, when on a mundane shopping trip, 'one dreary Saturday morning in 1971', she saw a copy of *Picnic at Hanging Rock* tossed out at a discount from a local second-hand store and newsagency.[15] Lovell optioned the rights to Lindsay's novel after reading it — by putting down the last $100 in her bank account. Despite her accomplishments as a performer in front of television cameras, she had no experience in producing a full-length film. So she decided to cut her teeth with a documentary on the opening of the Sydney Opera House. The documentary was directed by another stalwart of the Australian film revival, Bruce Beresford. With her colleagues on the Today show both encouraging and pestering her to either produce the film or move on (she said herself that she was becoming boring, constantly talking about how to transform the book to the screen) Lovell passed the book on to Peter Weir, whose short films, *Michael* and *Holmesdale*, had so impressed her. Weir had also worked (as a stage hand) at ATN7 in Sydney. By the time Lovell approached him about *Picnic at Hanging Rock*, Peter Weir had graduated from NIDA (Sydney's National Institute of Dramatic Arts) and had accumulated film credits in the Commonwealth Film Unit. Phillip Adams gave Lovell encouragement and industry contacts, whilst prolific playwright and successful screen-writer, David Williamson, showed initial interest in the project. Martin Sharp, who in the words of Marsha Rowe, 'gave the 1960s counterculture its visual expression', was fascinated by the story and the film-making.[16] Recently returned from London, where he had survived both charges of obscenity over his artwork in the magazine Oz, and life in the communal space of Chelsea's 'Pheasantry' with Australian artists and English pop stars, Sharp approached the production team with 'marvellous visualisations' representing the film's many 'complex undercurrents', and over one hundred pages of plot analysis.[17]

Don Dunstan's opening night caution may well have been justified. Peter Weir had worked on documentary films for the Commonwealth Film Unit, before turning his hand to short horror pieces; *Count Vim's Last Exercise* (1967) and then his black comedy, *Holmesdale* (1971). He then turned out an even darker full-length movie, *The Cars that Ate Paris* (1974). His distinctive style quickly attracted a cult following, without reaching a broad mass audience. Peter Weir, like Lovell, was struck by the cinematic possibilities of Lindsay's picnic and disappearance. Together, he and Lovell set out on several futile searches for funding for the film. Some money eventually came from the Australian Film Development Corporation, as Dunstan later indicated. After several painful, not to say humiliating rejections, the pair of aspiring film-makers eventually found private sponsorship through David Williams of Greater Union cinemas, to make up a final budget of $443,000. The support of the South Australian Film Corporation was probably only secured because Lovell had brought on board the McElroy twins, whose involvement and experience seemed to satisfy risk-averse state financiers.

Peter Weir recollected that as a young director in his late twenties, surrounded by a crew more or less of the same age, and with the McElroy brothers barely older, just how new they were to the whole business of film-making.[18] Undeterred, Weir embraced the mysteries of the novel. In turning the book into a film, he chose to exaggerate its mystic possibilities, rather than hewing to the factual claims of the book, although he and others promoting the film remained coy about its historical authenticity. As he later recalled, in an interview shortly after the film's American release, his approach stressed the mysterious moodiness of the narrative, whereas Joan Lindsay had written in something of an ironic, even parodic mode. Weir remembered his caution when Joan Lindsay saw the film. His discussion with her revolved around the change in tone between novel and film, with Peter Weir explaining that in any such transition between written text and cinematic image, such change was inevitable.[19] He did though agree with Joan Lindsay on the futility of trying to distinguish fact from fiction. As he made clear, his work with the Commonwealth Film Unit had left him with a healthy suspicion of documentary, or in other words, film-making which made a claim on fact.[20]

On their first Victorian visit to explore the film's location, the two Sydneysiders, Lovell and Weir, got lost, and ended up in Bacchus Marsh. Skirting around Melbourne's western and northern fringes, they thought about giving up on Hanging Rock altogether, and simply shooting outdoor sequences in the more familiar Blue Mountains of NSW. Then, just when they thought themselves lost, they drove over a rise and saw before them Hanging Rock. Lovell reflected on this moment, which seemed to cement the film as a unique opportunity, one they just had to grasp:

> Deep in discussion and a bit lost, we suddenly drove over a rise and there on the plain below us was an eerie mass of boulders spewing out of the earth with trees emerging at strange angles from the top. Hovering over this was a single cloud. There were no other clouds in sight. It was chilling to come upon it (Hanging Rock) this way[21]

Weir kept up an illusion of mystery throughout filming. When the cast arrived for their very brief time on location, before setting off for the mandatory South Australian shooting, he persuaded all those on the team about the mysterious and spiritual qualities of the Rock.[22] His cast included well-regarded Englishman, Dominic Guard, the child actor in *The Go-Between* (1971). Veteran English star, Rachel Roberts, filled the role of Mrs Appleyard. She had only been cast at the last minute due to first choice, Vivien Merchant's, illness. Roberts, by then based in the United States, had made her name in the gritty 'kitchen sink' realist dramas, which sparked a film revival in England. She won acclaim for lead roles in *Saturday Night and Sunday Morning* (1960) and *This Sporting Life* (1963). Moving from her characters in the working-class milieu of northern English towns, to play the headmistress in an Australian private college, fazed her not one bit. Rachel Roberts looked on her role as Mrs Appleyard as a great opportunity. She was also excited to be filming in what was then, far-off Australia. And a lead role in a film at the forefront of a promising new national film industry, seemed a worthy challenge for her acting skills. Rachel Roberts acted out her two-week stint with aplomb, pocketed $9,500 US for her time, and went back to the United States,

where, as it turned out, her life would be blighted by addiction and depression.[23] Weir cast bright young actors from stage and television in Australia for other key roles. Several went on to illustrious careers. Amongst them were Helen Morse, John Jarratt and Jackie Weaver. Popular television comedian Gary McDonald, whose later career included significant dramatic roles, took on a small but striking cameo role as a Woodend police constable.

The schoolgirls were almost all amateurs, and it was only revealed more than three decades after the film's release, that their voices had been dubbed by professionals.[24] One of these was Barbara Llewellyn. Llewellyn was already an Australian icon in her own right, since she had starred in an advertisement familiar to generations of Australians, the Aeroplane Jelly television commercial.[25] After filming, just as he was forced to do for the American release of *Cars that Ate Paris*, Weir synchronised the voices, kept dialogue to a minimum, and filmed his unknown young women in a style perfectly suited to his rich imagery of turn-of-the-century upper-class schoolgirls. The director searched through photographic collections of Victorian and Edwardian portraits, identifying qualities which distinguished their subjects. Faces in these photographs seemed heavier. They possessed a distinguishing calmness, a quality he continued to seek out in his screen tests.[26] Weir later explained that he had reviewed five hundred screen tests across three states for the parts of the Appleyard College students, trying to match the particular 'look' of the era.

For decades fans have been engrossed by the film's mystery, trying by any means available to explain the disappearances of Miranda and friends. Peter Weir never directly addressed the question of the film's historical truth. Although he did hint at its historical authenticity.[27] For all the attempts to deflect suspicions about the film's fictional origins, *Picnic at Hanging Rock's* standing as a classic of Australian and global cinema, depends on far more than mysterious disappearances. Weir's crafting of intricate scenes, and a consistency in settings, and camera angle, established a mood for the film. And it is mood rather than narrative drive that has won over audiences. The film's ambience is partially a consequence of the music chosen by Weir and his production team, in particular the pan-pipes. Peter Weir wanted these for their 'pre-Christian' qualities.[28] Eventually, the director settled on the pipe music of Romanian pan flute master Gheorge Zamfir. Musical director Bruce Smeaton's own composition, 'Ascent to the Rock', was also essential to the film, with its strange intermingling of harpsichords and flute, along with a mellotron. These blended with Weir's adaptation of Beethoven and other classical compositions, producing a musical score unlike any other in the Australian film revival.[29]

Peter Weir kept up the illusion of otherworldliness in front of his crew and cast. He built up the mystery of the lost schoolgirls long before his team reached Hanging Rock. Weir prepared for the day's filming in a manner that left cast and crew under the impression that they were about to reconstruct an actual disappearance. Anne Lambert, the actor who played Miranda, was probably the only member of the schoolgirl cast able to bring professional acting experience to the filming. Lambert recalled that, even with the best efforts of Weir, in trying to build up an unsettling mood, the shooting process, with so little time available, was too hectic for mystery.[30] There were some uncanny incidents, all the same. At one stage Patricia Lovell's watch kept stopping. She also recollected that alarm clocks would go off at different times, throwing out any attempts to co-ordinate arrivals at the Rock. Even years later, Lovell thought there was something mysterious about the Rock itself.[31] Besides exaggerating this eerie ambience in the film, in part by relying on non-professional actors, and then overdubbing voices with professional performers, Weir made sure that the film was distinctively edited. He looked back on the shooting process reflecting that he constantly altered camera speeds.[32] The structure of the film relied, as Anne-Marie Cook pointed out, on an editing process which slowed frames and used sharply contrasting montage. This technique allowed Weir to create a consistent antipathy between Appleyard College and Hanging Rock.[33]

Peter Weir's crew were forced to work swiftly at Hanging Rock, because of the commitment to spend most of the time available in South Australia. As Anne Lambert, who played Miranda, recalled forty years later ' when a film crew arrives, it's like a herd of elephants — there's a lot of people, there's a lot of equipment, there's action and coming and going and all the relationships and politics and carry on of any film (which) sort of took over the place for a while'.[34] Confusion extended to a helicopter dropping one of the generators used to power the lights and camera, problems with shadows from the Rock, and crude attempts at inserting counter-balance to the harsh light in an Australian summer. The principal outdoor scenes were shot within a few days at Hanging Rock during a hot February. Director of photography, Russell Boyd, remembered that he had to settle for a lightweight camera. Because they had to cart equipment up and down the Rock he relied on only one camera. Boyd used gauze over the camera lens to diffuse the light for the crucial picnic scene. Other critical scenes could only be shot for an hour or so each day, otherwise shadow and contrast would ruin the consistency of the final shots. Boyd turned to polystyrene sheeting to balance light for many of the shots. Eventually the winds around the Rock smashed his sheets and blew them across the picnic ground. Even so, Russell Boyd reflected that 'I would hate to think that if we were to make the film now that I would treat it any differently.'[35]

HANGING ROCK AS MOVIE STAR

When critics looked beyond the disappearance of Miranda and friends, or set aside the music and mystery, they often concluded that Weir's subtlety, and completeness in constructing composition and props for each shot, along with Cliff Green's minimalist dialogue, made the film. All the same, the film would have completely missed the mark were it not for Hanging Rock itself. The Rock's presence, awesome, eerie and eccentric, was fixed firmly in the opening scenes of the film. Russell Boyd looked back on this magical establishing shot. He knew that, in the helter-skelter of filming in a difficult location, away from any studio, it was almost entirely by chance that they were able capture such a mesmerising scene. Boyd, many years later, reflected on his journey from Macedon to Hanging Rock on a unique day in filming. He remembered that as he and Peter Weir were driving towards Hanging Rock, early one morning, they came over a hill, just as the sinister Rock loomed out through morning mist.[36] Russell Boyd flagged down the camera truck and began to film. Once the fog had lifted, the crew then reshot the Rock, this time in a clear light. This opening scene established Hanging Rock there and then, as a principal character in the film. It ensured that the cinematic, eerie Rock, rather than the Rock of racegoers or picnickers, would be reflected around the globe.[37]

Peter Weir opens the film with this panorama of Hanging Rock. But from that point onwards, the Rock and the Reserve diverge from common filmic tropes of Australians in the landscape. Other films of the Australian 'New Wave', many of them released at about the same time as *Picnic at Hanging Rock*, often adopted an entirely expansive view of the Australian outback, whereas *Picnic at Hanging Rock* has a near urban setting. In launching Weir's film, Don Dunstan looked back approvingly, and unfairly, to *Sunday Too Far Away* (1975) another of the SAFC productions, and one released only a short time before Weir's movie. Dunstan liked to think that his SAFC had complete artistic control over *Sunday Too Far Away*. Shot in the Flinders Ranges, the film played on the openness and emptiness of the Australian inland. It revisited heroes of the Australian bush legend, tough men working in shearing sheds and carousing in pubs. Many of the Australian 'New Wave' films, Gillian Armstrong's *My Brilliant Career* (1979) for example, worked in similar fashion, with several of them owing a debt to the style of *The Overlanders* (1946, Director Harry Watts) a post-war co-production with Britain's Ealing Studios. When it came to popular rather than critical acclaim, these differences may not have mattered all that much. The film critic, John Hinde, reminded his readers that the so-called 'ocker comedies', amongst the most respected, *Alvin Purple and The Adventures of Barry Mackenzie*, though panned by broadsheet writers, were runaway successes with audiences. They attracted far wider popular enthusiasm, at least in their initial release, than did either *Sunday Too Far Away* or *Picnic at Hanging Rock*.[38]

Hanging Rock, as captured in Boyd's opening shot, may have appeared on the screen as both sinister and beautiful. The film is equally coloured by the over-stuffed, not to say cloying interiors, and schoolgirls' conceits of Appleyard College. For, in *Picnic at Hanging Rock*, the Rock and its unique contours, can seem secondary to the carefully composed interiors of the school, and the headmistress's office in particular. The Fitzhubert estate, so significant to the novel, occupies a marginal role in the film. Weir uses the estate's gardens and lake, for a tableau outdoor party scene, included in the film to symbolise the misplaced, superficial and fragile order of British gentility in the colonies. Apart from this scene, his film for the most part, and to a far greater extent than Lindsay's novel, is played out between Hanging Rock and Appleyard College. Once the girls disappear, the audience's gaze is more intensely centred on Appleyard College and its tragic headmistress. The panorama of the Rock gives way to the claustrophobia of the school. Alexander Walker, film critic and biographer of Rachel Roberts, was certain that by juxtaposing school and rock, Weir (whom he dubbed an Antipodean Antonioni) was establishing, and then extending, a distinctly eerie mood, as well as commenting on the fragility of colonial identities.[39]

To emphasise the contrast between natural landform and planted college, Boyd filmed the College as a symmetrical structure. Consistently, the schoolgirls appear in neat and balanced rows on the screen, the very opposite to the Rock's asymmetry. Shot from middle distance, or further, the neo-classical block of the South Australian heritage structure, which stood in for Appleyard College, is always centred and balanced, a model of symmetry, order and planned control. The garden is neat and regulated. In contrast to the dreamy, diffused light of the picnic scenes at the Rock, Weir used high contrast lighting in many of these interior scenes, with the impression of dark surrounds heightened by the repeated use of spot light below or to the side of, the faces of his actors. In this construction, Mrs Appleyard's office, with its crowded desk and portraits covering walls, provides the perfect contrast to the openness and disorder of the Rock and its picnic ground. The film ends with Mrs Appleyard's withdrawal

Picnic at Hanging Rock. Bruce Petty, 1975.
Cartoon. This refers to the 1975 Australian
Government constitutional crisis.

Republished in *The Australian*, May 30, 2014.

from the world around her, although unlike the final pages of Joan Lindsay's account, we do not see her fall from the Rock. Instead Boyd's cameras capture the college headmistress dressed in funereal black, sitting fixedly beneath the portrait of Queen Victoria, another women who, in 1900, had only a few months of life left to her.[40]

The scenes that were shot at Hanging Rock might have seemed overwrought and melodramatic, were it not for Boyd's photography and Weir's composition. Boyd's clever use of the available light, softened by the gauze over his camera lens, produced an idyllic picnic ensemble. It is composed around the white dresses of the schoolgirls, designed in Sydney, straw hats shipped in from a theatrical costume maker in London, and the schoolgirls framed by the coloured parasols of the teachers. Once Miranda and friends decide to climb the Rock, we see them through bright spyholes and highly-contrasted deep grey rocks. The camera tracks them as they move between boulders and ever upwards towards the Summit. They move easily and inquisitively around and through the Rock. At least one European reviewer thought that the film lost its charm after the girls disappeared. Robert Johnstone, writing in Belfast's *Fortnight*, thought that the film promised more than it delivered. The first half he found 'superb, a haunting, restrained, perfectly judged evocation of the girls' boarding school'.[41] Once the camera focused on the male searchers rather than the schoolgirls, 'the lightness of touch of the female half of the film becomes a cruder and less convincing male insistence'.[42] All the same, Johnstone advised his Belfast readers to head off to The Avenue theatre, where the film was showing. Despite the weaknesses, it was 'well worth a visit'.

As Johnstone notes, in the film's transition from disappearance to searching, Hanging Rock also changes. The Rock starts to appear ugly, murky and awkward. The camera looks down on the climbers, who struggle to make their way up pathways. Male searchers are made to look ridiculous, in contrast to the assured journey upwards of the schoolgirls. Weir gathers together a search party of men with grappling hooks and a ludicrous periscope. Only once is the silhouette of a successful searcher pictured atop the Rock's summit.

HANGING ROCK: AN AUSTRALIAN OR GLOBAL CLASSIC?

Despite his disappointment with later sequences, Robert Johnstone praised Peter Weir for confronting 'the ancient enigma of the new continent' as symbolised by Hanging Rock itself. When the film was shown in the United States, critics also understood Hanging Rock, the eerie majestic monolith, as the central image for the film. One appreciative reviewer reflected on the Rock as the central point of both film and the landscape around it.[43] Ed Roginski commented that

> It is the monolith that dominates all other images on the screen in precisely the same way it looms above objects in its surrounding countryside — it is the focal point for the world around it, the measure of everyone and everything in view.[44]

And yet, whilst the film has moulded Hanging Rock and the Reserve into icons of a global popular culture, and although critics have sought to constantly return the film to some role in an unsettled Australian post-colonial engagement with the environment (a theme in which Peter Weir seemed singularly uninterested) the Rock is never quite the central character. Rather, Peter Weir's mood settings and music, combined with the exquisite Edwardian costumes and artifacts, are able to shape the film. They suffuse through any lingering memory.

In making this unparalleled film, Peter Weir, relying on a brilliant script by Cliff Green, and unique cinematography by Russell Boyd, seems to have stood apart from the revision of 'Australian' identities at the heart of other films in the New Wave. Ken Hannan's reconstructed shearers in *Sunday Too Far Away*, for example, reflect an enduring Australian stereotype. Hannan queries their legendary status whilst placing his characters in a recognisable, expansive outback. Here, they are players in the drama of Australian labour history.[45] Peter Weir was more concerned with time rather than place, pointing to the mid-1960s as a turning point in which the old Europe vanished from Australia. He claimed on one occasion that the overpowering context of the film was the youth culture of the 1960s.[46]

195

The music composer for the film, Bruce Smeaton, once remarked that

> I remember Peter [Weir] saying that if the film had come out six months earlier or later it might have bombed completely...It just happened to be the right film at the right moment and gave Australians a different view of themselves than the old one.[47]

Despite Peter Weir's reservations, this timing no doubt explains some part of the film's popularity. It captured a long repressed popular desire to explore Australian identities and to recognise the limitations of a British and colonial world. If Don Dunstan was measured in his account of the film, critics afterwards were enthusiasts, more so when it won acclaim in Europe, after its showing at Cannes and in London. At the 1976 Cannes film festival the American critic Rex Reed recalled 'poking around the outlying cinemas' and discovering *Picnic at Hanging Rock*. Comparing the direction and camerawork to Bo Widerberg's *Elvira Madigan* (1967) this reviewer identified the movie's enduring uniqueness; its succinct balancing of the 'delicate' with the 'chilling and hypnotic'.[48] Despite its initial failure to win mass market release in the United States, Weir pointed to the fact that it eventually attracted a passionate audience on the US college film circuit. Once a shorter version of the film was shown across the United States, it did win a broad and diverse popular audience. This was a film then, which both won popular acclaim (for a budget of less than $500,000 it has grossed about $5 million) and subsequently won critical acceptance. 'A few faults but still a most splendid film' claimed the *Canberra Times* critic.[49] The revered Melbourne film critic Colin Bennett, placed Weir's film it in the top ten world movies of 1975.[50] Others had reservations. A few thought that the film's weaknesses were most obvious in Weir's changing of frame speed and in his resort to stereotypical montage shots and extended dissolves. Accepting that the disappearances were 'derived from an actual incident', some reviewers saw the major success of the film as lying in its capacity, in the face of a supposed historical authenticity, to maintain the mystery of disappearance.[51]

When the film eventually won a release in the United States and despite the anger of commercial distributors at its non-closure, Ed Roginski noted its power, deriving in particular from Hanging Rock itself.[52] For Roginksi, it was a sense of paganism and animism which overwhelmed his viewing. To American reviewers, *Picnic at Hanging Rock* could automatically be placed in the vast movie genre of 'horror', the place from which director Peter Weir emerged.[53] Vincent Canby reviewed the film as a superior example of the horror genre. Weir's later (1977) *The Last Wave* had beaten *Picnic* to American screens (and *The Last Wave*, unlike *Picnic*, trod the now familiar path of placing an American actor, in this case Richard Chamberlain, in a lead role). Canby thought that *Picnic at Hanging Rock* exposed the weaknesses of the later film, in which Weir resolves the mysteries for his audience. He did acknowledge that Hanging Rock itself was crucial to the film, comparable to the role of the New England countryside in Nathaniel Hawthorne's writing for example.[54] In the end, however, Canby, unlike Roginski, was less interested in the role of Hanging Rock. He saw the success of the film as depending on the fact that Weir and Cliff Green had made 'a movie composed almost entirely of clues'.[55]

Picnic at Hanging Rock was shown on Australian television in 1980, when it outrated all other offerings on television in Sydney. It was released on video and DVD with eventually a director's cut available (and perhaps uniquely for such productions it was a director's cut which was actually shorter than the original film). Since then there have been eulogies on the fortieth anniversary and showings at Hanging Rock on each St Valentine's Day. There remains an ongoing debate about the absence of Aboriginal life in the film (how could anyone expect otherwise in the Australia of the early 1970s, when the only guide to Aboriginality on screen was to be found in Charles Chauvel's well-meaning but mechanistic *Jedda*).[56] Some critics are transfixed by the hints at a subtextual homoeroticism in at least the initial scenes. Despite the tedious academic debates about Australian identity that have followed Weir's film, the dominant on-screen location is the very Edwardian and English girls' college.[57] The child lost in the bush seems the key theme to others. Yet, Miranda is not lost at all. She climbs up the Rock knowing exactly where she is going.

She is deliberately escaping from the suffocation of Appleyard College. And despite the constant attempt to position the film in a European fine art rather than populist tradition, if anything, *Picnic at Hanging Rock* defers to Hollywood, with John Wayne's threatening persona in *The Searchers* (1956, Director, John Ford), an inevitable shadow to the hunt for the disappeared girls on Hanging Rock.[58] All the same, for fans of the film, especially for those who travel across the globe to come to Hanging Rock, it is the Rock itself, and the universality of the story, with its challenge to a time-bound modernity, which have held up over forty years. Such are the characterisations in the National Film and Sound Archives online exhibition and recent events surrounding the 40th anniversary of the film.[59]

Just as had Patricia Lovell, on her dreary Saturday-morning shopping trip in 1971, Russell Boyd discovered a Hanging Rock story, in a second-hand book shop. On one vaguely recalled day, he picked up a copy of a book in which the Shire of Macedon Ranges had fused stills from the movie with Joan Lindsay's text. As Boyd pointed out, just as in his discovered book, the material place, Hanging Rock, and its cinematic image, are now difficult to disentangle. Hanging Rock has become much more than a recreation reserve. The film has diffused Hanging Rock around the planet, and simultaneously brought new life and enthusiasms to the picnic ground itself. In doing so it has marginalised even further, the buildings and landscape of car parks, racetrack and picnic tables. The sites that Boyd and his crew could not allow to appear on screen.

Picnic at Hanging Rock has gone on and rightly so, to win recognition as a critical turning point for the Australian film industry. It demonstrated that an Australian director could not only handle, but remodel, the plot themes and the scene construction acceptable in long established film industries elsewhere around the globe. *Picnic at Hanging Rock* was able at the same time to capture the enthusiasms of a popular audience in Australia and beyond. Equally, it demonstrated a respect for the Australian environment, along with a deeply-embedded ability to interpret and manipulate that environment, in

its representative icon, Hanging Rock. It launched Peter Weir onto a global stage as a fully-fledged 'auteur' (the Antipodean Antonioni no less) and undeniably established the skills of Australian actors. As it did so, it radically transformed Hanging Rock Reserve. Anyone looking closely at the scenes captured by the camera crew of Boyd, Geoff Burton and John Seale, would have noticed a sharply eroded Hanging Rock. In scene after scene, the actors moved over barren open spaces, eroded gullies and bare soil, most of it cleared of any ground cover. Steps up the pathway looked worn down and crumbling. This tired picnic ground, best known for its very occasional horse race meetings, suddenly had to accommodate a broadening stream of curious visitors. Receipts for visits to the Reserve highlight this new interest, stimulated by the film. Total receipts in 1974, the year prior to the film's release, came to $7,572. In 1976, the year following the premiere, income had jumped to $ 17,911.[60] Paradoxically, *Picnic at Hanging Rock*, by playing on some nineteenth-century images of the Rock's untameable wildness, eventually meant that Hanging Rock would be managed in a bureaucratic, structured and thoroughly tamed manner. Patricia Lovell reflected on the change, after one visit in 1985:

> Unfortunately since the release of the film it (Hanging Rock) has become a tourist attraction with parking fees and a souvenir shop. When I revisited the Rock in 1985 it gave me the horrors and I had to leave quickly. All of those old stones seemed so alive and I felt guilty for the endless stream of people clambering over them ... I seriously felt the Rock might take retribution for what I've done.[61]

In creating a menacing landscape within the 'Hanging Rock Picnic Ground', film-makers had of course, to avoid broad swathes of the real Reserve around the Rock itself. Boyd's small team framed their shots so as to exclude entrance roadways and exotic plantings. They avoided filming the racetrack (where the stewards' rooms became the production office). Ironically, these images from the film, of a landscape that was inherently wild and untamed, but one eroded and worn-down, provided the impetus for transforming the Rock into the very opposite of wild nature. ❁

Filming of the TV mini-series of *Picnic at Hanging Rock* by FreemantleMedia Australia for Foxtel, April, 2017. Photograph by Matthew Nickson

Endnotes

Cliff Green, *Picnic at Hanging Rock*: a film, Photographs, David Kynoch, Melbourne, Cheshire, 1975.

[2] Phillip Adams, 'Time Out for Picnickers', *Weekend Australian*, 29 December 2001: 28.

[3] Don Dunstan, Premier South Australia, 'Address on the occasion of the opening of the Hindley Cinemas and the world Premiere of 'Picnic at Hanging Rock', 7 August 1975, DUN/Speeches/2739, Dunstan Collection, Special Collections, Flinders University Library, Adelaide.

[4] Patricia Lovell, *No Picnic an autobiography*, Pan McMillan, New York, 1995.

[5] Don Dunstan, Premier South Australia, 'Address on the occasion of the opening of the Hindley Cinemas and the world Premiere of 'Picnic at Hanging Rock', 7 August 1975.

[6] Don Dunstan, Premier South Australia, 'Address on the occasion of the opening of the Hindley Cinemas and the world Premiere of 'Picnic at Hanging Rock', 7 August 1975.

[7] Don Dunstan, Premier South Australia, 'Address on the occasion of the opening of the Hindley Cinemas and the world Premiere of 'Picnic at Hanging Rock', 7 August 1975.

[8] Hal McElroy to McCleod, Australian Film Commission, 6 April 1976, Patricia Lovell Papers, MLMSS 9085/1, Mitchell Library Manuscripts, State Library of NSW.

[9] Lovell, *No picnic*, p. 163 Patricia Lovell Papers concerning film-making in Australia, Mitchell Library Manuscripts, MLMSS 9085/Box 1, Mitchell Library Manuscripts.

[10] 'Picnic at Hanging Rock', *The Australian Women's Weekly*, 1 October 1975: 152.

[11] 'Theatrette Aids Patriotic Funds', Sunshine *Advocate*, 22 November 1940: 8.

[12] At the time, a highly imaginative and insightful thirteen-year-old Melbourne Grammar student, Tony Ingram had begun filming *The Day of St Valentine* in 1969, within two years of the novel's publication. http://archive.li/WkQ0w . A few minutes of his footage can be seen on Youtube, with a voice over by Anthony S. Ingram. https://www.youtube.com/watch?v=CMwQYrq1jlo (viewed January 2017). 'Cheshire initially saw no difficulties with the students' film, so long as it was only shown 'privately'. Joan Lindsay also wrote along the same lines to Tony Ingram. By this stage the young director–producer had contacted friends at Clyde and the school itself, about roles for students, and space to work and stay at Macedon. From correspondence in possession of Tony Ingram.

[13] Lovell, *No picnic*: 164.

[14] 'Grande dame of film, TV', *Sydney Morning Herald*, 4 February 2013.

[15] Lovell, *No picnic*: xiii.

[16] Marsha Rowe, 'Martin Sharp Obituary', *Guardian*, 7 December 2013, (https://www.theguardian.com/artanddesign/2013/dec/06/martin-sharp, (viewed online September 2017). The familiar details to the film's creation have been canvassed many times. Patricia Lovell's recounting in *No Picnic* remains perhaps the most vivid reconstruction of the people and complex events involved.

[17] Letter, copy, Hal McElroy to J. McLeod, Commissioner, Australian Film Commission, 6 April 1976, Patricia Lovell Papers concerning film-making in Australia, MLMSS 9085/Box 1, Mitchell Library Manuscripts.

[18] John C. Tibbetts, 'Interview with Peter Weir', *Peter Weir, Interviews*, University of Mississippi Press, Jackson, Miss., 2014: 63.

[19] Michael Dempsey and Peter Weir, 'Inexplicable Feelings: An interview with Peter Weir', *Film Quarterly*, vol 33, no. 4, Summer 1980: 2-11.

[20] Dempsey and Weir, 'Inexplicable Feelings: An interview with Peter Weir'.

[21] Lovell, *No picnic*: 137.

[22] Some cast members recalled that he kept up the Appleyard College discipline even when the cameras stopped rolling, with students not allowed to speak to staff. The British star, Rachel Roberts (Mrs Appleyard) had no intention of talking to Australian children in any case.

[23] Alexander Walker, ed., *No Bells on Sunday: the Journals of Rachel Roberts*, Pavilion, New York, 1984: 118-120.

[24] 'Picnic at Hanging Rock- The unseen voices', The BrightLight Café, brightlightmedia.com,(viewed online February 2017).

[25] 'Picnic at Hanging Rock- The unseen voices', brightlightmedia.com.

[26] Dempsey and Weir,'Interview', *Film Quarterly*: 8.

[27] Dempsey and Weir,'Interview', *Film Quarterly*: 9.

[28] John C. Tibbetts, 'Interview with Peter Weir': 73.

[29] Picnic at Hanging Rock, 40th anniversary, ABC News, http://www.abc.net.au/news/2015-08-06/picnic-at-hanging-rock-mystery-keeps-people-guessing-40-years-on/6671684 , viewed July 2017.

[30] Ann-Marie Cook , 'Terra Firma: Manufacturing and Marketing: the horrors of the Bush in Picnic at Hanging Rock', in Graeme Harper and Jonathan Rayner, eds, *Film Landscapes: Cinema Environment and Visual Culture*, Cambridge Scholars, Newcastle U.K., 2013.

[31] 'Interview with Patricia Lovell' Newspaper clipping, Hanging Rock Box, Mt Macedon and District Historical Society, Gisborne.

[32] Weir and Dempsey, 'Interview', *Film Quarterly*, 1980: 8.

[33] Ann-Marie Cook , 'Terra Firma: Manufacturing and Marketing'.

[34] Picnic at Hanging Rock 40th anniversary, ABC News.

[35] '"I am your eyes" Interview with Russell Boyd, ACS, ASC', in Tibbetts, *Peter Weir Interviews*: 218.

[36] I am your eyes': 207.

[37] 'I am your eyes': 221.

[38] John Hinde, *Other People's Pictures*, ABC Books Sydney 1961.

[39] Walker, *No Bells on Sunday*: 118.

[40] Weir does not show us Mrs Appleyard's suicide. But the death of Rachel Roberts some years later bore uncanny resemblances to events in the film. As Rebecca Harkins-Cross pointed out. Roberts killed herself at home in Los Angeles and fell through plants and a glass door in doing

so. Rebecca Harkins-Cross, 'The Shadow of the Rock', first published in *Island Magazine*, no 141, July 2015 and then in Australian Film Critics Association, http://www.afca.org.au/the-shadow-of-the-rock.html , (viewed online March 2017).

[41] Robert Johnstone, 'Choc Ice in Burning Black', *Fortnight*, no. 154, 30 September-13 October 1977: 16.

[42] Johnstone, 'Choc Ice': 16.

[43] Ed Roginski, 'Picnic at Hanging Rock Review', *Film Quarterly*, vol. 32, no. 4, Summer 1979: 22-26.

[44] Ed Roginski, 'Picnic at Hanging Rock Review': 22-26.

[45] Peter Wilshire, 'Of Myths and Men: "Sunday Too Far Away"', *Metro Magazine: Media & Education Magazine*, no. 150, 2006:154.

[46] Tibbetts, *Peter Weir Interviews*.

[47] Hanging Rock 40th Anniversary, ABC.

[48] Rex Reed, 'Cannes –it's really crazy, but it works', *New York Sunday News*, 30 May 1976.

[49] Canberra *Times*, 22 October 1975:15.

[50] Melbourne *Age*, 23 November 1975.

[51] Canberra *Times*, 22 October 1975:15.

[52] Ed Roginski, Picnic at Hanging Rock Review': 22-26.

[53] Roginski, 'Picnic at Hanging Rock Review': 25.

54 Vincent Canby, 'Review Picnic at Hanging Rock;, first published *New York Times*, 1979 and then in The Criterion Collection, https://www.criterion.com/current/posts/40-picnic-at-hanging-rock , (viewed online March 2017).

[55] Canby, 'Picnic at Hanging Rock'.

[56] Suneeti Rekhari, , 'The "Other" in Film: Exclusions of Aboriginal Identity from Australian Cinema', *Visual anthropology*, vol. 21(2), 2008): 125-35.

[57] Brian McFarlane, 'The long shadow of Hanging Rock', *Screen Education* 75, 2014: 108-12; Lauren Harris, 'Paranoid Australia: Alone in a "Strangerland"', *Metro Magazine: Media & Education Magazine*, vol. 186, 2015: 56; Livio Dobrez, 'Old myths and new delusions: Peter Weir's Australia', *Kunapipi*, vol. 4, no.2, 2014: 10.

[58] Arthur M. Eckstein, and Peter Lehman. *The searchers: essays and reflections on John Ford's classic western*. Wayne State University Press, Detroit, 2004.

[59] Picnic at Hanging Rock, online exhibition, National Film and Sound Archives, Australia, https://www.nfsa.gov.au/collection/online-exhibition/picnic-at-hanging-rock , (viewed July 2017).

[60] Hanging Rock Committee of Management, Hanging Rock Reserve Cash Book, Original held at the Shire of Macedon Ranges Office.

[61] Lovell, *No picnic*: 138.

Leonard Cohen at Hanging Rock. 2010. Photograph by Martin Philbey / Redferns / Getty Images

Rock Icons

'. . .At the Hanging Rock RESERVE, at King's Booth
There is sure to be plenty of Music and Dancing.
. . . Everybody and two or three other people are going to hear
the Christy Minstrel's at King's Booth'

Advertisement, Kyneton Guardian 18 December 1869

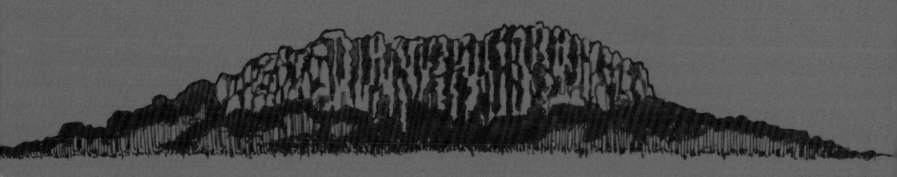

One cold spring night in 2010, a star descended on Hanging Rock. Leonard Cohen, the Canadian poet turned musician, who had once trained to become a Zen Buddhist monk, took his music onstage in the East Paddock. Cohen had returned to touring after a break of more than a decade, his rock renewal only ensured by the discovery that a former manager had emptied his bank accounts. On this 2010 tour, the 76-year-old Cohen played at Glastonbury's legendary festival outside London. He performed at the wonderfully restored Royal Hospital, Kilmainham, in Dublin, and at Piazza San Marco in Venice. Hanging Rock now joined these iconic locales as a backdrop to Cohen's music. As the sun began to sink behind the Rock, and the moon rose above the 12,000 crowd, Cohen thanked his fans for inviting him to 'this sacred place'. With such a legend of rock music on stage, supported by names familiar across the Australian popular music scene, Paul Kelly, Clare Bowditch and Dan Sultan, a new mythology grew around Hanging Rock. *Sydney Morning Herald* journalist, John Mangan, wrote that Cohen, whom he described as a 'singer-poet', stood before the 'brightly-regaled audience' in a grey suit, with the Rock behind him. Mangan went on to point out that a Leonard Cohen concert was typically centred on the star performer. At Hanging Rock however, it was the spectacle of the Rock which left audiences in awe. [1]

Leonard Cohen won Live Performance Australia's 2011 Helpmann Award for the best international contemporary concert.[2] Almost single-handedly, Leonard Cohen, in his award-winning appearance in the East Paddock, had introduced a vast new audience to Hanging Rock.

Already known around the planet through literature and film, Hanging Rock now entered a select list of shrines dedicated to rock music heroes. Along with that expanding fame has come new demands on the Reserve, its flora and fauna, and in the end, on its managers and the local community.

TOP BILLING AT HANGING ROCK

Leonard Cohen's concert was the result of long years of work by Michael Gudinski and the music promotions company, Frontier Touring. For more than twenty years, Gudinski had lived at Mount Macedon, a ten minutes' drive from Hanging Rock, and he had taken a risk by bringing Leonard Cohen to play at the East Paddock.[3] Certainly Cohen was enthusiastic, and Gudinski explained that the 'singer-poet' had 'jumped at the chance to play Hanging Rock, remembering the eerie atmosphere of Peter Weir's film'.[4] There were also precedents for Gudinski's gamble. As the advertisement from the 1869 local newspaper above makes plain, international music stars were no strangers to the Rock. At the first Hanging Rock Christmas and New Year picnics, several of the publicans' booths employed performers like the Upson Christy's Minstrels to draw a crowd. The Minstrels, alongside other singers who came to the Rock in the nineteenth century, were touring colonial Australia's pubs and music halls. Bands and minstrel groups routinely enlivened annual Hanging Rock racedays with many of these performers drawn from the local region. Sometimes they did no more than recite the national anthem, although returned soldiers put on a concert for crowds after World War I. In 1928 six loudspeakers around the course broadcast Flemington races to racegoers. In between each race, popular music was played through the sound system to entertained punters. Local musicians in brass bands led holiday-makers out of Woodend and onto Hanging Rock for Tradesmen's Picnics in the 1860s. For decades afterwards, their successors amongst local musicians were always on hand for special days at Hanging Rock. These ranged from visits by colonial and state governors, and celebrations for the federation of the Australian states, to incidental music for post-war picnics and festivals, or for carnivals promoted by local residents' associations. Frontier Touring were able to revive Hanging Rock's musical traditions in part because of Gudinski's drive and Cohen's interest in adding this outdoor performance to his tour dates. Other pieces had fallen into place also. Crucially, managers of Hanging Rock were searching for new revenues, and the Shire of Macedon Ranges wanted to expand the Rock's role in local tourist attractions. It would take several years for these interests to coincide.

Leonard Cohen at Hanging Rock. 2010.
Photograph by Martin Philbey
/ Redferns / Getty Images

The Band entertains the Visitors during the interval. Hanging Rock Races (Woodend) 2 January, 1905. Punch, 5 January, 1905.

State Library of Victoria

AN EXPANDED RESERVE

When the Hanging Rock management committee met on 17 October 1989, its working party returned a much-anticipated report on future directions for Hanging Rock Reserve.[5] The working party had been confronted with a difficult task. They had to try to find a balance between the many diverse popular interests and organised groups using Hanging Rock Reserve, with the demands for the increased revenue needed to upgrade pathways and buildings. Then, a 1993 Loder and Bayly report on management structures again pointed out the Reserve's dire need for more income. This too presented plans for the future of the Reserve, and whilst much of their report focused on conserving natural aspects of the Rock, Loder and Bayly certainly recognised the financial obstacles in the way of restoration and improvement. Anyone reading either report would quickly be convinced that profitable public events would need to fill a major role in the future of the Reserve. Over the following decade as a result, the Hanging Rock committee of management turned to varied music and festival events to fund upgrades in the Reserve.

Concert or festival proposals at the end of the twentieth century had their origins in these attempts to bring in new revenue. Music concerts, which for a time were combined with Harvest Festivals, brought local and a few overseas musicians to Hanging Rock in the 1990s. Whereas the racecourse was seen initially as a perfect site for outdoor concerts, proposals soon turned to a possible new site on an expanded Reserve. The committee of management had, by then, already turned its eyes to expanding the Reserve to the east.[6] Funding an expansion and restoring the existing Reserve was to prove a difficult balancing act around which the committee struggled for more than a decade. These grew more complex once the Reserve took in the East Paddock.[7] The greatly expanded Reserve, now including the flat and open expanse to the east of the Rock, seemed the perfect site for open-air concerts. It also placed a new financial strain on the Reserve management. In addition, local police raised concerns about safety and emergency exits for masses of people who might be attracted to concerts at Hanging Rock.[8] Concert promoters could, of course, point to the years

of massive crowds able to access and exit the site at race meetings.

Local entrepreneur Andrew Pattison ran a very successful event on the racecourse in 1992. His concert line-up was headed by The Seekers and Shane Howard. So popular was the event that it led to a proposal for a two-day festival in 1993, to be held at the end of February.[9] With local crafts and arts on display, food sold by Gisborne Gourmet Deli and wine from the Macedon region wineries, the festival was much more than a straightforward outdoor concert. It also brought together an eclectic list of international and local performers. Brent Parlane, Greg Champion and other local musicians filled much of the bill. Familiar if fading names from the global music scene – John Prine, Dave Van Ronk and Peter Starstedt, then headlined the festival.[10] This 1993 event didn't bring in the money expected, so that the attractions of local food, wine and crafts were separated from popular music, and both took on lives of their own. In 2007 Hanging Rock hosted the first 'Owning Our Lot' festival with Australian musicians Tex Perkins and Cruel Sea. These artists returned in later years to be joined by local bands Crosswind, Rex Wicked and Rock Child. Harvest Festivals were also turned into highly successful community events. They were, at the same time, an opportunity for the wider region to promote the new artisanal food produce of Macedon and the Central Highlands. The 'Harvest Picnic' had become one of Victoria's longest-running community events, when organisers decided to close it down in 2013. After 25 years the picnic lost a major sponsor. Moreover, as executive officer Kirsty Hunt pointed out, so commonplace were farmers markets across the towns of the Macedon region, that people no longer needed one event, like the Harvest Picnic, to locate specialist produce.[11] The last picnic in 2013 gave visitors a choice of more than one hundred local wines as well as ales and preserves. Several Melbourne chefs along with famed Mildura-based food guru, Stefano de Pieri were on hand and James Reyne provided the music.[12] Other events came and went, although none survived for as long as the Harvest Picnic. Classical music concerts were held in 1994. In October 2017 a 'Hanging Rock Makers Market' planned to promote and sell the works of local artisans. These musical and food and wine festivities were

THE INAUGURAL

HANGING ROCK
WINE & MUSIC
FESTIVAL

SATURDAY MARCH 14TH

1 9 9 2

10.00 am to 7.00 pm

MUSIC.....

3 stages featuring
CONTEMPORARY
TRADITIONAL
DIXIELAND
CLASSICAL•COUNTRY
SWING•BLUES•FOLK

and children's entertainment.

WINE...

WINERIES OF
THE MACEDON REGION
Meet the winemakers...over 50 wines for
sale by the glass, bottle and case.

FOOD...

PRESIDED OVER BY
GISBORNE GOURMET DELI
BEERS AT McCOY'S BAR

ARTS, CRAFTS,
& LOCAL PRODUCE MARKET.

THE SEEKERS

featuring Karen Knowles

SHANE HOWARD
MIKE McCLELLAN
TED EGAN
MARTYN WYNDHAM-READ
BRODERICK SMITH BAND
ALEHOUSE 7 + 1
YVONNE JOHNS
CHRIS DUFFY & DAVID KRYCER
BRUCE WATSON
AL WARD, & more...

**TICKETS SELLING FAST...
BOOK NOW & SAVE!**

Adults $17.50. Children (6-16) $10,
Family (2+4) $45

EARLYBIRD DISCOUNTS...
BEFORE MARCH 1: prices $15, $5, $35

Mail Bookings: send stamped addressed
envelope & cheque to
Box 36, Lancefield 3435. (Ph (054) 291 217)
or book through BASS (plus fees)
008 338 998 or (03) 11500.

Gates open 9.00am.

CAR PARKING $5.

THE SEEKERS

SHANE HOWARD

MIKE McCLELLAN

TED EGAN

MARTYN WYNDHAM-READ

BRODERICK SMITH

Hanging Rock is
55 minutes drive from
Melbourne via
The Calder Highway
& Woodend.

**FOR FURTHER
INFORMATION**
'PHONE 744 2291
OR (054) 291 217

Outdoor concerts!...bring your sun gear, wet weather gear, jumpers, picnic rugs, etc.!
PLEASE DO NOT BRING LIQUOR INTO THE FESTIVAL... food & drinks all at very reasonable prices.

*Poster for The Inaugural Hanging
Rock Wine & Music Festival*, 1992.
Courtesy of Andrew Pattison

Harvest Picnic Festival. c.2005. Photographs by Matthew Nickson

eventually dwarfed, when legendary performers, such as Leonard Cohen, began to arrive and play at Hanging Rock. A sense of local communal belonging made way for the anonymity of mass audiences and their global rock heroes.

HANGING ROCK ON STAGE

None of the local concerts and festivals, complex to stage in themselves, demanded the massive technical infrastructure essential to a 21st century concert by global stars, particularly one like Leonard Cohen. But then, so well received was the Cohen concert, that some of the great, if perhaps gradually receding names of rock music, were happy to follow in his footsteps. Frontier Touring initially held a license for several concerts, with Leonard Cohen followed by Rod Stewart and Bruce Springsteen.[13] So successful were these that the Shire of Macedon Ranges extended the permit to the company for an

additional five years. Quickly winning acclaim amongst music fans, Frontier Touring's concerts are now by and large accepted as part of the annual cycle of events at Hanging Rock. They are critical to the income of the Reserve and to local businesses. Bruce Springsteen's first two concerts were thought to have brought in ten million dollars to local businesses as well as providing a hefty income increase for Hanging Rock Reserve.

Occasionally, Michael Gudinski, the Australian rock industry pioneer, invited touring artists to his Macedon home. Bands could retreat there from touring mayhem, to relax and work on music. Their host, Gudinski, had begun promoting rock music in his teenage years. When he launched Mushroom Records, one of the company's first forays into the world of vinyl releases was a three-disc compilation of Australia's then most famous outdoor concert — the Sunbury Festival, held as

Leonard Cohen and Michael Gudinski, 2010. Unknown photographer.

it happened, not far from Hanging Rock. Gudinski had great success with local bands, Skyhooks and Split Enz. After Frontier was formed in 1979, Gudinski and this new company then took a plunge, by bringing emerging international acts to Australia. The first of these was U.K. Squeeze, in January-February 1980.[14] Soon afterwards Frontier ran a tour by The Police. By 1986 Frontier had climbed to new heights, touring some of the biggest names in rock music. Their 1986 tour list included Bob Dylan and Sting. Frontier at the same time continued to support local acts, best known amongst them were probably Jimmy Barnes and Crowded House. Venturing into a different musical field in 1989, Gudinski turned his promotional skills away from rock music. Frontier took on a tour by long-standing crooners, Frank Sinatra, Liza Minnelli and Sammy Davis Jnr.[15]

Michael Gudinski had often wondered about holding outdoor concerts somewhere beneath the Rock. Gudinski had not only survived for decades, but eventually prospered, in the tough and precarious world of popular music promotion. The recording company with which he is most often associated, Mushroom Records, had been built up into perhaps the best-known label in Australia. Gudinski always retained, in his mind's eye, a picture of Hanging Rock as a music venue; the perfect place for an Australian site to rival Red Rocks in Colorado, made famous by a U2 concert and film in 1983.[16] Hanging Rock thought Michael Gudinski, might even one day be so famous that it could feature on a Qantas advertisement! In August 2010 the Shire of Macedon Ranges approved a series of four concerts. Frontier Touring Company lined up established, though not quite elderly global megastars for each one.[17] Following Leonard Cohen, Frontier Touring booked Rod Stewart to perform at Hanging Rock.[18] Like Cohen, Stewart announced that he was keen to perform there because he was a great admirer of the movie Picnic at Hanging Rock. When Rod Stewart and his 15-member band followed Leonard Cohen, and performed at the second Frontier Hanging Rock concert in 2012, he was 66 years old, and expecting his first grandchild.[19] Council approval for these events was only the start of a long challenge for Frontier as it was for Hanging Rock's managers and staff. Before any concerts could go ahead, a

new road, sufficiently strong to take the weight of the pantechnicons supporting the massive temporary stage, had to be carved into the East Paddock. Work crews installed temporary lighting, put fencing in place and connected sewerage. Not that any of this deterred Frontier Touring or rock fans.

To test the roads, parking, sewerage, lighting, and most importantly sound qualities of Hanging Rock, only 12,000 tickets were sold for the Leonard Cohen concert, whereas the site could have accommodated more than 20,000.[20] Once Frontier Touring and the Shire of Macedon Ranges were convinced that the events would run smoothly, it was expected that later concerts could be expanded to fit in 20,000 ticket holders. And from the very start these events were recognised as offering much more than a spectacle for music fans. The Cohen concert opened the way for a new wave of visitors to Hanging Rock and for tourist dollars to be spent across the Macedon Ranges region. So successful were Frontier's concerts that state and federal governments offered a grant of up to 4.5 million dollars to upgrade the East Paddock so as to ensure further concerts could go ahead.[21] However most of the funds were needed for basic infrastructure to support long-term plans for the Reserve, rather than specifically to enable the concerts to go ahead.[22] The concert series were on the way to becoming, not just a famous cultural event, but also a turning point for the tourist industry in towns around Hanging Rock. There remained one catch. Two members of the threatened Powerful Owl species nested at Hanging Rock from April onwards. Performers, road crew, audience, stage fencing and temporary power had to be off the East Paddock before the owls started nesting in April.[23]

Undeterred by the owls, megastars of rock music lined up to follow in Leonard Cohen's and Rod Stewart's footsteps. Bruce Springsteen took to the stage for two concerts over Easter 2013. Combined numbers for both events was 34,000. He too came back with his E Street Band, most recently in 2017. When Bruce Springsteen turned up at Hanging Rock again in 2017 so too did a couple of Victorian cabinet ministers. And like rock's royalty they arrived in chauffeur-driven cars, drawing the ire of parliamentary opponents.

Outdoor concerts are never easy to promote. Co-ordinating stars who had established international reputations decades earlier, individuals and groups with enormous global fan networks, and who travelled with an army of managers and staff, was never going to be a simple task. Chance events could upset the most carefully planned event at any time, as Frontier found on two occasions in trying to bring the Rolling Stones to Hanging Rock.[24] The consistently proclaimed 'Greatest Rock 'n' Roll Band in the World' arrived in Perth for a long-awaited tour in March 2014.[25] In the midst of local promotions the band was told that, L'Wren Scott, girlfriend of lead singer (Sir) Mick Jagger, had been found dead in her New York apartment. Frontier Touring had no choice but to postpone the entire Rolling Stones tour.[26] The Stones did come back to Australia in November that year, landing again with their army of support staff, fifty containers of equipment, and with a Hanging Rock show once more listed as a key date on their tour. For a second time, the Rolling Stones had to call off their Hanging Rock concert, this time because Jagger, the veteran of nearly six decades of live stage shows, had come down with laryngitis. Under 'strict doctors' orders' he apologised to fans and thanked them for their messages of support. Not all were so forgiving. Those who had already travelled from interstate to Hanging Rock had to turn around and go home. Local businesses lost out on accommodation, bookings, food and drink. Such was the precarious world of popular music, to which the Macedon region had now tied itself. Whilst Mick Jagger recovered, and disgruntled Stones fans turned for home, local businesses counted their costs. The journey towards converting Hanging Rock into Australia's Red Rocks was not going to be straightforward after all.

Undaunted, Frontier continued to bring the global stars of rock music to Hanging Rock. In May 2014 the Eagles were announced as the next act for the East Paddock, as part of their 'History of the Eagles' tour to Australia and New Zealand.[27] Hanging Rock hosted a concert by the Eagles in 2015. The band, reformed in 1994, and much altered since their original 1971 line-up, went on stage after the crowd had watched lightning flash across Hanging Rock. The Eagles began their first set on a warm night at the end of summer 2015, with thunder

It all went wrong
I'll stand before the Lord of Song
With nothing on my tongue
but Hallelujah

HALLELUJAH HALLELUJAH HALLELUJAH HALLELUJAH Hallelujah Hallelujah Hallelujah Hallelujah Hallelujah
HALLELUJAH HALLELUJAH HALLELUJAH HALLELUJAH

to Michael and Sue, with affection and gratitude
Hanging Rock was an inspired location
We were honoured to play here
Thank you!
Leonard Cohen

Calligraphy. Donna Lee, 2010. Print. 41 cm x 57 cm. Image courtesy of the artist, and Michael and Sue Gudinski.

still rumbling in the distance. After the first few songs, lightning lit the Rock once more, and then a storm swept the crowd. Suddenly the stage shook, a screen fell; then the band ran. The Eagles returned to finish the concert. They left fans awestruck by both the music, and the image of Hanging Rock, shining beneath the glow of an electrical storm.[28]

In 2015, the concerts at Hanging Rock took on a different character. Alongside transnational megastars, Frontier Touring announced their first Hanging Rock concert to be headlined by an Australian band. In fact Cold Chisel were listed as heading an 'All-Victorian' concert line-up.[29] Supporting acts included Mark Seymour, Living End and the local band formed in Darraweit Guim, Stonefield. In amplifying the supernatural image of Hanging Rock, these concerts at the same time expanded the Rock's commercial possibilities, and so raised questions about the management of the Reserve. The conflict over these uses returned to an older contest between a modernising and a natural Hanging Rock. Rival visions came to the surface when English performer Ed Sheeran decided to film a music video, not in the East Paddock where Cohen and others performed, but atop the Rock itself.

WILDLIFE AND SOCIAL MEDIA

As it turned out, a select, 'intimate' concert, by a rising global superstar rather than any ageing rock veteran, brought conflicts between music and nature to a head. And it was not because of the concerts at East Paddock. Instead the rising rock luminary, Ed Sheeran, performed for a small crowd at the top of the Rock rather than on the flat below.[30] There had always been occasional carping about rock concerts in Hanging Rock Reserve, most of them because of the impact of cars and crowds on natural habitat. Some feared that the concerts were so successful that they would become all-year round events, with permanent stages and seating. The Ed Sheeran event did not attract these sorts of criticisms because it was so intimate. Sheeran had walked up the Rock with Gudinski (on a dull, rainy day) and immediately grasped its unique qualities. Sheeran, awarded an MBE (Member of the British Empire) at only 27 years of age, has

become one of the superstars of the music world, his reputation linked intimately to social media and digital technology. His one very brief, filmed performance, in front of a small select audience, transposed Hanging Rock into this digital world.

In 2017, Sheeran performed at twilight, for an audience numbering less than 100 and for only half an hour. The pinnacles of Hanging Rock were merely providing a background for his music video, which he planned to broadcast digitally to millions of fans. From the viewpoint of the Shire of Macedon Ranges, this low-key event could do no harm to the Rock, and would undeniably swell tourist interest in the region. Whereas the Frontier concerts in the East Paddock appealed best to an older audience that had 'grown up', and often elderly, alongside the performers, Sheeran opened a door to a younger generation. And besides, Sheeran had touched local teenagers by taking a bit part in the Australian television soap opera *Home and Away*. Here was an opportunity to win over an entire new generation of tourists, drawn through Ed Sheeran's music, the Hanging Rock backdrop, and circulated through vidcasts and social media.

Predictably, a concert at the Summit of Hanging Rock raised the ire of several local groups, especially those whose interest in Hanging Rock revolved around the protection of habitat for animals and birds. To local environmentalists, the Sheeran video seemed regulated by few of the environmental safeguards complied with in Frontier Touring's East Paddock concerts. There had already been murmerings about the Frontier concerts, with one irate letter writer demanding that Gudinski hand over any profits to protect habitat restoration at Hanging Rock.[31] But by moving to the Rock itself, and performing on the Summit, Sheeran's event seemed to pose a different set of risks.[32] Most of the significant environmental values of Hanging Rock Reserve were attached to the Rock, rather than the picnic grounds below. And the Rock had already been identified as providing a valuable link between nearby zones with surviving natural habitat.[33] Local environmentalists complained that there were a number of species 'just hanging on at Hanging Rock' and that the Sheeran concert was a threat to their

at Hanging Rock' and that the Sheeran concert was a threat to their survival. One local defender of the Rock wondered if authorities would allow Uluru to be used for such an event.[34]

Anyone familiar with the history of Hanging Rock would quickly realise that there was little new in these conflicts. Promoters justified such spectacular events because the wealth generated by these concerts spread through the region, with estimates in the tens of millions for the value of each concert. Early in the twentieth century, battlelines over the rebuilt racetrack had set the lovers of the 'picturesque' against 'the fourteen or fifteen thousand who attend their favourite sport'.[35] Without crowds drawn into such spectacualr events such as the race meeting, local businesses would surely suffer, as Jack Murray reminded opponents of the expanded racing club in 1905-6.[36] The conflict between those wanting solitude and a natural uniqueness had always run up against promoters of the first picnics, racing's expansionist plans, and a drive to modernise the Reserve.

And yet, in the 21st century, deeper fears underlay anger at the Sheeran event. Whereas the East Paddock concerts had to both conform to the natural rhythms of the Reserve, and be widely publicised, Ed Sheeran's video seemed the very opposite. It was kept a secret for as long as possible. Shire of Macedon Ranges staff assured critics that there were strict conditions attached to the permit, and that an inspection after the event showed no damage to the Rock and no disturbance to animals and birds. Nonetheless, there was again a clear demarcation, between those seeing Hanging Rock as a resource to be modernised and commercialised for the economic benefit of the region as a whole, and others who placed preserving natural habitat and a personal enjoyment of nature as the prime, and often the only, legitimate goal, of the Reserve's management.

In 2017, more concerts are planned for Hanging Rock, though in the East Paddock rather than on the Summit. As part of their 'Great Circle' tour, Frontier announced a Hanging Rock concert headed by Midnight Oil, for November 2017. The Great Circle would be Midnight

Oil's first tour for twenty years, and within an hour of tickets going on sale they had sold out. Despite an outcry from fans, there was to be no second Midnight Oil concert at Hanging Rock. The Rock might be eerie, majestic and inspiring, but the band was already locked into dates at places with lesser claims on such qualities: Sunshine Coast, Wodonga and Wollongong. When 'faddists'and 'ramblers' had tried to stymie the racing club's expansion at the start of the twentieth century, they failed, in the face of the enormous popularity of horseracing. Opponents of rock concerts seem likely to meet with similar failures. Protections for the natural environment at Hanging Rock are far more entrenched now than one hundred years ago. At the same time the economic benefits to the region, of even one or two events a year, are far more alluring than when the racing club had sought to expand at Hanging Rock in 1905.

Occasionally, the disappointments of nature-lovers are matched by those of nostalgic rock fans. When one Leonard Cohen concert-goer complained about plastic chairs covering the East Paddock, and asked why the fans could not just lounge on the grass as they did years ago, she probably represented a minority sentiment amongst the enraptured audience. In 2017, ageing rock fans (in other words many of spectators at these concerts) may be well beyond lounging around on grass. The generation of fans who have 'grown up', alongside Rod Stewart, as much as the superstars they adulate, now need somewhere to sit down. From time to time then, and despite rapturous ovations and reporting, Frontier Touring's Hanging Rock concerts have unavoidably succumbed to a relatively decorous tone. Moreover, the enormous enthusiasm and popular awareness of concerts at Hanging Rock have brought their own set of regulations to the Reserve. Ticket-holders are warned that they are not permitted to enter the venue with eskies, umbrellas or folding chairs. They prepare themselves to be searched by security on arrival. They are warned that police will monitor their departures down the roads around Hanging Rock. Rock concerts bring with them a nostalgia for freedom and adventure. Like the Rock itself, the legendary performers are imagined as timeless. When these grandfatherly legends finally appear on stage, figures

majestic setting as Hanging Rock, they still manage to conjure up the limitless energies and broken boundaries of rock's pioneering days. And although Hanging Rock itself might be timeless, the stars and fans are not. Great artists eventually do run out of time. Amongst those who performed at Hanging Rock, Leonard Cohen died after a fall at his home in Los Angeles in November 2016.

As with most other events at Hanging Rock, concerts must be policed, regulated, orderly, and often sedate. Taken together, an ageing audience, and minute regulation, have changed the nature of outdoor rock music events. And not just those at Hanging Rock. When Upton's Christy Minstrels performed at King's liquor booth at the Hanging Rock races, more than a century ago, they faced a crowd shaped by very few rules. The crowds at Hanging Rock in 1869, were a much wilder lot than those turning up sit on plastic chairs and listen to music in 2017. It is certainly true that Frontier Touring, Michael Gudinski and their legendary performers have added a remarkable new chapter to the history of Hanging Rock. At every one of these events, fans turn up in their thousands, hoping not just to listen to music, but to catch an echo of their youth. The location, Hanging Rock, also fascinates them because of its mythical, timeless past. The concerts on the other hand, are now performed in a regulated present, ordered by multiple rules, and with the performers depending on the technical accuracy of sound equipment, stage construction and lighting mechanics. There is no doubt that fans go away from a Hanging Rock concert, certain they have shared in a ritual with some irreplaceable qualities. At the same time, the spectacular concerts are events in which promoters, musicians and audience are linked together, subject to order, precision and regularity. These are the very hallmarks of the modernity that, in the 21st century, has come to characterise Hanging Rock Reserve. ✹

Leonard Cohen at Hanging Rock. 2010. Photograph by Bruce Hedge

Leonard Cohen at Hanging Rock. 2010. Photograph by Travis McCue / Newspix

Bruce Springsteen at Hanging Rock. 2017. Photograph by Brett Schewitz

Endnotes

[1] John Mangan, 'Leonard Cohen at Hanging Rock', *Sydney Morning Herald*, 21 November 2010, http://www.smh.com.au/entertainment/music/leonard-cohen-20101120-181wz.html (viewed online June 2017)

[2] Mushroom Promotions, http://mushroompromotions.com/press-releases/leonard-cohen-hanging-rock-concert-wins-helpmann-award-best-international-contemporary-concert-the-legendary-rod-stewart-to-play-at-the-iconic-venue/, (viewed online July 2017)

[3] Leonard Cohen fans wrote positively about the Hanging Rock performance, although one did complain about the 'acres of plastic chairs', remembering other outdoor events in which the crowd relaxed on the grass, Leonard Cohen Forum, http://www.leonardcohenforum.com/viewtopic.php?f=44&t=23713 (viewed online March 2017)

[4] Mangan, 'Leonard Cohen'. Cohen was born in 1934, in Quebec. His first tour as a musician rather than poet was in 1970. After several breaks he returned for a tour which extended from 2008 to 2010, when he performed at Hanging Rock. His last live performance appears to have been in Auckland, New Zealand in 2013. Leonard Cohen died, 7 November 2016, at his home in Los Angeles.

[5] Working Party Report, 1989, Hanging Rock Committee of Management, Minutes, September 1989.

[6] Committee of Management, Minutes, June-December 1978.

[7] Committee of Management, Minutes, Minutes, 1987-95.

[8] Committee of Management, Minutes, 20 October 1987.

[9] Correspondence, 7 September 1992. Committee of ManagementMinutes.

[10] See Peter Starstedt, obituary, *Guardian* online 9 January 2017. https://www.theguardian.com/music/2017/jan/08/singer-songwriter-peter-sarstedt-dies-aged-75, (viewed online, January 2016).

[11] Alyssa Allen, 'Harvest Picnic festival calls it a day after 25 years', 22 October 2013, ABC Radio Melbourne, http://www.abc.net.au/local/stories/2013/10/22/3874310.htm, (viewed online December 2016)

[12] Barry Kennedy, 'Hanging Rock, tasty picnic', *Sunbury Macedon Leader*, 19 February 2013: 14.

[13] Christie Eliezer,' More Shows for Hanging Rock', *Beat magazine*, http://www.beat.com.au/music/more-shows-hanging-rock, (viewed online June 2017).

[14] 'Frontier Touring Master List', original held by Frontier. U.K. Squeeze, emerging from the same South London music scene as Dire Straits, were known in Britain as 'Squeeze', but toured Australia as U.K. Squeeze because of conflicts with an existing group name.

[15] 'Frontier Master List'.

[16] *U2: Live at Red Rocks. Under a Blood Red Sky* (1983). In common with Hanging Rock, the Red Rocks Amphitheatre had staged music performance for over one hundred years, it was located in an area of geological significance and lay within a natural environment which attracted city residents looking for a relaxation from the nearby urban sprawl (Denver). The Beatles performed at Red Rocks in 1964 and it was the site of the 'Riot at Red Rocks' during a 1971 Jethro Tull concert, after which rock acts were banned for several years.

[17] Frontier also took on other community-oriented tasks such as the 2009 Sound Relief concerts at the Melbourne and Sydney Cricket Grounds, held to raise funds for the victims of the 2009 Victorian bushfires.

[18] *Sunbury Macedon Ranges Leader*, 2 August 2011: 7.

[19] Sir Roderick Stewart, CBE, (A.K.A. 'Rod the Mod') was originally lead singer in the Jeff Beck group. He then fronted the Faces, and performed with English blues star Long John Baldry. His solo career took off in the late 1970s and with few breaks he has continued on as a solo performer.

[20] *Sunbury Macedon Ranges Leader*, 2 August 2011: 7.

[21] *Sunbury and Macedon Ranges Leader*, 11 June 2013: 5.

[22] Shire of Macedon Ranges, *Regional Development Australia, Application*, 11 April 2013.

[23] On the threatened status of the owl see generally, Bird Life Australia, Powerful Owl Project, http://birdlife.org.au/projects/powerful-owl-project (viewed online).

[24] Stuart Cope, 'It's Only Rock'n' Roll', *Weekend Australian Magazine*, 2015.

[25] The group had first toured Australia in 1965 when its original line-up included guitarist Brian Jones. They followed with other tours in the 1970s and 1980s and then Jagger toured as a solo act. The band returned again in the 1990s and in 2003, when they played in some smaller venues such as the Enmore Theatre in Sydney. By the time they toured in 2014 Bill Wyman had retired from touring and several key supporting musicians, including Ian Stewart and Billy Preston were no longer alive. Bobby Keys, long-time supporting saxophonist, died in December 2014.

[26] Stuart Cope, 'It's Only Rock'n' Roll', *Weekend Australian Magazine*, 2015.

[27] Angela Valente, 'Eagles at Hanging Rock', *Sunbury and Macedon Weekly*, 27 May 2014: 9

[28] Adam Holmes, 'One of those crazy nights at Hanging Rock', *Bendigo Advertiser*, 1 March 2015.

[29] Matt Crossman, Interview, *Sunbury and Macedon Ranges Weekly*, 11 August 2015:9. Jimmy Barnes lead singer of Cold Chisel was in fact born in Glasgow Scotland and grew up in Adelaide, working for South Australian Railways before turning to rock music.

[30] *Sunbury Macedon Ranges Leader*, 14 February 2017:3.

[31] *Macedon Ranges Weekly*, 28 February 2012: 13.

[32] *Sunbury and Macedon Ranges Weekly*, 14 February 2017: 3.

[33] *Central Victorian Biolinks Workshop, Report*, July 2012, Bendigo Victoria.

[34] 'Ed Sheeran's Hanging Rock gig draws criticism from green group', *Sunbury Leader*, 13 February 2017, http://www.heraldsun.com.au/leader/north-west/ed-sheerans-hanging-rock-gig-draws-criticism-from-green-group/news-story/968e95139be155ee25bd7b1bcd77a158, (viewed online July 2017).

[35] 'True Sportsman', *Argus*, 12 July 1909: 4.

[36] See above: ch 5.

Ed Sherran at Hanging Rock. 2017. Photograph by Jayden Ostwald

Hanging Rock 1976-80. Fred Williams. Oil on canvas, 85.5 X 95.5 cm. Fred Williams Estate/me

Red Tape and Renewal

'The land upon which Hanging Rock is situated . . .by a ridiculous blunder or almost culpable want of forethought, was sold about twenty years ago. A deputation . . .interviewed Mr Tucker the Minister of Lands, with a request that the Rock be permanently reserved for the use of the public . . . Mr Tucker decided that a surveyor should be sent from the Lands Department to mark off not less than 50 acres, the price to be paid being £20 per acre.'

Melbourne Leader, 8 December 1883: 29

When rock climbers charted routes up the ramparts of Hanging Rock in 1974, they did so without any enthusiasm. 'In winter' announced the standard guide to climbing in central Victoria, the 'cliffs are green and dripping and a pall of mist makes Hanging Rock even more depressing than usual'.[1] Climbers were to cause more than a few dilemmas for the Reserve's managers over the years that followed. But their assessment of the Rock in 1974 seems accurate, as Hanging Rock certainly suffered in the post-war decades. And although rock climbers were by and large disappointed in the environment around Hanging Rock, many Victorians disagreed with them. Not long after the climbers wrote off the Reserve in such damming terms, new problems appeared. Crowds who had seen *Picnic at Hanging Rock* began to turn up at the Reserve, curious about the site of the great 'College Mystery'. New laws to protect flora and fauna reflected a widening popular interest in Australia's natural wonders, Hanging Rock included. As well as catering to film fans and nature lovers, the Reserve eventually played host to thousands gathered for concerts. As fringe suburbs of Melbourne edged northwards, new housing estates brought many more weekend excursionists within an easy drive of Hanging Rock. Satisfying racing fans, cricket, football or tennis players, the longstanding users of Hanging Rock, and at the same time catering to new waves of visitors, has become a complex task. It is a challenge that grows no easier, as visitor numbers increase, finances are stretched, and fanciful commercial projects are floated. Hanging Rock can easily fall victim to its rapidly expanding popularity. A review of the recent history of managing Hanging Rock may indicate some of the more promising ways to safeguard this special place.

RENEWING THE ROCK

When nine members of the revamped committee of management for Hanging Rock Reserve met in June 1978, they faced more pressing issues than those posed by rock climbers. The Hanging Rock Ranger had presented the meeting with a scathing assessment of the condition of the Reserve. He complained that 'no effort had been made to repair the damage done to the Reserve by cars and human wear and tear'.[2] Water flows were silting up lower levels of the Reserve.

An illegal gate had been cut into one of the fences, cars were still parking on areas that had to be resown with grass, and flooding had devastated some flat land.[3] So bad was the weather damage that when Channel Nine Television later approached the committee wanting to put together a news special on the devastation, storms prevented them from getting their film crew onto the Reserve. At the following meeting the Ranger sounded even more exasperated. 'The area continues to be downgraded and the Committee does nothing' he charged.[4]

The shire engineer of Newham and Woodend also visited Hanging Rock. He too found the Reserve in a sorry state. Paths were poor, if not outright dangerous, toilets often overflowed, whilst the many attractions of the site were largely untended and deteriorating. There was a general air of neglect, and in some places, danger, especially on the pathways up to the Rock's plateau.[5] Branches had fallen onto cars whilst erosion and crumbling drains meant that road access only added to the seemingly insurmountable tasks facing the committee. The shire engineer's 1978 report was unequivocal. At Hanging Rock, a generally dilapidated and degraded character reflected a range of quite specific failings.[6]

Visitors themselves sometimes compounded the dangers. Several carloads had to be banished from the Reserve because of loud music played through 'car transistors'. A courageous Ranger also admonished 'around ten' bikies who had parked their bikes in the women's toilets. Some visitors had let dogs run wild. Echoes of the unruly early days of Hanging Rock tourism still caused difficulties, with rowdy day-trippers drinking and carousing right through the summer holidays.[7] The Reserve was still home to a racetrack and in 1986 an athletics carnival was proposed for the Rock, with the straight of the racecourse seen as a suitable venue.[8] These gatherings, reminiscent of the first picnics at the nineteenth-century Rock, did not fit well with the more environmentally sensitive leisure pursuits of the 1970s and 1980s.

With the Reserve as a whole now rapidly deteriorating, sports clubs were forced to relocate home games. Even as they did so, casual visitors were continuing to damage the playing surfaces of the 'smaller ovals'.[9] The Hesket Football Club was told that they could not use the ground in 1978, as the committee of management set out to upgrade change rooms and club facilities. That year the club amalgamated with Woodend and turned to playing home games at the Gilbert Gordon Oval. The racing club wanted new work at the northern end of the track, and hoped to upgrade its buildings. The club was looking for funds for a female jockeys' room in 1989.[10] After a schoolgirl fell from the Rock in 1975, the committee found itself caught up in detailed and lengthy exchanges about public liability, a conversation which eventually resulted in severe restrictions on climbers, and more worries about visitor numbers and safety.[11] All in all, Hanging Rock Reserve was showing the signs of a long steady decline. As the last decades of the twentieth century approached, almost every corner of the place was gradually wearing down.

MONEY AND THE ROCK

Restoring this distinctive landscape certainly seemed to strain the resources of one local government authority and its management committee. Attempts to win commonwealth government support through National Estate listing had proved fruitless. At the same time, various efforts, several of them sponsored by Digby Crozier, Minister for Lands and for a time, for State Development, Environment and Tourism, ensured public awareness, whilst Crozier sought out support from colleagues in the state Liberal Party. Fortunately for the future of Hanging Rock Reserve, a premier who took the new community interest in the environment and public recreational space seriously, now led the Victoria state government. Rather than the bulldozer and chainsaw approach to the natural environment, much admired by his predecessors, an urbane new premier, Dick Hamer, sought improvements in the quality of the Victorian natural environment.[12] He and his senior ministers, co-operated with the Labor government in Canberra, to enforce provisions of the Environment Protection Act 1970. In 1975 they introduced the Victorian Wildlife Act.[13] Victorians responded to the new environmental protections by flocking to places

like Hanging Rock. As well, enterprising tour operators began to include Hanging Rock in Melbourne Cup packages sold to inter-state visitors.

At the start of 1979, the year in which Picnic at Hanging Rock was released in the United States, the State of Victoria handed over $125,000 for what was labelled a 'Facelift' to Hanging Rock Reserve. Digby Crozier, as minister for state development, announced a grant from the state tourist fund of $83,334 to be topped up by shire funds.[14] As it turned out, 'Facelift' was probably the most apt description for the scope of restoration made possible by the grant. The money secured by Digby Crozier, though very welcome, did not seem to be enough to repair pathways to the Summit. Years later the committee noted that whilst funding had vastly improved things at the base of the Rock, masses of visitors climbing up and down the worn tracks to the Summit had continued to degrade the upper levels of Hanging Rock.[15]

Occasionally, private proposals could seem the answer to cash shortfalls. One such scheme, an 'Origins of Man' Prehistory Park (known locally as the 'Dino Park') was proposed for a site near to Hanging Rock. After receiving more than 100 objections, the shire council rejected the Dino Park. It did though encourage the visionary behind the scheme to look for another site within the shire. The Dino Park instead was proposed for another small rural shire. The promoter behind this scheme won approval from the Shire of Ballan for a site along the Western Highway at Gordon. 'Origins of Man', despite its sweeping comprehension of planetary history, and its worthy educational commitment, went the way of other dreams at Hanging Rock.[16] It vanished.

EXPANDING THE RESERVE

In 1985 the Shire of Newham and Woodend received a professional assessment of the 'conservation values' of the shire as a whole.[17] In this, Hanging Rock, figured highly, even though clearly degraded by 'heavy visitor pressure'.[18] As the shire tried to respond to the damage wrought by 1983 bushfires, it also sought to assess shortcomings

225

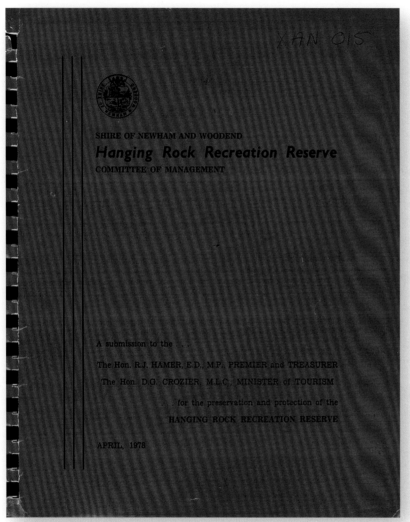

XAN OIS

SHIRE OF NEWHAM AND WOODEND
Hanging Rock Recreation Reserve
COMMITTEE OF MANAGEMENT

A submission to the . . .

The Hon. R.J. HAMER, E.D., M.P., PREMIER and TREASURER

The Hon. D.G. CROZIER, M.L.C., MINISTER of TOURISM

. . . for the preservation and protection of the
HANGING ROCK RECREATION RESERVE

APRIL, 1978

Submission from the Hanging Rock Committee of Management April 1978,
to the Victorian Government *"for the preservation and protection of
the Hanging Rock Recreation Reserve"*.
Woodend and District Heritage Society

Apparent conflicts existing at present are :

* THE TENDENCY OF SMALL NUMBERS OF IRRESPONSIBLE
  SIGHTSEERS TO THROW ROCKS AND BOTTLES FROM THE
  TOP OF THE CLIFFS, REGARDLESS OF THE DANGER TO
  CLIMBERS AND OTHER WALKERS BELOW.

* THE ENCLOSURE OF THE RESERVE BY HOBBY FARMS
  BEING DEVELOPED ON WHAT MERELY MUST BE TERMED
  INAPPROPRIATE SUBDIVISIONS THAT HAVE OCCURRED,
  PARTICULARLY ON THE "ROCKS" WESTERN BOUNDARY.

* DOGS: THESE ARE A PROBLEM GENERATED BY HOBBY
  FARMS. PICNICKERS, WALKERS, CLIMBERS AND DOGS
  DO NOT MIX.

* FIRES: PICNICKERS RARELY APPRECIATE THE NEED
  TO CONTROL FIRES IN A COUNTRY AREA. THEY PERSIST
  IN LIGHTING FIRES ON WHICH TO BARBECUE. THE
  COMMITTEE OF MANAGEMENT, IN AN ENDEAVOUR TO LESSEN
  THE FIRE RISK, HAS BANNED ALL FIRES WITHIN THE
  RESERVE DURING THE DECLARED C.F.A. FIRE DANGER
  PERIOD.

* MINI-BIKES ARE EXCLUDED FROM THE RESERVE FOR
  REASONS OF NOISE AND EROSION.

"CONFLICTS" page 7 from the submission.
Woodend and District Heritage Society

Hanging Rock. William Delafield Cook, 1985. Acrylic on canvas 122.3 x 198 cm.
Gift of Eva Besen and Narc Been AO 2001.

Tarrawarra Musuem of Art Collection

in controls at the Rock (the 1983 fires had done little damage to the Reserve but burnt out neighbouring farmlands). Again in 1986 the shire engineer reported on the condition of Hanging Rock. This time it was not so much the state of the Reserve itself that troubled him, but the shape of the management body. The Reserve needed, in his view:

> A proper management plan [that could] incorporate objectives to enhance the attractiveness of Hanging Rock while at the same time conserving many of the assets and reverse much of the degradation which has occurred in the upper areas of the Rock in particular. (The plan) would clearly indicate w[h]ere Hanging Rock's future lay.[19]

Hanging Rock Reserve, created in response to the nineteenth century's relaxed free-for-all around publican's booths, kept in the public eye through horseracing, school picnics and car club 'runs', and then displayed to the world in film and novel, was about to be brought under orderly and bureaucratic management, systems manipulated within newly-formed and rapidly professionalised tourism and conservation industries.[20]

In 1987, a comprehensive tourist brochure tried to explain the varied attractions of Hanging Rock. Announcing Hanging Rock as 'A Place of Mystery and Nature' the brochure advised anyone on a day out at the Reserve that they could 'climb pinnacles, squeeze through crevices, scramble up and down slopes, admire the bush and take in panoramic views'.[21] With the Hanging Rock Hotel now long gone, visitors could instead relax at the Reserve's Tearoom with its famed Devonshire Teas. Weekend visitors could take a pony ride. The more adventurous could embark on a climb up towards the Rock's pinnacles. And in a sign of the new environmental curiosity bringing tourists to the Rock, visitors were also told about which birds and rare marsupials could be seen on a walk around Hanging Rock.

Was it even possible for the Reserve to safely accommodate so many potentially clashing recreations in one small place? Clearly, not all of these activities were entirely compatible, and the daring rock climbers were the first to face eviction. Rock climbers as we have seen earlier,

were exploring the Rock in the 1960s, using metal bolts to create routes up the rock walls and with little detailed supervision. Following the death of a climber and a coronial inquiry in 1990, the committee had imposed new restrictions on schools and individuals wanting to use the Rock for climbing or abseiling.[22] A climbing ban was extended in June 1991. As the committee pointed out in response to Education Department requests that schools be permitted to continue using Hanging Rock:

> Regrettably rock climbers have caused erosion problems but not one climber or organisation has come forward with an offer to help restore the eroded areas. The Committee finds that to be a very sad situation.[23]

Although the Hanging Rock management committee had decided to ban rock climbing, in 1993 they discussed a new rock climbing/abseiling strategy.[24] Whilst not 'actively promot[ing]' the sport, the committee would now allow 'commercial/instructional climbing' so long as instructors were properly accredited.[25] Over the years that followed even this freedom was withdrawn. The rock climbers could hardly complain about these precautions. After all, they had been the first to point out the dangers of climbing up Hanging Rock. Their 1974 guide, as well as noting that several climbs at the Reserve were 'complete rubbish', warned that at Hanging Rock the trachyte walls were not easily handled even by experienced climbers. Handholds could easily crumble and bolts driven into the rock might not support those ascending the rock face. Technically the climbs posed few challenges to experienced climbers but the make-up of the rocks made climbing in the Reserve a challenge for anyone without a 'cool head'.[26]

A NATURAL RESERVE
'The reserve must expand to protect itself' councillor Alcock had noted at one meeting in 1978. A report on tourist crowding in 2000 was to eventually conclude that changes had to be made to retain an acceptable 'comfort level' for visitors.[27] For years before then, the committee had tried to minimise crowding by expanding boundaries either to the east or west of the Reserve.[28] In 1986, plans were afoot

to buy up farmland along one boundary of the Reserve.[29] The Reserve managers, as a first step, were intent on preventing subdivisions in this area. A newly formed 'Friends of Hanging Rock' emerged, following the report on natural landscape values, submitted to the shire by Nathan Alexander.[30] The Friends sought formal recognition and approached the committee asking that a special 'Friends of Hanging Rock Membership Card' could be sold, with proceeds from sale of the card devoted to ongoing maintenance within the Reserve. Friends of Hanging Rock took up several issues, amongst them the question of planning permits issued for buildings when they obscured sight lines to Hanging Rock.[31] Soon afterwards, in a sure sign that natural heritage values were about to play a far greater role in the Reserve's future, the committee met with the Victorian Conservation Trust, to discuss means of protecting the natural conservation characteristics of their Reserve. Acknowledging the different popular interests in Hanging Rock, the secretary reminded his fellow committee members that 'there can be conflicting demands for a reserve such as Hanging Rock because of its diverse attractions'.[32]

By the meeting of August 1991 the Hanging Rock Reserve was at last listed on the Register of the National Estate.[33] This long-delayed recognition took place following a detailed breakdown of the discrete natural characteristics of Hanging Rock. Whilst nineteenth-century illustrators and journalists had generally seen the Rock as a singular monolith, the Friends of Hanging Rock sought to break down distinct and contributory landscape qualities. This meant a more detailed focus on the elements of height, the verticality of the rock walls, separation of pinnacles, and the tactile and visual experiences of visitors moving through the spaces of the Rock with its rare orienting landmarks. The Rock and its pinnacles were pictured as both 'abstract and sculptural'. Hanging Rock was then, as Alexanders's study made plain, 'not just a monolith but is composed of many small elements that together sensually engage the person'.[34] The guide then went on to detail the animal and birdlife of the Reserve. But its importance really lay in updating the nineteenth-century metaphorical imagery of the Rock; breaking down the singular monolith and describing

Hanging Rock as someone moving towards the Summit might experience the distinct aspects making up the Reserve's environment.

As it turned out, a comprehensive management report in response to the committee's earlier tender for consultants, rather than any delayed management restructure, set Hanging Rock on a new course. The 1993 Loder and Bayly Report with the racing club in mind, recognised that existing and historic users of the Reserve deserved a place in future plans. At the same time, Loder and Bayly foregrounded the natural environment. All 'invasive non-indigenous plant species [were to] be progressively removed over a period of ten years' wrote the consultants.[35] Only significant oaks in the racecourse enclosure, and cypress, willows, poplars and non-indigenous eucalypts in the core picnic area were to survive.[36] The habitat value of Hanging Rock was to be maximised to the extent of making some areas off limits as 'core habitat'.

For years the committee had wrestled with the use of firearms in the Reserve (hunters in the 1970s had come in specifically to shoot koalas). Dogs on and off leash posed problems. So too did horse riders near the picnic areas.[37] The management plan was now unequivocal. Firearms were banned; horse riding was restricted to the racetrack. Dog walkers were further restricted and 'unregistered nuisance dogs and foxes [were to be] shot'.[38] Fencing would be used to control pedestrian movements, whilst lower slopes of the Rock itself were to have formed pathways with interpretive signage. Haphazard track patterns, created over decades, had to be 'rationalised'.

Loder and Bayly's plans also rejected proposals for an upper limit to visitor numbers. Such limits were initially floated as a way of preserving the 'wilderness experience' of a climb to the Summit. In resisting this idea, (and thus contradicting more than a century of image-making in which an ascetic climb was opposed to picnic area festivities) the consultants reasoned that there could be no 'wilderness effect' on days when the Reserve was crowded below, on the grassy flats. While little in the way of recognised historic structures had

Hanging Rock. c.1970s.
Photograph by Chris Baxter.
Black Hill / by Michael Hampton.
Camels Hump; Hanging Rock /
by Chris Baxter.
Wild Publications, 1991

Hanging Rock. 2017. Photograph by Bruce Hedge

survived on the Reserve, the management plan did recommend a consistent design strategy (for which sketches were appended) before turning to the vexed issue of rock climbers. Here the consultants seemed ready to challenge years of discussion, and simply asserted that any 'threat of potential litigation should not be a reason ... for banning climbing'.[39]

THE MANAGED WILDERNESS

These changes worked their way slowly through strategies for the future of Hanging Rock. A Hanging Rock Development Advisory Committee, as recommended in the Loder and Bayly report, was created in 1996 and recast in 2009. Its role was to assist the Shire of Macedon Ranges in assessing any development proposals for Hanging Rock, and to ensure consistent responses to the Loder and Bayly Report.[40] The call for engagement of local groups also led to practical research and maintenance activities within the grounds of the Reserve. The Macedon Ranges Conservation Society began conducting bird-watching excursions and wildlife counts within the Reserve.[41] Friends of Hanging Rock, along with local bird observers; groups conducted 'bird identification walks' at Hanging Rock in 2013. 'Above all it's an excuse to have a day in the bush . . . you never know what you're going to see and there is a level of excitement', observed one bird club member.[42] Planting and weed clearing became, as the management plan proposed, the task of local volunteers. Since its formation in 2004, the Newham and District Landcare Group has raised significant funding and planted over 9,000 trees, shrubs and grasses, including varieties such as candlebark, manna gums, swamp gums and blackwood, as well as prickly moses and ti-tree.

The tragedy of the Reserve's koalas was final proof that an emphasis on nature conservation had come just in time. There had been 270 koalas counted at Hanging Rock in the 1970s. But by 2007 less than ten survived in the park. Guido, the Hanging Rock ranger thought that disease and the practice of scientists moving infected koalas to Hanging Rock had caused a collapse in numbers. Although he thought that there was sufficient food and water in the Reserve to support

more koalas, he also blamed car drivers who ran over injured and ill animals.[43] Sick koalas unable to climb up trees, became easy prey for foxes and wild dogs. Annual koala counts supported by the Shire of Macedon Ranges and engaging local groups became an annual conservation activity in the Reserve.

THE RENEWED ROCK

Patricia Lovell, as we have seen, was not at all impressed by the new, systematically managed Hanging Rock Reserve when she encountered it for the first time in 1985.[44] Had Lovell returned in the early 21st century, perhaps she would have been confused by later changes at Hanging Rock. As the new century dawned, Hanging Rock was already set on a new path. Whereas the 1970s saw uncertain restrictions on dogs, motor-cyclists and shooters, even those who shot koalas, there was now an organised koala count and controls on dogs, with all shooting banned. These were welcome changes. However, in the process of protecting fauna and flora, the natural wildness of the Rock was to be corralled, by core habitat definition, systematic and monitored tree plantings, and exclusion of invasive animals and plants. As these strategies transform popular heritage sites such as Hanging Rock from places known, admired but degraded, to a point where they are listed in state and national registers, overarching bureaucratic management and commercial manipulation seem inevitable. At Hanging Rock, the change is made more dramatic because the Reserve encompasses expansive sites for sporting activities, the imagined spaces of cinema fans, and performance arenas for global music legends and their fans.

Commercial dreams have never entirely vanished from Hanging Rock. In 2013 the commonwealth government announced a grant of two million dollars to upgrade tourist facilities in the Reserve.[45] Not that this halted new development schemes. Most recently the Shire of Macedon Ranges was presented with an alluring vision of a 'Wellness Centre' within the Reserve. This would have an 'adventure-based nature activity' focus, together with a convention centre and an hotel with one hundred rooms. Nature it seems could be commercialised

232

just as readily as a racetrack or concert arena. Even though the Hanging Rock Action Group demonstrated that, in 2012-13, the Reserve had generated more than half a million dollars, the Wellness Centre captured the imagination of several planners. Only with the intervention by minister for planning for Victoria, Matthew Guy, was the vision speedily brought back to reality. Following in the footsteps of premier Jack Murray, in adjudicating on the racing club in 1905, as well as Alfred Deakin and Albert Tucker in expanding the Reserve in 1884, Matthew Guy came up to Hanging Rock to see for himself. After climbing Hanging Rock, Guy was convinced that the environment had to be protected. He indicated state government support for restoration and upgrading was on the way. As well as setting up a new rolling fund to enable ongoing works, Guy also raised the possibility of rezoning to protect the Rock. 'More people will be able to enjoy the natural beauty … with proper funding now guaranteed', he predicted. He also suggested that he would work with the shire to update management plans for Hanging Rock.[46] When the Rock and Reserve (excluding the East Paddock) were subsequently listed on the Victoria Heritage Register, a new level of protection was provided to the Rock and the picnic grounds. In leaving out the East Paddock from their listing, however, the Heritage Council left the way open for potential change.[47]

Matthew Guy's initiative probably hastened other changes at Hanging Rock. Visions for a natural health centre, even one with 'adventure-oriented nature activity', vanished as speedily as they appeared. But they had one direct result. The plans drew together a wide network of lovers of Hanging Rock, who now realised the need for a continued monitoring of commercial proposals. Meeting in the Petanque Club building at Hanging Rock Reserve, several networks, amongst them Friends of Hanging Rock and the Hanging Rock Action Group, resolved to keep up an unbroken surveillance of new plans. They listened to Anne Lambert, the star of the film that had launched Hanging Rock onto global cinema screens. Anne Lambert reflected on the 'strange, mysterious beauty about the place which is really difficult to define'.[48]

DEEP MEANINGS AT HANGING ROCK

It is this deep quality, reiterated over and over again, rather than any proposed commercialised well-being, which as Anne Lambert rightly pointed out, continues to draw people to Hanging Rock. Hanging Rock Reserve now has a management plan, an advisory group and the Shire of Macedon Ranges has made a commitment to community consultation on any changes at Hanging Rock. An extensive 2015 review of management acknowledged the challenges facing one site which hosted a range of different, even conflicting activities, within a Reserve with significant natural values.[49] The review reinforced the need for 'stakeholder' involvement, in seeking a balance between competing interests. In 2016 a new Victorian Labor government continued to promote ideas for a new masterplan. After reviewing the difficulties faced by the Reserve's managers, the state environment minister, Lisa Neville, announced that the Shire of Macedon Ranges would continue to manage the Reserve. The shire in turn decided to hold off on any major works in the Reserve until the state government could put a new masterplan on the table.[50] Some months later the MLA for Macedon, Mary-Anne Thomas reminded members of the Victorian legislative assembly that

> one of the first things this government (ALP) did was to move to ensure that Hanging Rock will be protected now and into the future by ensuring that there is proper community consultation in place and proper care of Hanging Rock's environmental values.[51]

NEW AND OLD HANGING ROCK

Engaging with the cultural values of Hanging Rock may throw up more difficulties than protecting the natural environment or engaging community groups. For these cultural values are never fixed. Artists and photographers return to Hanging Rock all the time, constantly reworking the meanings of rock walls and pinnacles. Joan Lindsay's novel has gone from written text and cinema screen to become a stage play. Theatre audiences, it seems, no longer share in the confident nationalism, or sense of place common to readers in 1967, or cinema-goers in 1975. Tom Wright, in adapting the novel to the stage, reflected on the 'psycho-social neurosis' underlying the politics of the Australian environment and which seemed unavoidable in any reflection on Hanging Rock's past and future.[52]

The historian Tom Griffiths noted that nineteenth-century Australians sought a reflected English landscape in the natural wonders of the Australian bush. As he wrote 'European romantic sensibilities found suggestions of antiquity in primeval nature, seeing pillars of rock as ancient and abandoned castles'.[53] German cultural critic, Andreas Huyssen, also reflected on our fascination with ruins in nature. He once remarked that 'the cult of ruins has accompanied Western modernity in waves since the eighteenth century'.[54] These metaphors of ruin have accompanied the modernising Rock for more than 150 years now. They symbolise more than anything the ongoing tensions about the place; between modernising and conserving, between image-making and material reality, and between the solitude of the Summit and the crowding of the flats below. Whatever image of the Rock is most loved by visitors and locals, there remains a sense of attachment to some deeper significance. In the 21st century, visitors often attempt to come to terms with an Aboriginal custodianship at Hanging Rock. Still others seek out a natural Rock, untouched by human alterations.

Whenever writers or artists attempt a metaphorical connection to Hanging Rock, the place somehow comes to reflect social divisions and networks. Usually these are to do with the vast chasm separating the raucous, commercialised Rock at the base, the place of noise, picnickers, racetrack gamblers or music fans, and the solitude of the Summit. The Summit and the Rock itself are typified as the resort of the reflective, educated and sensitive nature lover, seeking respite from the city-like turmoil below. One account designed for travellers and published in an English newspaper in 1993, captured this commonly drawn contrast. After summarising Joan Lindsay's 'grisly tale', the writer noted the crowds of picnickers at the base whereas up towards the Rock he saw a couple of koalas 'just beyond beer-can-hurling range' and hidden from the crowds with their with rock music blaring out across the Reserve.[55] 'If the background is epic poetry, the

foreground is squalid prose' he remarked.[56] And, in looking out from the Summit, he wondered at the vast panorama, empty but for the occasional cluster of farmhouse and sheds.[57] There are echoes here of narratives presented by climbers in the 1870s and repeated across the twentieth century. And yet, as more and more people come to Hanging Rock it becomes difficult to maintain this contrast. The place of the Reserve in Aboriginal history now has moved towards the centre of planning strategy. And as managers reflect on traditional uses of the place, many more day-trippers keep turning up at the Rock for their first visit. Picnickers, rock fans and racegoers all become admirers of the Rock's majesty. The crowd below moves inexorably to the Summit, and, as it does so, it blurs old divisions, forcing new demands on the Rock, its Friends, and its managers.

FUTURE HANGING ROCK

From its highest points, Hanging Rock can still exert some supernatural, perhaps 'spectral' force. It still reminds visitors of a ruined castle. Music, drinking and fun still colour the flat below; solitude, nature and spiritual energy, the Summit above. And yet as more people arrive on holidays these once clear contrasts begin to break down. Modernity, as Huyssen remarked, demands a contrast with the historic, and always reduces the past to ruin. By a mixture of luck, intervention by Victoria's leaders, and wide community love for its landscape, Hanging Rock has so far escaped large-scale ruin. The Rock has been a fortunate place, securely removed from urban sprawl. In report after report, planners have sought to itemise the Rock's appeal, so as to work out strategies for protecting its enigmatic and special character. The most recent attempt sets out a series of *Visions for Hanging Rock*.[58] These now have to take in a landscape in which the emptiness scanned by the *Independent's* travel writer in the 1990s is vanishing. For Melbourne's northern suburbs are emerging as amongst the fastest-growing regions in Australia. In 2017 the Victorian state government announced seventeen new suburbs, several of them planned to the east of Hanging Rock. Sheltered away from the city to the north of Mount Macedon and lying between the crowded freeways heading to Bendigo and Sydney, Hanging Rock is

234

still set in the midst of a quiet rural neighbourhood. But for how much longer? The state government's new suburbs will include Lancefield Road and Beveridge, within easy reach of Hanging Rock.[59] New housing estates spread rapidly along the Calder Highway and on the fringes of the railway towns between Melbourne and Bendigo. For the moment, the many wineries around Hanging Rock and Macedon point to a rich and enduring agricultural tradition. The horse breeding pioneered by Edward Dryden has its successors. Miranda Park Stud, near to Hanging Rock, has recently sold several yearlings at the Inglis bloodstock sales. The farmland that surrounds Hanging Rock seems prosperous enough, able to go on providing a secure cordon holding back housing estates. And yet the city expands relentlessly northwards, and there are few signs that the sprawl of Melbourne will be contained. Indeed, almost every attempt to construct a metropolitan boundary has failed miserably.[60] The several efforts at 'envisioning' Hanging Rock are imaginative and worthy. All the same, Melbourne is expanding so rapidly that suburbia may well have the final say in shaping Hanging Rock's future. Those familiar divisions favoured by observers, between the rowdies below and the aesthetes above, between racetrack gamblers, elderly punters at rock concerts and nature 'ramblers', or between a natural, and a humanised, modern Hanging Rock, will soon make little sense.

Difficult choices face any future manager of Hanging Rock. One common planning strategy is to respond to popular interest by identifying, and then consulting 'stakeholders'. Frequently, in a place such as Hanging Rock, which includes so many varied land uses, this can be a fraught process, since selecting and dividing up stakeholder interests can exaggerate differences and presage indecision. The history of the Rock has involved consolidating parcels of land into the one Reserve. Perhaps the diverse interests in the Reserve, might force a complete reconstruction: A managerial division between a natural Rock surrounding the peak itself, an active recreational base run by sports clubs, and a more commercialised, separately managed space in the East Paddock? Alternatively, just as has happened at Mt William, Hanging Rock could be handed back to its traditional owners,

to manage as custodians on their own terms. Whatever the case, the least likely future is for the Rock to be reinvented, rather than restored, as an imagined natural place, from which the accumulated human activities of 150 years, and their material remains, are permanently expelled.

Planners working in local government often face a hard task in ensuring conservation of public space. The survival of Hanging Rock Reserve, in the face of so many competing pressures, is testament to their efforts and successes over the years. It is perhaps unfair to town planners, to ask that they protect myth and legend as well as material form. And yet, the appeal of Hanging Rock is as much about its many legends as its rocks, flora and fauna. Perhaps history can aid planners wrestling with Hanging Rock's future? For the history of this place can be understood as emphasising common, rather than conflicting, interest, expressed through the hybrid cultural landscape of the Reserve. Hanging Rock has never been and can never become, an exclusive environment. Across its history, the Reserve has been modernised, without being taken over for commercial gain, and without destroying its most significant natural qualities. It is after all a humanised landscape, as it has been since long before Europeans arrived in Australia Felix. These various users of the Reserve are on the one hand rivals for space, but on the other, interdependent, and unable to safeguard the Rock without sharing in mutual support and ambition. Hanging Rock was always more than a material space, and over time its deeper meanings have come to fascinate visitors, even as they were constantly confused by the range of its metaphorical imagery. As suburbia encroaches on the rural world to the north of the Macedon Range, no doubt there will be more demands on Hanging Rock. On the one hand the urgent need for recreational space will mean a search for new sporting facilities. On the other, as an imagined remnant of a pre-European landscape, Hanging Rock will be increasingly prized for its natural habitat, with more strident efforts to protect and enhance these natural qualities.

For Sale. Tim Jones, 2014. Acrylic on MDF panel, 87 cm x 122 cm.
Image courtesy the artist and Roy Martin

When Hanging Rock Reserve was finally handed over to the Shire of Newham in 1884, one journalist proclaimed that 'the government may be congratulated upon regaining this fine property, which, it is to be hoped, will never again pass from the hands of the people'.[61] In reserving Hanging Rock for 'the people', Albert Tucker made clear that he wanted the Rock to be preserved to benefit a generalised 'public' rather than a few rent-seeking lease-holders. And he knew that the public or the 'people', would support his plan. And so they did. More than likely, they still do. On Good Friday 2017, just as at Easter and summer holidays since Tucker's 1884 decision, crowds gathered at Hanging Rock. By midday the Reserve car park was completely full. At the barbeques, Indian families ate and drank together, whilst boys wearing turbans played kick-to-kick with an Australian Rules football. Clusters of international students, many from China and Latin America, clambered up the Rock to take selfies, and shoot these instantly across the globe. The odd 'rambler' set off on a trail around the base of the Rock. Long lines surrounded the cafe, waiting patiently for coffee. A grey kangaroo lay down amongst them. Some in the long lines wondered about just which megastar would perform next in the East Paddock. This is the new and modernised Hanging Rock. It is colourful, hybrid and comfortable. It is the product of a rich human history. Its people don't seem stricken by any psycho-social angst. For the cultural landscape around them is not the world conjured up for novel, film and more recently, stage play. But then, neither can they easily fill roles as the planning profession's 'stakeholders'.

This gathering, on one of the major holidays of the year, was drawn from across Melbourne's northern suburbs. It reflected the diversity, and the commonality, of the Rock's new neighbours, the residents of housing estates on Melbourne's bulging frontier. Hanging Rock's diverse and loyal admirers spent Good Friday gathered around the pinnacles of Hanging Rock, sharing picnic tables, pathways, and sports ovals. They walked to the Summit and wondered at rock walls and crags. The crowds appeared comfortable, happy and stimulated in the Reserve's landscape. Protecting this landscape, for the people, or the public, is just as important now, as when Albert Tucker set aside a recreation reserve at Hanging Rock in 1884. ✸

Hanging Rock. Rick Amor, 1988. Oil on composition board, 58 cm x 90 cm. Image courtesy the artist and Niagara Galleries, Melbourne

Hanging Rock. 2013. Photograph by Bruce Hedge

Hanging Rock. 2014. Photograph by Bruce Hedge

Hanging Rock. 2010. Photograph by Bruce Hedge

Endnotes

[1] Chris Baxter, *The VCC Rock Climbing Guide Central Victoria*, VCC, Melbourne, 1974.

[2] Hanging Rock Reserve, Committee of Management, Minutes, 16 June 1978.

[3] Committee of Management, 16 June 1978.

[4] Committee of Management, 11 September 1978.

[5] Shire Engineer's Report to Committee of Management, 1978.

[6] Engineer's Report, 1978.

[7] 'Hanging Rock', 1987.

[8] Committee of Management, 17 June 1986.

[9] Committee of Management, 16 June 1978.

[10] Committee of Management, 21 November 1989.

[11] These discussions continued on from 1977 and took years to resolve, Committee of Management, Hanging Rock Reserve.

[12] On Hamer's career see Tim Colebatch, *Dick Hamer, the liberal Liberal*, Scribe, Brunswick, Vic., 2015. In most of these innovations he was closely supported by ministers in land management portfolios, Borthwick and Hunt.

[13] 'Wildlife Act', 1975, No. 8599, *Victoria Government Gazette*, 13 August 1975: 2925.

[14] 'Funds for Hanging Rock Reserve', *Canberra Times*, 13 January 1979: 11.

[15] Commitment of Management, Minutes, 1986.

[16] 'Hanging Rock Park Gets All-clear', *Sun*, 30 November 1976, Kyneton *Guardian*, 8 December 1976, *Age*, 14 December 1976.

[17] M.J. Allan, 'An assessment of conservation values in the Shire of Newham and Woodend', Arthur Rylah Institute for Environmental Research, August 1985.

[18] Allan, 'Environmental Assessment': 6.

[19] Hanging Rock Reserve C.O.M. 17 June 1986.

[20] Clipping file interview from *Royal Auto* 2014, Gisborne and Mt Macedon Districts Historical Society.

[21] 'Hanging Rock', 1987.

[22] Committee of management 19 November 1990.

[23] Copy letter D. Drew to Ministry of Education, Graham Willis 5 October 1990, committee of management Hanging Rock Reserve, Minutes 19 November 1990

[24] C.O.M. Hanging Rock Reserve, Minutes 9 November 1993.

[25] 'Banned/Closed Climbing Areas', Cliffcare, https://cliffcare.org.au/about/bannedclosed-climbing-areas/ (viewed 9 January 2017).

[26] Baxter, *The VCC Rock Climbing Guide Central Victoria*, 1974

[27] Damien Morgan, and Luke Lok. 'Assessment of a comfort indicator for natural tourist attractions: the case of visitors to Hanging Rock, Victoria', *Journal of Sustainable Tourism* 8, no. 5 (2000): 393-409.

[28] See Committee of Management, Minutes for several meetings in 1989.

[29] Committee of Management, Minutes 10 September 1985.

[30] See above ch 5.

[31] Objection to Planning Permit, Application Friends of Hanging Rock, Hanging Rock Box, Gisborne and Mt Macedon Districts Historical Society, Gisborne.

[32] Committee of Management 17 June 1986.

[33] Committee of Management Minutes 20 August 1990.

[34] Nathan Alexander, *Hanging Rock a Guide, for Friends of Hanging Rock*, 1991: 6-7 based on Nathan, Alexander, Spirit and Earth: Setting The Scene For Experiencing Hanging Rock, 1985

[35] Loder and Bayly, Management Plan, 1993.

[36] Loder and Bayly, Management Plan 1993: 4.

[37] Some of these issues had been dealt with in regulations formalised in 1979 but the new Management Plan sought to tighten some restrictions. See, 'Hanging Rock Reserve Amendments', *Victoria Government Gazette*, 15 August 1979.

[38] Loder and Bayly Report: 6.

[39] Loder and Bayly: 58

[40] Macedon Ranges Shire Council, Advisory Committee Charter, Hanging Rock Development Advisory Committee.

[41] Madedon Ranges Conservation Society Newsletter, July-August 2004.

[42] Angela Valente, 'Sticky Beaks at Hanging Rock', *Sunbury and Macedon Ranges Weekly*, 17 September 2013: 17.

[43] C. Ryan, 'Curtains for koalas?', Sunbury Macedon Ranges Leader, 27 November 2007: 405.

[44] Patricia Lovell, *No Picnic, An Autobiography*, McMillan 1995 Sydney:138.

[45] '$2 million upgrade at Hanging Rock', *ABC News*, 7 June 2013.

[46] 'Hanging Rock', *Sydney Morning Herald*,16 May 2014, http://www.smh.com.au/environment/hanging-rock-people-power-saves-icon-from-development-20140516-38dzt.html (viewed online March 2017) and ABC News, 16 May 2014, http://www.abc.net.au/news/2014-05-16/deal-struck-to-prevent-hanging-rock-development/5457024 (viewed online November 2017).

[47] Heritage Council Victoria, Determination, 28 October 2014.

[48] *Sunbury and Macedon Ranges Leader*, 25 February 2014: 8.

[49] PPB Advisory, *Review of Ownership and Management Arrangements of Hanging Rock Reserve and East Paddock*, 24 November 2015.

[50] 'New Masterplan mooted', *ABC News*, 24 February 2016.

[51] Mary-Anne Thomas, *Hansard, Victoria*, Assembly, 22 June 2016: 2793.

52 Tom Wright as quoted in Sonia Hartford, 'Return to Hanging Rock', Age, 20 February 2016, see too Tom Wright, *Picnic at Hanging Rock, Joan Lindsay, adapted by Tom Wright*, London, Nick Hern Books, 2017.

53 Tom Griffiths, *Hunters and Collectors: The antiquarian imagination in Australia*, Melbourne, Cambridge University Press, 1996.

54 Andreas Huyssen, 'Nostalgia for Ruins', *Grey Room*, no. 23, Spring 2006: 7.

55 Simon Calder,' Hanging Rock', *Independent*, 6 February 1993.

56 Simon Calder,' Hanging Rock', *Independent*, 6 February 1993.

57 Simon Calder,' Hanging Rock', *Independent*, 6 February 1993.

58 Village Well, Aspect Studios, *Hanging Rock Vision Paper*, 2016.

59 Property Council of Australia, Melbourne's New Suburbs, 2 March 2017, https://www.propertycouncil.com.au/Web/Content/News/VIC/2017/Melbourne_s_new_suburbs.aspx , (viewed online July 2017).

60. Bob Birrell, Virginia Rapson, Ernest Healy, and Kevin O'Connor. *Melbourne 2030: Planning rhetoric versus urban reality.* Monash University ePress, Melbourne 2005.

61 'Purchase of Hanging Rock Reserve', *Mt Alexander Mail*, 13 October 1884: 2.

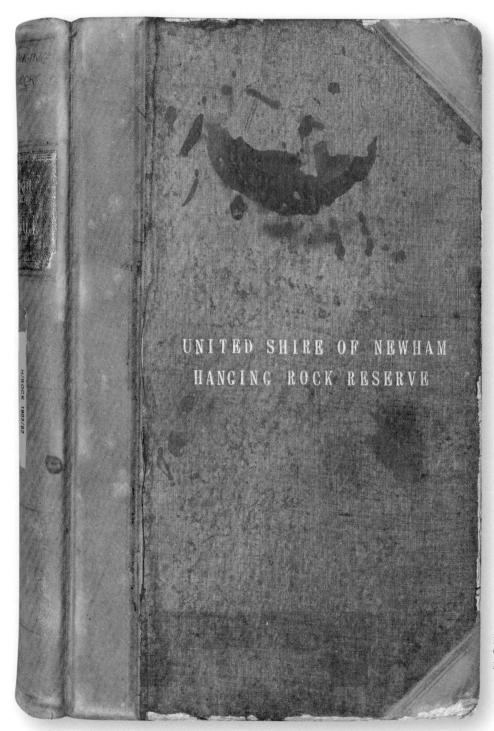

Hanging Rock Committee of Management
Cash Book, Dec. 1903 – Sept. 1982.
Macedon Ranges Shire Council

Bibliography

Bibliography

MANUSCRIPT

PUBLIC RECORD OFFICE VICTORIA

Coronial Inquests.

Field Books Survey Department.

Inwards Correspondence. Chief Protector of Aborigines.

Lands Department. Correspondence.

Probate Files.

Shire Council Meetings. Minute Book. United Shire of Newham and Woodend.

SHIRE OF MACEDON RANGES

Hanging Rock Committee of Management. Hanging Rock Reserve Cash Book.

Hanging Rock Recreation Reserve. Committee of Management. Minutes.

Woodend and District Heritage Society

Hanging Rock Petanque Club File.

Hanging Rock Racing Club Collection.

Hanging Rock Recreation Reserve. Management Plan. Report to the Committee by Loder and Bayly.

Macedon Ranges Tourist Booklet. 1922.

United Shire of Newham and Woodend. Outward Correspondence.

Transcribed Interviews. Visits to Hanging Rock.

Gisborne and Mount Macedon Districts Historical Society

Cuttings. Notices. Hanging Rock Box.

Letters to Minister of Lands.

Shire Council to Commissioner of Lands.

Typescripts. Hanging Rock file.

OTHER

Coles Hotel Index. State Library of Victoria.

Don Dunstan. 'Address on the occasion of the opening of the Hindley Cinemas and the world Premiere of 'Picnic at Hanging Rock, 7 August 1975. DUN/Speeches/2739. Dunstan Collection, Special Collections. Flinders University Library. Adelaide.

Donaldson, Elizabeth. 'I remember well'. Typescript. bound folio. Manuscripts. State Library of Victoria.

von Guérard, Eugene. Sketch Books. State Library of New South Wales.

Letters. Purchase of Hanging Rock. Hanging Rock Archive. Monash University Library.

Knights, P.S. authorised by John R Parker, Surveyor General. 'Rivers and Their Impact on Cadestral Boundaries'. Typescript. Victoria. October 1996.

Lovell, Patricia. Papers concerning Film-making in Australia, Mitchell Library, Manuscripts. State Library of NSW.

Tanner, R. '"What Aborigines". The History of the Gunung Willam Balluk of the Macedon Region: Pre-settlement to the Year 2001'. Bachelor of Arts Honours Thesis. Monash University. 2001. Manuscripts. State Library of Victoria

PRINTED GOVERNMENT SOURCES

'Return of Stations', Western Port District. Occupants of Crown Lands, Victoria 1853. Return to Legislative Council. Victoria Parliament Printing, Melbourne, 1853.

Annual Report for the Secretary of Mines. Victoria 1907.

Australian Bureau of Statistics. Census of the Commonwealth of Australia, 2011. Regional Data. Macedon Region.

Census for the Commonwealth of Australia. 1911.

Census Return, 15 March 1877. Royal Commission on the Aborigines, Report, Minutes of Evidence and Appendices. Parliament of Victoria. 1877.

Crown Lands. Crown Land Licences. 1851. Parliament of Victoria Legislative Council 1856. John Ferries. Victoria Government Printer. Melbourne. 1851.

Government Gazette. NSW.

Government Gazette. Victoria.

Heritage Branch Victoria. Victoria Heritage Database. Former Kerrie Primary School, 1290. Entry H1631. Government of Victoria.

Heritage Council Victoria. Victoria Heritage Database Report. Hanging Rock Reserve. VHR number H2339. Government of Victoria.

North Central Catchment Management Authority, Victoria. Five Mile Creek Waterway Action Plan. Government of Victoria. 2004.

Parliament, Victoria. Report from the Wattle Bark Board of Inquiry 1878. Victoria Parliamentary Papers, 1878.

Practical Ecology. Hanging Rock Reserve Environmental Management Plan Part 1: Background report. Macedon Ranges Shire Council October 2015.

Proceedings of the Committee Inquiring in to the Aborigines. Legislative Council. Victoria. 1859.

Report of the Committee on Aborigines in the Colony. Legislative Council. Victoria.1859.

Selwyn, Alfred. Notes on the Physical Geography, Geology and Minerology of Victoria. Geological Survey. Victoria.1859.

Skeats, E.W. and Summers, H. S. 'The Geology and Petrology of the Macedon District'. Bulletins of the Geological Survey of Victoria. Number 24. Department of

Mines. Melbourne. 1912.

Victoria Department of Agriculture. *Minutes of the Proceedings taken at a Conference on Horse Breeding.* 7 September 1900. Department of Agriculture. Melbourne.1900.

Victoria. Legislative Assembly. *Hansard.*

NEWSPAPERS AND JOURNALS
(unless otherwise stated, all viewed online via Trove, NLA)

Age.

Argus.

Australasian.

Australasian Sketcher.

Australasian.

Australian Town and Country Journal Sydney.

Ballarat Star.

Burnie Advocate.

Canberra Times.

Cluthan. (Hard copy, State Library of Victoria).

Farmers Advocate.

Geelong Advertiser.

Herald Sun.

Illustrated New for Home Readers.

Kilmore Free Press.

Kyneton Guardian. (Online and Woodend and District Heritage Society clippings)

Maitland Mercury and Hunter River Advertiser.

McIvor Times and Rodney Advertiser.

Mount Alexander Mail.

Overland. (hard copy Research Collecion Victoria University Library Footscray Park Campus. Footscray)

Port Melbourne Standard.

Port Phillip Gazette.

Prahran Telegraph.

Romsey Examiner.

South Australian Colonist and Settlers' Weekly Record .

South Bourke Standard.

South Bourke and Mornington Journal.

Sunbury News. (Hard copy).

Sunshine Advocate.

Sydney Morning Herald. (Hard copy. State Library of Victoria).

Table Talk.

The Australian Women's Weekly.

The McIvor Times and Rodney Advertiser.

Victoria Racing Calendar. (Hard copy. State Library of Victoria)

Wagga Wagga Advertiser.

Weekend Australian.

Weekly Times.

Western Mail.

Williamstown Chronicle.

Woodend Star.

PRIMARY SOURCES BOOKS

Blandowski, W. *Personal Observations in Victoria.* Goodhugh and Trembath. Melbourne. 1855.

Bonney, T.G. Volcanoes. London. 1899.

Gregory, J.W. *The geography of Victoria, historical, physical and political.* Whitcomb and Tombs. Melbourne. 1903.

Hills, E.S. *The Physiography of Victoria.* Whitcombe and Tombs. Melbourne. 1940.

Hinde, J. *Other People's Pictures.* ABC Books. Sydney. 1981.

Hovell, W.H. Answer to the preface to the second edition of Mr Hamilton Hume's *'A Brief Statement of Facts' in connection with an overland expedition from Lake George to Port Phillip in 1824.* J. Ferguson. Sydney.1874.

Howitt, A.W. *The Native Tribes of South-East Australia.* Macmillan. London.1904.

Hume, H. *A Brief Statement of Facts in Connection with an Overland Expedition from Lake George to Port Phillip in 1824.* J. J. Brown. Yass, NSW.1874.

Lyell, C. *Principles of Geology: or the modern changes of the earth and its inhabitants as illustrative of Geology.* John Murray. London. 1833.

Mitchell, T. *Three Expeditions into the Interior of Eastern Australia: with descriptions of the recently explored region of Australia Felix and of the present colony of New South Wales.* T.W. Boone. London. 1839.

RACV. *Touring Guide.* RACV. Melbourne. N.d.

PRIMARY SOURCES, PRINTED ARTICLES

Dunn, J. and Mahony, D. J. 'Biographical sketch of the founders of the Geological Survey of Victoria'. Victorian Geological Survey. *Bulletin*. 23. 1910.

Gregory, J.W. *Proceedings of the Royal Society of Victoria*. vol xiv. New Series Pt 2: 201. 1902.

Johnstone, R. 'Choc Ice in Burning Black'. *Fortnight*. No. 154. 30 September-13 October 1977.

Jones, W. 'Newham', in Shire of Newham and Woodend. *A Century of Local Government*. 1962.

Lyell, C. 'On craters of denudation, with observations on the structure and growth of volcanic cones'. *Quarterly Journal of the Geological Society 6*. No. 1-2 (1850): 207-234.

Reports. Field Naturalists Club of Victoria. *The Victoria Naturalist*, 15 April 1909. Vol. 25. No. 304.

Roginski, E. 'Picnic at Hanging Rock Review'. *Film Quarterly*. Vol. 32. No.4. Summer 1979: 22-26.

Victorian Climbing Club. Newsletter. *Argus*. April 1965.

Wheeler. R. 'Bird Notes from Macedon Victoria'. *Emu*. Vol. XLIII. 1944: 187.

SECONDARY SOURCES

ARTICLES AND CHAPTERS

Allen, H. ed. 'Introduction'. In *William Blandowski's Illustrated Encyclopedia*. Aboriginal Studies Press ANU. Canberra. 2012.

Cook , A-M. 'Terra Firma: Manufacturing and Marketing: the horrors of the Bush in Picnic at Hanging Rock'. In Harper, Graeme and Jonathan Rayner, eds. *Film Landscapes: Cinema Environment and Visual Culture*. Cambridge Scholars. Newcastle U.K.2014:25-42.

Daalder, J. 'The Brave New Feminist World of Joan Lindsay's "Picnic at Hanging Rock"'. *Gulliver*. no 23, 1988 : 121-134.

Dempsey. M. and Weir, P. 'Inexplicable Feelings: An interview with Peter Weir'. *Film Quarterly*. Vol. 33. No. 4. Summer 1980: 2-11

Dobrez, L. 'Old myths and new delusions: Peter Weir's Australia', *Kunapipi*, Vol. 4. No.2. 2014.

Dow, C. 'In search of the picturesque'. *Tourism Culture & Communication*. No. 2. 1999: 111-22.

Huyssen, Andreas. 'Nostalgia for Ruins', *Grey Room*. 23, Spring 2006: 6-21.

Mackay, M. 'Singularity and the Sublime in Australian Landscape Representation', *Literature & Aesthetics*. No. 8, 2011:113-27.

Mackay, M. 'Sleeping Tigers of the South: Volcanoes and the Sublime'. *Australian Journal of Art*, Vol. 13. No. 1. 1996: 93-113.

McBryde, I 'Kulin greenstone quarries: the social contexts of production and distribution for the Mt William site', *World Archaeology*. Vol. 16. No. 2: 267-85.

McBryde, I. 'Exchange in south eastern Australia: an ethnohistorical perspective'. *Aboriginal History*. 1984: 132-153.

McBryde, I. and Watchman, A. 'The distribution of greenstone axes in southeastern Australia: a preliminary report', *The Australian Journal of Anthropology*. Vol. 10. No.3.

McFarlane, B. 'The long shadow of Hanging Rock'. *Screen Education*. No. 75. 2014: 108-12. Harris, L. 'Paranoid Australia: Alone in a "Strangerland"'. *Metro Magazine: Media & Education Magazine*. Vol. 186. 2015:56-61.

Menkhorst, P. 'Blandowski's Mammals: Clues to a Lost World', *Proceedings of the Royal Society of Victoria*. Vol. 12 No. 1, 2009: 61-89

Michon, L., et. al. 'Explosive activity of the summit cone of Piton de la Fournaise volcano (La Réunion island): a historical and geological review'. *Journal of Volcanology and Geothermal Research*. No. 264. 2013: 117-33.

O'Neill, T. 'Joan Lindsay A time for everything'. *Latrobe Journal*. Vol. 83. May 2009: 46-48.

Peltier, A. et. al. 'Internal structure and building of basaltic shield volcanoes: the example of the Piton de La Fournaise terminal cone (La Réunion)'. *Bulletin of volcanology*. Vol. 74, No. 8. 2012: 1881-97.

Presland, P. 'How Aboriginal Studies ceased to be part of natural history'. *Victorian Naturalist*, 124, no. 3, 2007: 157-62.

Rekhari, S. 'The "Other" in Film: Exclusions of Aboriginal Identity from Australian Cinema', *Visual anthropology*. Vol. 21. No. 2. 2008: 125-35.

Rudwick, M. J. S. 'Lyell and the Principles of Geology', Geological Society. London. *Special Publications*. 143. No. 1. 1998: 1-15.

Scaramellini, G. 'The picturesque and the sublime in nature and the landscape: Writing and iconography in the romantic voyaging in the Alps', *GeoJournal*. Vol. 38 No. 1.1996: 49-57

Tibbetts, J. C, 'Snapshots in Time,Interview with Peter Weir', in *Peter Weir, Interviews*, University of Mississippi Press, Jackson. 2014: 6-39.

Tilley, E. 'The uses of fear: spatial politics in the Australian white-vanishing trope', paper in a special issue, *Fear in Australian Literature and Film*. O'Reilly, N. and Jean-Francois Vernay, J-F. eds. *Antipodes*. Vol. 23. No. 11. June 2009: 33-41.

Varcoe-Cocks, M. 'A Brush with Fidelity: Three works by Eugène von Guérard'. National Gallery of Victoria.

Wellman, P. 'Hotspot Volcanism in Australia and New Zealand: Cainozoic and Mid-

Mesozoic', *Tectonophysics*. 1993: 225-43

Wellman, P. and McDougall, I. 'Cainozoic Igneous Activity in Eastern Australia'. *Tectonophysics*, No. 23, 1974: 49-65.

Wilshire, M. 'Of Myths and Men: "Sunday Too Far Away"', *Metro Magazine: Media & Education Magazine*, No. 150, 2006: 154-57.

BOOKS

A brief history of the National Country Party of Australia. National Country Party. Canberra. 1979. Ellis, U. *A History of the Australian Country Party*. Melbourne University Press. Melbourne. 1963.

Allen, H. *William Blandowski's Illustrated Encyclopaedia of Aboriginal Australia*. Aboriginal Studies Press. Canberra. 2010.

Baker, D. W. The Civilised Surveyor: *Thomas Mitchell and the Australian Aborigines*. Melbourne University Press. Melbourne. 1997.

Barned, B.J. *My side of the mountain, a history of Hesket, Cherokee and Kerrie*. Lowden. Kilmore. Vic..1983.

Billis, R. V. and Kenyon, A. S. *Pastoral Pioneers of Victoria*. McMillan. Melbourne. 1932.

Bland, W. ed. *Journal of Discovery to Port Phillip*. Queensberry Hill Press. Carlton South. 1985.

Broome, R. *Aboriginal Victorians: A history since 1800*. Allen and Unwin. Crows Nest. NSW. 2005.

Bruce, C., Cornstock, E. and McDonald. F. *Eugene von Guerard: a German Romantic in the Antipodes*. Alister Taylor. Martinborough NZ. 1982.

Boxshall, S. *Beyond the Black Forest*. Woodend and District Heritage Society. 2017

Buggy, H. *The Real John Wren*. Widescope edition. Melbourne. 1977.

Cahir, F. *Black gold: Aboriginal people on the goldfields of Victoria. 1850-1870*. ANU Press. Canberra. 2013.

Cato, J. *The Story of the Camera in Australia*. Angus and Robertson. Melbourne, 1955.

Clark, I.D. ed. *An Historical Geography of Tourism in Victoria: Case Studies*. De Gruyter. Berlin. 2014.

Clemens, V. P. *Interesting Facts of the Hanging Rock near Newham and Woodend*. Kyneton, Vic. 1974.

Eckstein, A.E. and Peter Lehman, P. *The searchers: essays and reflections on John Ford's classic Western*. Wayne State University Press, Detroit. 2004.

Fuery, W. *Dream within a Dream*. Mobius. Wodonga Vic. 2010.

Gammage, W. *The Biggest Estate on Earth: How Aborigines made Australia*. Allen and Unwin. Sydney. 2011.

Gardiner, L. *Thomas Mitchell*. Oxford University Press. Melbourne. 1962.

Gisborne and Mount Macedon Districts Historical Society Inc. *Pictorial Hanging Rock: A Journey Through Time*. Gisborne and Mount Macedon Districts Historical Society Inc. Mount Macedon, 2012.

Griffiths, S. *A Rolling Stone Gathers No Moss*. Angus and Robertson, Sydney. 1933.

Guile, M. *Clyde School, 1910-1975*: An uncommon history. Clyde School Old Girls' Association, South Yarra. 2008.

Haldane, R. *The people's force: a history of the Victoria Police*. Melbourne University Press. Melbourne. 1986.

Hay, O.J. in collaboration with Reed, M.O. *The Chronicles of Clyde*. Brown, Prior Anderson. Melbourne. 1966.

Hewitt, R. *Map of a Nation: a biography of the Ordnance Survey*, Granta. London. 2010.

Holth, J. illustrated Moreland, J. *Forging History: a history of blacksmiths in the Woodend and Newham Districts*. Woodend and District Heritage Society. Woodend. 2008.

Hutton. M. *The Hanging Rock*. Mt Macedon Historical Society. Mt Macedon. 1991.

Jones, M. A. *A sunny place for shady people: The real Gold Coast story*. George Allen & Unwin, Sydney, 1986.

Lindsay, J. *Fact Soft and Hard*. Melbourne, Cheshire, 1964.

Lindsay, J. *Picnic at Hanging Rock*. first published Cheshire, Melbourne, 1967, Penguin edition. 2008.

Lindsay, J. *Time Without Clocks*. Cheshire. Melbourne, 1962.

Lovell, P. *No Picnic an autobiography*. Pan McMillan. New York. 1995.

Lynch, B. and Valerie Heath, V. *Picnic at Hanging Rock: playscript*, Lyncon. South Yarra, Vic. 2003.

McKenzie. C. *Newham Primary School Centenary*. C. McKenzie. Newham Vic. 1977.

Moreland, J. *Time Gentlemen Please: Hotels of Woodend and surrounding district*. Woodend and District Heritage Society. Woodend. 2013.

Pacini, J. *A Century Galloped By: The First Hundred Years of the Victoria Racing Club*. VRC. Melbourne. 1988.

Peeters, T. *Peter Weir and His Films: a critical bibliography*. Australian Film Institute Research and Information. Melbourne. 1983.

Pitkethly, A. and D. *N.J. Caire, landscape photographer*. The authors. Rosanna. 1988.

Pollard, J. *A Racegoer's Companion to the Australian Turf: Australian Horseracing*. Angus and Robertson. Melbourne.1988.

Poulter, J. *Sharing heritage in Kulin Country: lessons in reconciliation from our first contact history*. Red Hen. Melbourne. 2011.

Randell, J. O. *Pastoral Settlement in Northern Victoria*. 2 vols. Chandos Publishing. Burwood, Vic. 1982.

Roberts, V. Scottish Settlement in *Newham*. Valerie Roberts. Melbourne. 2009

Rousseau, Y. *The Secret of Hanging Rock: Joan Lindsay's Final Chapter*. with an Introduction by John Taylor and commentary by Yvonne Rousseau. Angus and Robertson. North Ryde. 1987. Rousseau, Y. *The Murders at Hanging Rock*. Scribe. Fitzroy. 1980.

Stawell Times. *Stawell and the Grampians visitors guide and directory*. Stawell Times News. Stawell. 1970.

Theobold, Marjorie. *Knowing Women: Origins of women's education in nineteenth-century Australia*, Cambridge University Press. Melbourne. 1996.

Tibbets, J.C. *Peter Weir: Interviews*. University Press of Mississippi. Jackson. 2014.

Walker, A. ed., *No Bells on Sunday: the Journals of Rachel Roberts*. Harper Collins. New York. 1984.

White. R. *Courses for Horses, the story of Victorian and Riverina Racecourses*. Hawthorn. 1965.

Williams, J. Echoes of the Past: *A history of Newham and Cobaw*. Woodend and District Heritage Society. Woodend. 2004.

Woodend and District Heritage Society. *Memories of Newham*. Woodend and District Heritage Society. Woodend. 1999.

Yarwood, A. T. *Walers, Australian Horses Abroad*. Melbourne University Press. Carlton. 1989.

THESIS

Sarah Frith, 'Fact and Fiction in Joan Lindsay's Picnic at Hanging Rock', Master of Education Thesis. University of Melbourne. 1990.

ONLINE

'Picnic at Hanging Rock- The unseen voices', The BrightLight Café. brightlightmedia.com.

'Unearthing Lancefield's Megafauna', *Latrobe University News*, no. 11, November 2016. 2016, http://www.latrobe.edu.au/news/articles/2016/release/unearthing-lancefields-megafauna.

Archives of Tasmania Names Index, 1468471, Series CS01/1/872, file number 18447. Archives of Tasmania, name index, 544402, Series POL459/1/2 p.24. The Archives of Tasmania Name Index at https://talis.ent.sirsidynix.net.au/client/en_AU/names/

Australian Dictionary of Biography, National Centre of Biography, Australian National University, http://adb.anu.edu.au/biography.

Bladen, V. 'The Rock and the Void: Pastoral and Loss in Joan Lindsay's *Picnic at Hanging Rock* and Peter Weir's film adaptation', University of Queensland library espace, https://espace.library.uq.edu.au/data/UQ .

Canby, V. 'Review Picnic at Hanging Rock;, first published *New York Times*, 1979 and then in The Criterion Collection, https://www.criterion.com/current/posts/40-picnic-at-hanging-rock,

Carroll, Khadija von Zinnenburg. 'What would Indigenous Taxonomy Look Like? The Case of Blandowski's Australia', *Arcadia*. Vol. 12. 2014. Rachel Carson Center for Environment and Society, http://www.environmentandsociety.org/node/6292,

Davison, G. 'Motor Cars', *e-Melbourne Encyclopedia of Melbourne*, http://www.emelbourne.net.au/biogs/EM01017b.htm.

Dr Vincent Clark and Associates, 'Hanging Rock Archaeology', http://vincentclark.com.au/2013/11/archaeology-at-hanging-rock/ .

Flynn, Peter 'Racing: Mad Dog Morgan, Lord Lucan, Jack Styring...It's a Great Cast at Hanging Rock'. *Footy Almanac*. 30 October 2014. http://www.footyalmanac.com.au/racing-mad-dog-morgan-lord-lucan-jack-styring-its-a-great-cast-at-hanging-rock/.

Foxtel Press Release, 6 September 2016. https://www.foxtel.com.au/got/whats-on/foxtel-insider/foxtel/picnic-at-hanging-rock.html.

Harkins-Cross, R. 'The Shadow of the Rock'. first published in *Island Magazine*. No. 141. July 2015 and then in Australian Film Critics Association. http://www.afca.org.au/the-shadow-of-the-rock.html.

Hulbert, A. 'The Precarity of the Inarticulate: Two Kinds of Silences in Joan Lindsay's Picnic at Hanging Rock', *Philament Journal* online, no 22, December 2016: 27-56. http://www.philamentjournal.com/wp-content/uploads/2016/12/Philament-22-Precarity-BOOK-FINAL-1.pdf.

Macedon Ranges Shire Council. *Organisational Protocols for Recognising Traditional Owners/Custodians*, n.d. http://www.mrsc.vic.gov.au/Home

National Gallery Australia, 'McCubbin,"Last Impressions" 1907-17', exhibition and BioArtistIRN=15672&mystartrow=37&realstartrow=37&MNUID=3&ViewID=2.

Picnic at Hanging Rock, online exhibition, National Film and Sound Archives, Australia, https://www.nfsa.gov.au/collection/online-exhibition/picnic-at-hanging-rock, viewed July 2017.

Racing.com> https://www.racing.com/news/2009-07-14/kyneton-and-hanging-rock-clubs-merge.

The Day of St Valentine, 1969. http://archive.li/WkQ0w. https://www.youtube.com/watch?v=CMwQYrq1jIo

The National Film and Sound Archives online exhibition. https://www.nfsa.gov.au/collection/online-exhibition/picnic-at-hanging-rock.

The Paranormal Guide. http://www.theparanormalguide.com/blog/garth-homestead-misery-and-death.

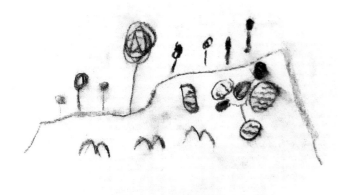

Hanging Rock. 2003. Charles Nickson

The Lyell family of Gisborne having a picnic at Hanging Rock. c.1900.
Unknown photographer.
Gisborne and Mount Macedon Districts Historical Society

Index

Hanging Rock 1, 1991. Tim Jones, Wood engraving, 7.2 x 5.0 cm.